Separating Fools From Their Money

Separating Fools From Their Money

A History of American Financial Scandals

Scott B. MacDonald
and Jane E. Hughes

Transaction Publishers
New Brunswick (U.S.A.) and London (U.K.)

Library of Congress Catalog Number: 2006044482
ISBN: 0-7658-0356-9
Printed in the United States of America

Library of Congress Cataloging-in-Publication Data

MacDonald, Scott B.
    Separating fools from their money : a history of American financial scandals
/ Scott B. MacDonald & Jane E. Hughes.
        p. cm.
    Includes bibliographical references and index.
    ISBN 0-7658-0356-9 (cloth : alk. paper)
        1. Commercial crimes—United States—History. 2. White collar crimes—
United States—History. I. Hughes, Jane E. (Jane Elizabeth) II. Title.

HV6769.M33   2007
364.16'80973—dc22   2006044482

Contents

Preface

"Out of every crisis, every tribulation, every disaster, mankind rises with some share of greater knowledge, of higher decency, of purer purpose. Today we shall have come through a period of loose thinking, descending morals, an era of selfishness, of individual men and women and of whole nations. Blame not governments alone for this. Blame ourselves in equal share. Let us be frank in acknowledgement of the truth that many amongst us have made obeisance to Mammon, that profits of speculation, the easy road without toil, have lured us from the old barricades. To return to higher standards we must abandon the false prophets and seek new leaders of our own choosing."—Franklin Delano Roosevelt, Chicago, July 2, 1932

Franklin Delano Roosevelt spoke these words upon accepting the Democratic presidential nomination in the dark days of the Great Depression, but his words have an echo in the years that followed the great bull market of the 1990s and early 2000s. In FDR's day, Americans clearly had worshipped long and hard at the altar of Mammon and then spent the early part of the twenty-first century paying for it. During the 2001-2003 period, Americans watched once again as the stock market plunged from dizzying heights to bruising lows; a parade of once-revered corporate leaders was discredited, shamed, and even jailed; and the personal fortunes and retirement dreams of many Americans evaporated along with the companies and pension plans on which so much depended.

Although the economic downturn following the end of the 1990s great bull market was not as gut-wrenching as that which followed the 1929 market crash, it left many Americans pondering what exactly had transpired. Much like the go-go 1920s, the go-go 1990s were a turbo-charged decade, when the rise of the stock market captured the public's interest. Leadership of corporate America had been lionized in the press as dynamic, innovative, and inspirational. In the aftermath of market downturns came the series of scandals that shocked and dismayed the American public. America's corporate leadership was now pilloried as greedy, overpaid, deceitful, and insensitive.

In many regards the history of great American financial scandals is cyclical. That cycle encompasses a period of technological and financial innovation, economic boom, public excitement and support of the new prosperity, and giddy riches, followed by a bust in which the market crashes, the economy slides downhill, and the public revolts against the greed that warped men's values. As historian Kevin Phillips noted: "In the U.S. more than elsewhere, the political economy has moved to such rhythms; the major periods of progressivism and reform have followed burst speculative bubbles or other severe economic disillusionment. Speculative heydays pull in large middle-class participation, fueling themes about the democratization of money and investment, at least until the bubble pops. Then comes the disillusionment."[1] The linkages between boom and bust, speculative explosion and speculative implosion, are evident with railroads in the second half of the nineteenth century, autos, electricity and aviation in the 1920s, and high technology and the Internet in the 1990s.

Inevitably, the boom/bust cycle is followed by a period of greater regulation and public caution, as well as an effort on the part of business to function at a higher standard. As Marjorie Kelly, editor of *Business Ethics* magazine noted in 2005 of the new corporate environment: "There is a new kind of Puritanism, replacing what was an era of arrogance and ignorance, an attitude that boys will be boys."[2] What could be said in 2005, could be said with equal relevance in 1932.

The purpose of this book is to provide a brief history of these great American financial scandals—that is, the major financial scandals that rocked the United States from its earliest period to the latest. A combination of technological and financial innovations—which marked the economic development of the United States—has also opened and reopened the door to scandals that are defined by a package of greed, personal and institutional connections, hubris, and an overconfident belief in the magic of the marketplace. (Indeed, the American marketplace has weaved its magic by transforming the United States into the world's leading economy. But the marketplace has also provided a stage for those who twist and abuse the free market for their own advantage.) There are many lessons to be learned—that history does repeat itself, that advances in the financial industry and capitalism are closely linked to aggressive envelope-pushers, and today's heroes can easily become tomorrow's goats.

The following pages are the product of several years of research that included trips to Jim Fisk's grave in Brattleboro, Vermont; Jay Gould's estate, Lyndhurst, in Tarrytown, New York; Theodore Roosevelt's New York City birthplace (28 East 20th Street); President Ulysses S. Grant's tomb in New York City; the John Jay Homestead in Katonah, New York;

and Franklin Delano Roosevelt's home in Hyde Park, New York. Although our guides might not have known it, they helped provide a better understanding of the times and people of their particular periods. These trips clearly helped provide an additional perspective beyond reading through historical documents. The authors would also like to thank the following for their assistance: Kristin Aguilera, communications director, Museum of American Financial History (in supplying articles and other useful documents), Kieran Lyons, Mike Carroll, and Martin Nance from Aladdin Capital Management for their helpful editorial assistance and viewpoints, and Professor Lawson Bowling III from Manhattanville College's history department for his critical comments. The authors would be remiss in forgetting to thank Irving Louis Horowitz, Mary Curtis, and Michael Paley for their encouragement and hard work, which made Transaction an excellent publisher for our project. Finally, the authors wish to thank their families for that most precious of commodities, time. Without support from parents, spouses, and children this book would all the less. While the assistance of many is deeply appreciated, ultimate responsibility for the contents of the book and the accuracy of the facts is wholly with the authors.

Notes

1.   Kevin Phillips, *Wealth and Democracy: A Political History of the American Rich* (New York: Broadway Books, 2003), p. xxi.
2.   Landon Thomas, Jr., "On Wall Street, a Rise in Dismissals Over Ethics," *New York Times*, March 29, 2005, p. C9.

1

Introduction

"What is the chief end of man?—to get rich. In what way?—dishonestly if we can, honestly if we must."—Mark Twain, 1871

It was January 6, 1872, late on a cold winter day in New York. The man was nervous and irritable. Over lunch at Delmonico's, a well-known haunt of the wealthy and famous, he had learned that a grand jury had acted to indict him on the charge of blackmail and that a warrant was out for his arrest. High-strung, sensitive to insult, and quick to nurse a grudge, the court decision pushed him over the edge. He was waiting for his nemesis on the first stair landing of the Grand Central Hotel. In his hand was a four-chambered Colt pistol.

Considering his good looks, social standing, and wealth, Edward Stokes, familiarly known as Ned, should have been highly successful. Born in 1841, he came from one of New York's richest and most distinguished families, managed his own company (the Brooklyn Refinery Company), and had married a young and attractive wife, who was well connected in the city's social hierarchy. Instead Stokes was a deeply troubled individual, caught between the ups and downs of Wall Street, his compulsion to bet on the horses (usually the wrong ones), and his romantic liaison with the beautiful and calculating Helen Josephine "Josie" Mansfield. Indeed, the combination of these forces had brought him to his current tortured predicament, waiting in the dim light to strike as an assassin. The strange sequence of events that had brought him to this point began in 1869, when he was introduced to the flamboyant and rotund Jim Fisk, an ebullient Vermonter who had ridden into Wall Street following the end of the American Civil War in 1865 and become one of the major forces in the volatile and largely unregulated stock market. The meeting between Stokes and Fisk was to be a fateful event for both men. From that day forward, the time left in Fisk's life was running out.

While the two men became involved in a number of business deals, it was through Fisk in November 1869 that Stokes met Josie Mansfield, who was regarded as one of the most attractive women of her day. She had arrived in New York with little to her name, but had caught Fisk's eye. She was full-figured and energetic, with big dark eyes and long black hair. Although Fisk was married, his wife Lucy lived in Boston and rarely came to New York. (It was rumored behind closed doors that she was frigid or, more likely, that she preferred women.) The more hot-blooded and ambitious Josie soon became Fisk's mistress, eventually being put up in a four-story house in New York City, well-equipped with servants and a collection of jewelry and furs. Fisk was smitten.

Yet there was trouble brewing between Fisk and his mistress. Fisk was overweight and often preoccupied with his many businesses—running the Erie Railroad with partner Jay Gould, and presiding over an opera company and a steamship fleet. He was also a colonel of the Ninth Regiment of the New York State Militia. At the same time, Fisk was happy to be seen surrounded by some of the young starlets from his opera company—something that probably did not sit well with Josie.

In contrast to the rotund Vermonter, Stokes was handsome, sophisticated, and appeared to have ample leisure time at his disposal (despite running a business and being married with a child). According to a New York *Herald* reporter in 1871, Stokes was "a gentleman of about twenty-eight years of age, of slender but sinewy build, with dark eyes, dark hair and a charming black mustache. He was dressed in the height of fashion and looked to be a man of the world, perfectly self-possessed and well bred and wearing an expression of savior faire which takes well with the female sex."[1]

The affair soon became messy and acrimonious. The fact that the Stokes-Mansfield affair occurred in a house that Fisk had bought for his mistress did little to lessen the bitterness of the Wall Street mogul. In 1871, the couple decided to blackmail Fisk. Stokes apparently needed the money to pay off his debts incurred at the racetrack. As for Josie, she was willing to keep Stokes as her lover and have Fisk pay for it.

Although Fisk initially went along, he eventually decided that Stokes would not get the better of him. For all of his jolly exterior, Fisk was highly competitive and, when the occasion demanded, he could be ruthless. First Fisk involved Stokes in some speculative ventures that lost money. Then, Fisk announced that he was not going to pay any more to Josie. In response, the couple threatened to send Fisk's love letters to the press. Not to be outdone, Fisk obtained an injunction prohibiting their publication and Stokes and Mansfield ended up in court, threatened by a charge of blackmail. For her part, Mansfield testified to Fisk's "oriental tastes and desires," to give the public something to titter about. Fisk, however, was undeterred as he moved to ruin Stokes' business, the Brooklyn Refinery Company, threatening the blackmailer with bankruptcy by taking away the cheap rates his railroad, the Erie, had earlier given to the movement of its products. The train of events was hardly what Stokes had expected. He had picked the wrong man to threaten and now he was paying the price for his foolishness.

So here Stokes was pacing the stairway landing, waiting for Fisk, who he had learned was coming to the hotel to meet a widow and her family to whom he provided charity. When the time came, Fisk, a large man, made an easy target. Stokes aimed the four-chambered Colt at his nemesis, shouting, "I've got you now!" He squeezed the trigger twice, with both bullets ripping into Fisk, one being the mortal wound to the abdomen. The stricken man staggered backwards, shouting, "For God's sake will anybody save me?" Stokes turned and casually walked out of the building.

Fisk lingered painfully, dying the next day; Stokes was soon arrested and went to serve time at Sing-Sing Prison. In the end though, he cheated the hangman and went down in history as the murderer of one of the most colorful characters to ever have walked on Wall Street.

Fisk: The Barnum of Wall Street

Even after his death, Fisk still commands attention. Despite his association with some of Wall Street's more seedy exploits, Fisk was well-loved by the citizens of Brattleboro, Vermont, where he had spent part of his youth and became an important philanthropist. Upon his death the citizens of that southern Vermont town collected money and paid for a monument to Fisk. Located at Brattleboro's Prospect Cemetery, Jim Fisk's family plot sits to one side, shaded by a stand of leafy tall trees, but it is the center of attention—just as Fisk was in life.

Sculpted by the same artist who produced the Lincoln Monument at Springfield, Illinois, the Fisk monument too was created to make people remember Jim Fisk's larger-than-life persona. The monument is a shaft of marble with a portrait medallion of Fisk on its face. At each corner of the large base are four topless young women, each holding a plaque representing Fisk's main interests—railroads, shipping, the stage, and trade. Sadly, souvenir hunters have taken most of the fingers and toes of the scantily clad women, while time and acid rain have eroded the stone.

Although most Americans have forgotten the colorful Jim Fisk (and even more so his assassin Ned Stokes), Fisk's monument in a quiet corner of a Vermont cemetery casts a long shadow over U.S. financial history. Fisk, also known as the "Barnum of Wall Street," was an active participant in the largely unregulated and freewheeling rollercoaster of the U.S. stock market following the American Civil War (1861-1865). His exploits included the rough and tumble fight over control of the Erie Railroad, and the infamous attempt to corner the U.S. gold market in 1869 that led to Black Friday and a steep economic depression. A celebrity in his own right on Wall Street, he rubbed elbows with the likes of Jay Gould (his erstwhile partner), Daniel Drew, Cornelius Vanderbilt, Boss William Sweeny Tweed, and President Ulysses S. Grant.

A strong extrovert who enjoyed being in the public eye, Fisk was loved by those who benefited from his largesse (like the citizens of Brattleboro) and vilified by those who were on the short end of his financial maneuverings (like the unfortunate Ned Stokes). Although his wheeling and dealing in the stock market and much of his personal life lacked a certain moral compass, he was an essential cog in what made Wall Street work. He was ruthless, aggressive, flamboyant, and keen to exploit the gray areas between what was legal and what was illegal (though he was willing to bribe the right people to make things legal). Although he was not working for the public good, nonetheless, his actions helped set in motion forces that would shape Wall Street well into the next centuries. A genuine American success story, he rose up from relatively humble beginnings in Vermont and through hard work, daring, and luck became one of the wealthiest players on Wall Street. The same combination of ruthlessness, ability to exploit the gaps between what was permissible and what was not, and flamboyance has a strong historical echo in the scandals that would follow on Wall Street during the twentieth and twentieth-first centuries.

In Fisk we see the forerunner of Michael Milken, Kenneth Lay (and his cohorts at Enron), and other corporate leaders, who lived—at least until the party ended—larger than life. At the same time, it is important to note that Wall Street survived Fisk, as it did the others who followed. Indeed, Wall Street was to grow stronger, in part due to these scandals, making it an essential part of the financial system that keeps the global economy in motion. That is the tale of the following pages.

The Kabuki-Like Drama of Scandal

For all its august reputation and stately traditions, the history of American finance constructed around Wall Street resounds with repeated stories of scandals. Despite the shock and indignation, financial scandals have recurred with regularity. A list of colorful characters strides (or skulks) through the pages of this history. Along with these characters come some unforgettable images. Who can forget that aerial photograph of Jeffrey Skilling's magnificent Florida spread? Or the vodka-spouting statue at Dennis Kozlowski's birthday bash? Complicated relationships—both professional and personal—abound, from Wall Street's flashy and brash Fisk, shot by a rival lover for the actress Josie Mansfield in the dim stairwell of the Broadway Central Hotel, to Jack Welch—captain of industry and lecture circuit doyen, whose financial excesses were mercilessly exposed by that staple of soap opera fiction, a betrayed wife.

This book traces the history of financial scandals in the United States from the dawn of the republic to modern times, with a focus on three periods—the Gilded Age of the late nineteenth century, the Roaring Twenties, and, of course, the closing days of the twentieth century. The implosion of Enron at the close of the century ushered in an intense period of navel-gazing among the habitués of Wall Street—but it is important to understand that financial scandals are a constant factor, rather than an exception, in American history. As *New York Times* reporter Jack Hitt observed in 2004: "…once the scandal begins, there's a Kabuki-like quality to the drama. Every person enveloped by the scandal seems to assume an almost ritualized role. In fact, certain characters appear repeatedly: the fallen giant, the whistle-blower, the dogged journalist, the arrogant lieutenants, the little people left twisting in the wind."[2] What was true in 2004 was certainly true in 1792 and during the second half of the nineteenth century.

U.S. economic history is underwritten by the sometimes volatile mix of industrial and technological advances that paved the way for investment opportunities and financial innovations, which eventually shifted into destabilizing speculative booms. In this sense, there has been a certain Schumpeter-like creative chaos in the American capitalist spirit. While this process has incorporated a series of alarming and intense financial scandals that have left a shadow over Wall Street, much good has come from it. The spectacular success of the U.S. economy in its first two centuries can only be explained by the important role played by a vibrant and ever-growing capital market. Despite the gamblers, robber barons, and conmen, so easily depicted as representing all of Wall Street as a pool of sleaze, U.S. financial markets have provided crucial support for the world's largest economy. Clearly, Wall Street must have done something right, some of the time. In a sense, Wall Street has gained its legitimacy from delivering the goods in an efficient and innovative fashion.[3]

Consequently, this history is in no way an indictment of the many great and honest people who have populated the pages of American financial history. It is still true that the vast majority of Americans who have amassed fortunes over the past two centuries have done so the old-fashioned way: They earned it. Nonetheless, a small but significant minority have taken great joy in pilfering Wall Street, eroding public confidence, and gaining political influence. And this has real significance, considering the weight of the stock market on the U.S. economy by the late twentieth century. As veteran market watcher Roger Lowenstein aptly notes: "By the late 1990s, America had become more sensitive to markets, more *ruled* by markets, than any other country on earth."[4] This only underscores the importance of understanding the dark side of U.S. financial culture as it evolved through the various stages of the country's economic history.

The evolution of U.S. financial markets has been a Darwinian process. For all of the sleazier elements and scandals, there has been a very strong tradition of innovation. The potential for great rewards continues to provide a powerful incentive to assume great risks—including a willingness to transgress accepted rules and regulations. Along these lines, important lessons have been learned, new practices adopted, and a balance has been struck (at least for a while) between the competing forces of regulation, order, and creative chaos. And in some cases, those vilified as conmen and robber barons have eventually emerged as important innovators, individuals who have made a difference in revolutionizing American finance.

What, then, is a scandal? Perhaps it is defined by the eyes of the beholder—I know it when I see it, as the U.S. Supreme Court famously explained with regard to pornography.[5] But most observers could probably agree on a simple definition: A scandal is an act or sequence of events that is publicly perceived as shameful or disgraceful. A *financial* scandal occurs when financial players—brokers, private investors, banks, partnerships, or companies—become involved in something that is shameful or disgraceful, which entails a breach of the rules and regulations that define what is accepted as proper and ethical behavior by the larger community.

This also implies an erosion of trust in the financial system by a large number of participants. Financial markets work because most participants *trust* that the system works. Savers would shun banks if they could not trust them; investors would shun the New York Stock Exchange if they lost confidence in its ability to function as a level playing field. Without this confidence, markets, be they financial or otherwise, become dysfunctional.

One of the great strengths of American capitalism is that the system—that broad network of interconnected capital markets, investors, and companies—is widely perceived as fair. But what is "fair" in this context? Does it refer only to an untainted and rule-based system of regulation and justice? Or is it more broadly based, inferring that contracts are upheld, big and small investors enjoy equal rules and access to the market, and regulatory authorities function effectively as referees rather than interested participants? The track of American history that follows in these pages reflects the struggle over how fair Wall Street really is: What is myth, and what is reality.

Fundamental Themes

As the following section will reveal, four fundamental threads will weave through every story that this book tells. For all their differences, over a time and space continuum from Orange County, California in the 1990s to New York City in the 1790s, the extent of the commonalities underlying all of these scandals is truly remarkable. William Duer was the spiritual ancestor of Dennis Kozlowski; Credit Mobilier the forerunner of Drexel. The more things change, the more they stay the same.

1. You Gotta Have Friends

Friends in the right places feature prominently in every unsavory chapter of American financial history. Influence-peddling, government-business cronyism, and worse, play a central role in every scandal that we examine—not surprising when you consider how much it costs to run for office in the United States, and how much money the great financiers have to throw around. From the 1790s, when William Duer capitalized on his connections to Alexander Hamilton, through the 1990s when Enron chief Kenneth Lay enlisted President Bill Clinton to help Enron collect past-due accounts in India, politically savvy business honchos have fed from the government trough.

Political support for the corporate heavy-hitters runs the gamut from benign neglect to outright corruption. Government regulators generally play an especially interesting role in helping to lay the groundwork for financial scandals. Observers often wonder why scandals occur so regularly in the most transparent, best-regulated markets in the world. Wall Street, after all, is not Bangalore, or even Buenos Aires. Innocent investors are supposed to be protected by a sophisticated net of laws, regulations, and impartial referees who ensure that the system is fair. So why do things go wrong on such a regular basis? Why weren't widows and orphans protected from the machinations of Jay Gould or Ken Lay?

The impartial referees are human, of course, and can make mistakes. Many scandals do involve complex, innovative financial transactions that are not easily understood by supervisors or regulators (think derivatives), and wrongdoers can easily exploit this complexity. But more than that, the regulators too often become actual enablers of scandal, with their contributions ranging from willful blindness to neglect, and, in a few cases, actual complicity. Politicians, for their part, stand complacently on the sidelines, protecting and even cheering on their business buddies until everything comes crashing down and the pols run for the exits, clamoring for more regulation and jail terms for the fiends. A few unlucky souls actually wind up in jail, many of the politicians get reelected, and the cycle begins all over again.

2. The Swing of the Pendulum

Which brings us to our second theme: the cyclicality of financial scandals. For every action, there is a reaction, and for every era of financial scandal there is a new round of regulation and supervision as government seeks to reform the corrupt financial sector. The presidency of Franklin Delano Roosevelt, for example, was left to clean up from the excesses of the 1920s bull market that came to an abrupt end in 1929 on Black Friday. During the 1920s rules and regulations had been loosened, and prudent investment practices were quietly pushed to the sidelines. In response to all the scams and schemes, from Charles Mitchell's Cuban sugar bonds to Teapot Dome, came the Securities Exchange Act of 1934 (creating the U.S. Securities and Exchange Commission to oversee corporate governance in publicly traded companies) and the Glass-Steagall Act of 1933 (dividing commercial and investment banking operations). FDR summed up the mood of the times in his second inaugural address on January 20, 1937: "Old truths have been relearned; untruths have been unlearned. We have always known that heedless self-interest was bad morals; we know now that it is bad economics. Out of the collapse of a prosperity whose builders boasted their practicality has come the conviction that in the long run economic morality pays."

But history repeats itself. The 1980s and 1990s were, once again, an era of deregulation, new technological marvels, and financial innovations, setting the stage for another long bull market on Wall Street. After the bull market came to an abrupt end, punctured by revelations of wrongdoing entangling virtually every major financial institution, public trust in Wall Street was seriously undermined and politicians quickly found a reason to pound the table in moral indignation. Congress scrambled to re-regulate, and a few scapegoats (like domestic maven Martha Stewart) ended up on the wrong side of guilty verdicts. For every period of scandal, the answer is usually more regulation—at least in the twentieth century and beyond. This includes not just the government, but also self-regulation on the part of professional organizations like the National Association of Securities Dealers or the New York Stock Exchange.

The fact is that scandals beget regulation, which beget a backlash against regulation as times get better, which begets looser regulations, which beget more scandals. The cyclical flow seems inevitable, especially since it is closely tied to the business cycle. Boom times create a foundation for financial scandals, which unravel quickly when the business cycle declines—creating the foundation for even steeper recession. As long as we have booms and financial innovations, it seems, we will have scandals.

Especially when a fickle media is willing handmaiden to each swing of the pendulum. Most of our favorite wrongdoers are initially lionized by the press, which breathlessly records their every exploit and enthusiastically applauds their daring innovations and brilliant new ideas. (Michael Milken, for example, was lauded as the greatest American financier since J. P. Morgan; Enron's Ken Lay was picked for the vice president's elite commission tasked with rewriting U.S. energy policy.) Then the worm turns, and the press piles on, vilifying the very people and practices they had cheered on in the very recent past. The uncritical, unquestioning tendency of the press to follow, rather than lead; to parrot, rather than report; to swallow inanities rather than investigate, deepens and exaggerates each swing of the pendulum.

3. Hubris

Media reports on the heroes and villains of the financial world are especially appealing, since larger-than-life personality types tend to emerge. Financial scandals—like financial innovations—invariably revolve around people who are willing to test the boundaries of what is accepted behavior in the market—the guys who continually push the edge of the envelope. While most market players are careful to avoid crossing the line, others are willing to go beyond what is perceived as acceptable. Some of these individuals go on to redefine the "acceptable" and are regarded as important innovators, like Michael Milken, but most are just remembered as crooks.

They not only work hard, they play hard too. Every chapter in American financial scandals has a bacchanalian theme as well—wild parties, willing women, and orgiastic excesses as men with gargantuan appetites turn their money and attention to play (yes, they are almost all men until the very end of the twentieth century; no doubt women will take their rightful place too among the crooks of American finance as they move to the top ranks of the business world). Dennis Kozlowski threw a birthday party for his wife on the island of Sardinia that cost $2.1 million and featured a custom-made statue spouting vodka from its private parts. Michael Milken's Predators' Balls provided girls, girls, and more girls for its lucky attendees. And remember the colossal Newport "cottages" of the Gilded Age?

The appetite for partying among these men was only exceeded by their appetite for success. In examining the track record of those at the core of major financial scandals, a broad profile emerges of energetic, creative, ruthless, and highly aggressive, even hubristic, individuals. The very nature of high finance helps foster a business culture of creative aggressiveness. This is frustrating for those on the other side—the reformers and regulators—leading one financial journalist to comment in 2004: "Some even argue that attempts at reform are futile in a business where aggressively courting risk can pay out such rich rewards."[6]

4. The Magic of the Markets

Finally, financial scandals are always enabled by a fervent faith in the magic of free markets. President Ronald Reagan, for example, swept into office promising to get government off our backs so the markets could function most efficiently, and the delighted financial markets heeded his call. Deregulation was in, big government was out, and Ivan Boesky assured us that greed is good (at least he is credited with saying so). Reagan, like many others before and after him, was a true believer in the power of the markets—as are the authors of this book. But the problem is, Reagan et al. (including the editorial page of the *Wall Street Journal*) also believed that the no-free-lunch rule had been repealed. Lowering taxes was a magic bullet: He could goose the economy and ultimately earn higher government tax revenues without any pain. High rewards no longer required high risks—the magic of the market would take care of everything.

Unfortunately for Reagan and everyone else, the laws of free markets could not be swept away by wishful thinking or fervent faith. Deregulation is no more a magic bullet than tax cuts; in fact, deregulation without proper oversight is silly and dangerous (just look at post-1991 Russia to see the results). Even more fundamentally, Reagan failed to appreciate that free markets operate perfectly *only under certain, impossible assumptions* (freedom from all regulations, perfect information flows, perfectly rational actors, and so on). When these assumptions fail—as they inevitably do in the real world—blind faith in free markets must be tempered by careful tending and nurturing.

Excessive profits are a good example. When Joseph Jett, a trader at Kidder Peabody, earned fantastically high profits in the early 1990s by trading no-risk government instruments, his supervisors cheered him on rather than wondering whether this was, literally, too good to be true. Nick Leeson brought down the venerable Barings Bank a few years later in almost exactly the same way—showing impossibly huge (paper) profits on low-risk trading operations. Did supervisors and regulators assume that the risk/return tradeoff had been abolished? Or just temporarily suspended?

So blind faith in the magic of the markets—coupled with an imperfect understanding of how markets (or various financial products) actually work—turns out to be a dangerous combination, laying the groundwork for scandal upon scandal. In fact, markets are not magic; they cannot create massive rewards without massive risks, and big wins come at the expense of big losers.

Outline of the Book

This book explores those losses and many more, dating back to the earliest days of the American Republic. The first chapter tells the story of William Duer, one of the young Republic's most prominent figures, a signer of the Articles of Confederation and a noted patriot. He was also the father of the first major financial scandal in the United States, which led to the Panic of 1792. Following the chapter on Duer, the focus shifts to the Gilded Age—those years of tremendous economic transformation in the United States and the ensuing manias on Wall Street, which included the influence-peddling Credit Mobilier scandal, the seedy side of trading in railway stocks, efforts to corner the gold market, and the Panic of 1873, which left the United States mired in a lengthy depression.

The book then shifts to the 1920s, which encompassed the Teapot Dome scandal (involving both Washington and Wall Street), and the adventures of Samuel Insull, who created an empire of public utility holding companies across thirty states that suffered a spectacular crash in the Great Depression. Financial innovation, technological advances, hubris, and greed all played their part in these American dramas. We do not cover the numerous other scandals leading up to the stock market collapse in 1929 as this is well-tread material by many other works and does not fit as easily our view of "scandal."

We then leapfrog forward to the intertwined scandals of the 1980s: insider trading, savings and loan collapses, and junk bonds. We end with an in-depth examination of the many scandals that ended the boom of the 1990s with a bang, ushering in a new period of disillusionment and recrimination. The 1990s were a period of high-flying financial capitalism and rock star-like CEOs, who built palatial mansions while riding the crest of a wave of technological innovation and globalization. Hand in hand with financial liberalization was strong economic growth that brought a major upsurge in national wealth. Sadly, much of that wealth was constructed on weak soil, for the late 1990s also marked the ultimate victory of perception over reality in the financial world. (Or, in b-school jargon, rosy forecasts about future profits were more important than the long-term viability of the business model, the quality of management, and the ability to actually generate revenue.) The animal spirits of the bull market were difficult to resist, as the stock market became a national pastime.

After the tech and stock market bubbles burst, and the world had struggled through the shock of 9/11, many Americans were left looking for answers to painful questions regarding the loss of their personal wealth. The hard times that followed were marked by a surge in unemployment, a polarization in the nation's politics between the haves and have-nots, and the threatened shrinkage of the middle class. The crass display of inflated salaries and compensation by many corporate leaders and ensuing scandals at Enron, Adelphia, Tyco, WorldCom and others rubbed salt in the wounds of deflated retirement plans and worries about losing one's job to a computer or, worse, to an engineer in Bangalore. With all that came deep-rooted concerns that middle-class America was being diminished by the excessive greed of a few. And that is when the pendulum swung back in the other direction—with the attempted re-regulation of Wall Street, a bringing to justice of the financial scandal-makers, and a quest for other means of wealth.

We conclude by briefly examining the career of New York Attorney General Eliot Spitzer, the major crusading figure to emerge in the aftermath of the market crash in the early 2000s. Spitzer captures much of the public's indignation at the high jinks of America's financial big shots and has campaigned against the perceived wrongs done to the common man. In many regards, the rise of Spitzer reflects the attempted re-regulation of financial markets, following the deregulation and liberalization of financial markets that marked the Reagan, Bush I, and Clinton years. Along with the passage of the Sarbanes-Oxley Act and the U.S. Patriot Act in the U.S. Congress, Spitzer and other state attorney generals sought to give regulation the bite it once had, broadcasting to any potential transgressors that there is a price to pay for violating the letter and spirit of the law. All the same, only one thing is certain: no matter how many supervisors are hired and regulations enacted, the groundwork for the next round of financial scandals is in motion. Problems at Bayou Management and Refco in 2005 indicated that mischief can still be made—even in a world of enhanced supervision.

While we have worked to define what the book is about, we should also clarify what it is not. *Separating Fools from Their Money* is not an economics text, nor is it a finance textbook. It is meant to be a wide-ranging financial history, incorporating elements of history, finance, political science, and economics. It is also not an old-style financial history that concentrates mainly on the negatives and ignores the positives. Not every U.S. financial leader can be described as a robber baron; moreover, without many of those colorful characters, Wall Street and U.S. capital markets would not be the success story that they are. Above all else, it is meant to be informative as well as entertaining, putting the most recent round of financial scandals into a historical context that is accessible to both MBAs and non-MBAs alike.

Notes

1.   Quoted from the New York *Herald*, January 18, 1871, from John Steele Gordon, *The Scarlet Woman of Wall Street* (New York: Weidenfeld & Nicoloson, 1988), p. 302.
2.   Jack Hitt, "American Kabuki: The Ritual of Scandal," *New York Times*, July 18, 2004, Week in Review, p. 1.
3.   Journalist John Kay made a very similar point in examining the source of legitimacy for business leaders. As he stated: "The case for capitalism is not a moral one derived from abstract notions of freedom of contract but a pragmatic argument rooted in the success of the system in promoting efficiency and innovation. Modern business and the people who lead it achieve authority through, and only through, their success. The legitimacy of their authority is achieved—literally—by delivering the goods." John Kay, "Business Leaders Have No Natural Authority," *Financial Times*, April 5, 2005, p. 17.
4.   Roger Lowenstein, *Origins of the Crash: The Great Bubble and Its Undoing* (New York: Penguin Books, 2004), p. 3.

5.   *Jacobellis v. Ohio*, 378 U.S. 184, 197 (1964).
6.   Patrick McGeehan, "Masters of the Universe, Leashed (for Now)," *New York Times*, July 18, 2004, p. WK 3.

2

Wall Street Loses Its Innocence:
William Duer and the Panic of 1792

The mob gathered outside the prison on the island of Manhattan. They were in a surly mood. Having weathered the Revolutionary War, Manhattan was weathering another storm—the Panic of 1792. The mob consisted of angry New Yorkers who had lost money in the recent stock market collapse. There were also merchants, their commerce now strangled by a lack of credit. Rounding out the crowd of largely men were the usual ruffians, those with little to do who were attracted to any public disturbance as an opportunity for fun. The man who attracted the mob—William Duer—no doubt shuddered at the call of his name. A slight man with sharp features and a receding hairline, he had been placed in the city prison on March 23, decidedly bewildered by his fall from grace. It was now early April and people were still less than forgiving. Indeed, Duer had already received at least one challenge to settle the matter of honor with a brace of pistols (Duer had quietly paid the man.) Fortunately, it was a rainy April evening and the authorities were able to persuade the mob to disperse. As the sound of the mob faded, Duer must have sat and wondered how he had come to this situation.

William Duer, who became the father of the first major financial scandal to rock the United States, was an unlikely candidate for this dubious distinction. Duer enjoyed privilege and social position from his birth, and had made an impressive place for himself in the young American Republic. Duer's home in New York City had a reputation for fine wine, good food, and interesting conversation; George Washington gave away the bride at Duer's wedding.

And yet, Duer was to spend much of his final year of life in debtors' prison, demonized by Americans who blamed him for the Panic of 1792. Hundreds of New Yorkers marched to his prison chanting, "We will have Mr. Duer, he has gotten our money." While Duer was not single-handedly responsible for the Panic, of course, his financial machinations were the spark that lit the flame, and he occupies a very special position in the annals of financial infamy.

Through Duer's experiences we find a United States that was overwhelmingly agrarian, groping to define its institutions and largely suspicious and ignorant of Wall Street—such as it was in the early 1790s. The Jeffersonian wing of American politics, with an echo to modern times, had little love for the seemingly arcane and speculative nature of stock markets. In contrast, the Hamiltonian wing of American politics liked the idea of the stock market, viewing it as essential in modernizing the country's financial infrastructure, helping the government in debt management, and attracting foreign investment. It is important to emphasize the word "investment" over that of "speculation," as the former suggested prudent behavior with the intention of long-term societal gain, as opposed to the latter being an exercise in gambling, solely for individual gain and possibly at the cost of the rest of society. To the Hamiltonian school of thinking, the market was oblivious to class, status, and inherited social position, a view that would transform American society away from its oligarchical, agrarian social order and into a more industrial society characterized by change, growth, prosperity, and national strength.[1] And so the battle lines were drawn over the evolution of the U.S. stock market, a story in which Duer would cast a long shadow.

Who Was William Duer?

Duer's story begins in 1747 in the green, leafy idyll of Devonshire, England. His father, John Duer, was a successful Caribbean planter with properties in Antigua, while his mother was the daughter of Sir Frederick Frye, an accomplished naval commander in the West Indies. The union produced three boys—an heir, a spare, and the unlucky third son, William.

The country into which William was born was undergoing considerable change. London had overtaken Amsterdam as the world's financial center, the industrial revolution was transforming the economy, and the British Empire was well on its way to becoming the dominant global power. But none of this played much part in Duer's early years. Young William attended Eton, the school of well-to-do young Englishmen, many of whom were to march from its halls of learning into the far-flung world of the British Empire. As was typical for a young man of the privileged classes, William grew up in a narrow world of connections and wealth. Following Eton in 1762, family connections were tapped to get William an appointment as aide-de-camp to the august Lord Clive, who was on his way to India as governor of Bengal (he was also to go down in history as one of the major architects for the British conquest of the subcontinent). Although Duer went to India, his tenure at Clive's side was not lengthy. The young man suffered severely from the climate and Clive soon sent him back to England, where he stayed for the next five years until his father's death.

As the third son, William's inheritance was not substantial. So, like countless other youngest sons, he was soon packed off to the colonies—in this case, Antigua—to help one of his brothers manage the family planta-tion. William arrived in the Caribbean as an experienced traveler. That was a good thing, considering the fluid nature of Caribbean society, the harsh nature of the plantation system, and the constant threat of violence from slave rebellions or war with other European powers. The British had come to the Caribbean during the late sixteenth century, eventually cementing their control over a number of islands in the region, including Antigua. By the time that Duer arrived in the 1760s, the island was well established as a British sugar colony.

The sophisticated young Duer probably found life on a sugar island limiting. But the limitations of the plantation system, ironically, would prove to be his salvation. With its tremendous concentration on a single crop, Antigua always needed to import items ranging from clothing to tools. While Europe's ports fit some of those needs, the American colo-nies were far closer. Consequently, when Duer was given the opportunity to travel to New York and arrange for a regular and constant supply of lumber for the plantations in Antigua, he must have jumped at it.

Duer Meets His Destiny: New York

Duer visited New York for the first time in 1768. We can only imagine his delight and fascination when he disembarked at this bustling, thriving port, so different from the sleepy plantation life of Antigua. Located at the mouth of the Hudson River and connected to the surrounding colo-nies by a slowly improving system of roads, New York was beginning a trajectory that would allow it within a few decades to bypass Boston and Philadelphia. (Indeed, as early as the 1720s New York had already become a multicultural and multiracial community strongly imbued with an entrepreneurial spirit—some things never change.) It must have been ideal for an ambitious young man out to make his fortune.

Duer found colonial American society an easy place to access. As a member of the transatlantic upper class, he was readily accepted in colonial society, which had a well-defined oligarchy, much of it tied to the land. As historian Forrest McDonald commented of early American society: "Status derived not from the marketplace, where deeds and goods and virtues could be impartially valued, but from birthright. More precisely, status rested upon personal relations which rested upon family connections which in turn rested upon ownership of the land."[2] Along these lines, Duer's family ties stood him in good stead, as did his acquaintance with General Philip John Schuyler, who was one of the movers and shakers in colonial New York society. Schuyler had married well (marrying Catherine Van Rensselaer, a descendent of one of the leading Dutch settler families), climbed the ranks of the colonial military, and was established in local politics. And for whatever reason, he took a liking to Duer, opening doors to the young Englishman.

...And Wall Street

Duer began his New York financial career in the late 1760s in unremarkable fashion, by purchasing a large tract of land at Fort Miller and thus establishing himself in the local timber business. The land was on the upper Hudson and had abundant woodlands and waterfalls, which allowed him to construct sawmills. With this commercial/industrial base and the Schuyler connection, Duer was soon part of the community. He was quickly appointed colonel of the local militia, judge of the county courts, member of the New York provincial congress, and member of the Committee of Safety. It is doubtful that he gave returning to Antigua any serious consideration.

While Duer did maintain his ties to England (in 1773 he went to London and negotiated a contract to supply the Royal Navy with timber for its ships), he sided with the American colonies in 1776. Throughout the Revolutionary War, he actively served in a number of posts, including as a delegate to the Continental Congress. He also served as deputy adjutant general for the New York militia, securing stores for the troops. Like many others involved in such commerce, he was not above mixing his own business with that of the government's, something that he would repeat more than once in his career.

The Wall Street that emerged from the war was young and vibrant, with a limited but fast-growing menu of activities. Wall Street as a market was born under the Dutch and matured under the British, but activity was largely limited to the trading of wheat, tobacco, cotton, sugar, and sometimes slaves. By the end of the Revolutionary War, New York's "exchange" was still far less sophisticated than the older and more established bourses in Amsterdam and London. (In fact, New York's stock exchange had not emerged as the dominant exchange, considering Philadelphia's stock market.) In many regards it was one of the emerging markets of the time—not dissimilar to India or China in the latter part of the twentieth century—offering high reward to the brave investor, alongside high risk.

Wall Street was also the domain of a small, somewhat intimate group of players, many of them well respected members of New York and American society. Many of Wall Street's leading lights had served in the Revolutionary Army or had been involved in the creation of the Republic's political institutions. In a world without Bloomberg, email, or cell phones, information—and rumors—traveled by word of mouth or letter and were judged on the strength of a person's reputation. The coffeehouse or tavern often served as a melting-pot of market rumblings, where clever individuals were apt to raise or lower their voices, depending on what they wanted to convey and to whom. Yet, for all its inadequacies, Wall Street played an important role in helping to finance the early Republic.

And by the close of the war, Duer was well placed on the Street. Perhaps most important, his Revolutionary War service elevated Duer into the top echelons of the political class in the emerging Republic. Through his multiple roles as supply master and prominent New York politician, he was soon in close contact with George Washington, Alexander Hamilton, and others—and he demonstrated a fortunate knack for siding with the winners. During the ill-fated Conway Cabal, an attempt to sack Washington as commander-in-chief and replace him with General Horatio Gates, Duer demonstrated his loyalty to the general, playing a role in foiling the conspiracy. Shortly after the end of the war, Duer backed the federal position taken by Hamilton, James Madison, and John Jay, the authors of *The Federalist Papers*. Duer was also secretary of the Board of the Treasury (the forerunner of the U.S. Treasury Department) from 1786 to 1789, a position that gave him a well-informed insider's view of the nation's financial situation.

Reflecting his close connections to the new country's movers and shakers, as well as his proven ability as a contractor, Duer was one of the elite—valued by the new government and well on his way to the top. Duer's position was not hurt by the fact that the American government had decided to locate for a brief period in New York City. The city had recovered nicely from the dreary years of the British occupation and the outline of new buildings and streets was moving northwards, gradually overcoming the pastures and woodlands. Within this context, Wall Street assumed a growing importance as one of the nation's two exchanges. (The other, the Philadelphia Stock Exchange, was founded in 1790.)

What made Wall Street doubly important was the fact that Alexander Hamilton, the new secretary of the Treasury, resided at the corner of Wall and Water Streets in a house close to the Coffee House Slip on the East River. Not far from this was the City Hall, the temporary core of the U.S. government. Although the federal government left for Philadelphia in the summer of 1790, New York was by then well-established as a financial hub of growing significance. New York clearly had an advantage in that ships from Europe usually came to its harbor first, hence giving its speculators a slight advantage in terms of "hot" information that could help them beat the markets.

By 1790 Duer was, in the words of business historian Robert Sobel, "one of the social and economic arbiters of American society."[3] As Sobel further observed: "It was Duer who found the house that Washington occupied in New York, and he also arranged terms for its lease. It was Duer who helped organize the ill-fated but speculative Scioto Company, which planned massive speculations in land, international trade, currency, stocks and whatever else seemed to offer a rich return. More than any other American, save Robert Morris, Duer was known in European banking circles as a master of finance."[4] Duer was well-regarded by his fellow Americans, too. Future President John Adams described him as "…a very fine fellow, a man of sense, spirit and activity…exceeded by no man in his zeal."[5]

When Duer married Catherine Sterling (known as Kitty) in 1779, it was George Washington who gave the bride away. And Duer had chosen wisely: Kitty was of good family, being the second daughter of General William Alexander, the claimant of the Scottish earldom of Sterling. Kitty was also related to the Schuylers, Livingstons, and De Peysters—all pillars of upper class New York society.

Speculation both Good and Bad

While Duer was generally liked by the New York upper class and well-connected in the American government, some important players, such as Thomas Jefferson, did not hold him in the same high regard. The crux of the issue was that Duer was a speculator.

There was nothing wrong with being a speculator per se; what mattered was what kind of speculator he was. At the time there was not a lot to invest in, as the new country lacked "blue chip" companies and banks. Instead, the wealthy speculated in land, bills of trade, and joint stock companies. These areas of speculation were regarded as legitimate, since they were actually investments that allowed the community as a whole to augment its wealth. Along these lines, many of the leading Americans of the time, including Washington, Jefferson, and Madison, were involved in speculative land companies.[6] This was the acceptable face of speculation.

What was not acceptable was speculation in securities. As Jefferson wrote to Washington in 1792: "All the capital employed in paper specu-lation is barren and useless, producing, like that on a gambling table, no accession to itself, and is withdrawn from commerce and agricul-ture where it would have produced addition to the common mass... It nourishes in our citizens habits of vice and idleness instead of industry and morality... It has furnished effectual means of corrupting such a portion of the legislature as turns the balance between the honest voters whichever way it is directed."[7] Jefferson also likened securities specula-tion to a philosopher's stone that people believed would turn everything into gold. In many regards, Jefferson's views would presage those in the 1980s and early 2000s who viewed the Leveraged Buy Out (LBO) craze as the manipulation of paper over productive assets to the benefit of a handful, and at the cost of everyone else.

There was also another dimension of Duer's personality that was to have an impact on his involvement in America's first financial scandal. Although he was very ambitious and was filled with energy, he was also apt to take on too many challenges, leaving himself stretched thin, both financially and mentally. Despite his many efforts to strike it rich, his financial fortune was based on the shakiest of foundations. He was constantly launching schemes to make money, including providing war materials to both sides (or so he was charged) during the Revolution and currency speculation at the end of that conflict. Even in those cases where he might have had a good business idea, he was often unable to follow through with implementation. One of his biographers underscored Duer's "tendency...to spread himself thin, taking on more than he could possibly handle."[8] This might, in part, explain the curious observation of Gouverneur Morris, the influential one-legged New York politician and close friend of Washington, who noted of Duer: "He is volatile. He is communicative, unstable."[9]

Looking for the Philosopher's Stone

Duer was active in all forms of speculation—before the war, during the war, and after the war. Indeed, in the immediate postwar environment

markets he actively traded in Continental currency, government obligations, and bonds of local companies and banks. Needless to say, all of
this was very high risk (think Russian government bonds in 1996-98).
The new nation had yet to prove itself, prospects for business failures
were significant, and recourse to the law was relatively nonexistent. At
the same time, if the right gamble was made, the rewards could be ample.
This appears to have been the view of many Dutch bankers, who were
willing to take the risk and thus helped to finance much of the Revolutionary government's early debt.[10]

Duer was quick to jump in. Following the end of the war, Duer established his own firm with Daniel Parker, called Parker & Duer, which
soon became a funnel for foreign (mainly French and Dutch) investors
who were looking to invest in American securities. It seemed like a match
made in heaven: The Europeans had capital, and Parker & Duer had
Duer, who was not only a rising force in American financial circles, but
also a potential member of the new government (which meant possible
access to insider information). Since there were no rules against insider
trading, a well-placed leak could make well-connected people a fortune.
Consequently, when Duer accepted the post of assistant secretary of the
Treasury under his old friend Hamilton in 1789, there was a sense of
excitement among Parker & Duer's European associates as well as those
speculators in New York who knew him.

To this day, Duer remains one of the perplexing historical questions
surrounding Hamilton. Regarded as a sound judge of men, Hamilton
decidedly did not fully comprehend the depth of his friend's speculative
personality. Hamilton was above reproach in not mixing his personal
business and that of the government's. Duer was—well—quite different.
Yet, Hamilton hired Duer, no doubt taking into consideration his friend's
position as secretary to the Board of Treasury since 1786, which made
him one of the best-informed people in U.S. finance. And in many ways
they were compatible: Duer agreed with Hamilton, for instance, on the
need for a stronger federal government and on funding the public debt.
In addition, the two men had married cousins and both had spent time
in the Caribbean, Hamilton being born in the British colony of Nevis in
1757. All the same, Duer had a major flaw in that he "suffered a severe
case of moral myopia and always found rather blurry the line between
public service and private gain."[11] Prior to accepting Hamilton's offer
at the Treasury, for example, Duer had amassed a sizeable portfolio of
government securities, which he still maintained after taking his new
position. Moreover, Duer was not above gossiping about government

finances. This must have been most perplexing for Hamilton, who sought to prohibit such activities.

The Scioto Scheme

While Duer generally fulfilled his obligations during his brief tenure at the U.S. Treasury (six months), he did not stop his speculative activities. Indeed, he had little compunction in mingling his business with that of the government's, something that he had done during the Revolutionary War. One of the schemes that followed Duer into office was the Scioto Company. At the end of the war in 1783, the new nation turned its attention to settling the Ohio River Valley. Quite reasonably, the United States feared that if it did not move quickly enough, it would soon find itself boxed into the original thirteen colonies by the European powers, in particular the British (who were still in Canada).[12] The new government was not exactly well-endowed with capital to undertake such a venture. Consequently, it was willing to sell off the land rights to private groups that would undertake the venture.

In 1786 the Ohio Company of Associates was established in Boston for the purpose of purchasing and settling lands in the Ohio River Valley. One of the directors, Dr. Manasseh Cutler, went to New York to negotiate the purchase of the land. There he was introduced to Duer, who indicated that he had access to European investors who might be interested in such a venture. Duer and a group of investors, soon to be called the Scioto Company, convinced the U.S. government that it could also find settlers for the American public lands between the Scioto and Ohio rivers.

As Duer assumed his position at the U.S. Treasury in New York, the Scioto Company was officially organized in 1789 in Paris as the Compagnie du Scioto by Joel Barlow, the agent for Duer and his associates (six Frenchmen and one lone Englishman, the improbably named William Playfair). Duer and others, such as Cutler who wrote in 1789 an exaggerated pamphlet describing the Ohio lands as near-paradise, never actually intended to organize or fund a colony. Rather, they concocted a complicated scheme in which they would:

- buy cheap American securities held by European banks and investors, and
- use them to buy Scioto land to resell to French investors, who
- would be left to handle the "details" of conveying settlers across the Atlantic and to Ohio.

As historian William Howard Adams noted: "It was another one of those smoke and mirrors schemes of early capitalism that suffered from the public's lack of a clear understanding of what it was all about beyond the usual dreams of large profits."[13]

The problem in this scheme was that Barlow exceeded his mandate and sold small plots at retail, largely through false advertising. (Some of the unlucky purchasers were Royalists wishing to escape from France, then in the early stages of what was to become the blood-soaked French Revolution.) Although Barlow was able to sign up around 400 proprietors, he mismanaged the company so badly that it went bankrupt.

Despite Barlow's inept bungling, a group of 500 remarkably ill-suited French settlers ended up on the banks of the Ohio River in 1790—though their legal claim to the land was shaky, owing to the dishonest fashion in which the deeds were written.[14] As for the French settlers, the majority returned to the east. A small core group, however, remained and helped found the Ohio town of Gallipolis, which still proudly acknowledges their contribution. Complicating matters, Duer and his associates never received any funds back from Barlow. Yet, the U.S. government clearly expected the Scioto Company to pay up. Instead, the company went bankrupt in 1790, by which time Duer had left the Treasury and was looking for another philosopher's stone—this time in the stock market.

The Bull Market of 1791

The bull market of 1791 sprang from a number of changes engineered by the nation's first Treasury secretary, Alexander Hamilton. Hamilton was deeply concerned about the need to develop a more mature financial system for the young country. In 1781, a decade earlier, he wrote: "Our whole system is in disorder, our currency depreciated until, in many places, it will hardly (circulate). Public credit is at its lowest ebb, our army deficient in numbers and unprovided. The government in its present condition is unable to command the means to pay, clothe or feed their troops."[15] When independence was formally recognized in 1783, the new nation was $11 million in debt to foreigners ($4.4 million to France, $1.8 million to the Dutch government, $3.6 million to Dutch bankers, and $175,000 to the Spanish Treasury). Yet, there were no easy means to repay these debts.

Hamilton Sets the Stage

Hamilton's solution was to strengthen national finances through the creation of a national bank (i.e., a central bank as in the Netherlands,

Sweden, and England), a national debt (that was tradable), and a system of national taxation. None of this was going to be easy, considering the lengthy and acrimonious debate over what form the new government should take, how to achieve a balance of power between the federal and state governments, and political sensitivity over taxation. But Hamilton was persistent, and by 1790 the emerging political system was leaning towards a federal form of government. Consequently, the U.S. Congress was able (albeit after heated debates) to pass legislation that helped Hamilton create a more unified and modern financial system. In particular, the Funding Act of 1790 allowed the government to issue federal bonds in exchange for earlier issued debt (Confederation and Continental bonds). This allowed the government to consolidate its debt, lengthen its maturities, and broaden its means of finance.

Hamilton was not done. Despite fierce opposition to the creation of a national bank by Jefferson and others, the bank bill passed and the First Bank of the United States (BUS) was mandated in February 1791. The new institution was to be capitalized at $10 million (25,000 shares of $400 par value) and was to be located in Philadelphia. The government would own a fifth of the shares, with the rest being sold to the public. Hamilton financed the government's part of the deal by selling a bond issue overseas through the office of Hope & Co. of Amsterdam, with a smaller part coming from a loan from the Bank of North America (a private bank chartered in 1781).

Creation of the BUS, while well-intentioned, ultimately laid the groundwork for the Panic of 1792. Initially, the BUS imbued U.S. markets with a sense of heightened strength and stability, generating a higher degree of confidence among both local and European investors. In turn, this meant that the entire U.S. securities market now merited a second look from investors. Valuations were low; Hamilton's confidence building measures suddenly made them under-priced and attractive. With the advent of U.S. government bonds (and the consolidation of the national debt), as well as the stocks from BUS, funds flowed in and the market experienced a higher degree of liquidity.[16] As the BUS started selling its stock, foreign investors turned to the United States. Accordingly, Daniel Crommelin & Co. of Amsterdam sent over $1 million to its U.S. correspondent; Daniel Parker established sales outlets in London; and Theophile Cazenove, an ally of the French Claviere Group, came to America ready to trade.[17]

In addition, the market's momentum—like that of many future booms—was fueled by a new financial innovation. In this case, it was wager stock. Wager stock is created when speculators borrow stock from its owners, paying a fixed amount of money for the privilege and promising to return it within a set number of months.[18] The speculators would then sell the borrowed stock, using the proceeds to purchase other securities. When the due date came, the borrower would sell out his position and repurchase the borrowed stock in order to repay the original owner. If the price of the borrowed stock rose more slowly than that of the speculator's position in other securities, he made a profit; if not, he lost the difference. This could obviously be a dangerous business and required a speculator with remarkably good stock-picking ability.

The Hamilton measures, arrival of BUS stock, the growing use of wager stocks, and the inflow of funds from European investors added considerably to the volume traded in the market. Consequently, by July 1791, the U.S. securities market was enjoying a substantial uptick in business, with foreign money pushing both volume and prices to new heights. New York's traders (and speculators) were enjoying one of the country's first booms.

BUS or BUST?

The drama with the BUS percolated for several months. Hamilton initially intended to open the sale of the BUS stock on the first Monday in April 1791 in Philadelphia. The Treasury secretary, however, had not considered that the U.S. Congress would interfere. Within Congressional ranks, there was some concern that the new bank's owners would be too heavily concentrated in Philadelphia. Consequently, a supplementary act was passed in Congress to facilitate a wider distribution of shares. So Hamilton moved opening day for subscribers to July, and the initial payment was cut to $25, for which the subscribers would receive certificates or scrip, which entitled them to buy the stock subsequently at par. Hamilton also used the Treasury Department to facilitate additional subscriptions in Boston, New York, Baltimore, and Charleston.

With a great sense of expectation, BUS stock went on sale on July 4. By all accounts, the sale was a massive success, with a mob of investors swarming over the clerks. In less than an hour, BUS stock was oversubscribed; most of the buyers were non-Philadelphians, many of whom were observed heading back north to New York City in the sale's aftermath.

The BUS stock surge continued, as scrip purchased for $25 in July was selling for $325 by mid-August.[19] Watching from the Treasury, Hamilton was initially pleased with the turn of events. The inflow of foreign capital seemed to reflect overseas confidence in the young Republic, and the securities boom made the country appear confident and successful. The Treasury actually continued its buying of bonds. Considering the dark cloud that had hung over the nascent Republic's early financial picture, the transformation in 1791 into a success story was reassuring and satisfying. By early August, however, Hamilton had misgivings due to the growing mania over bank shares and anything else that could be traded. Indeed, the mania had spread to other securities, including the 6 percent government bonds, which had previously traded at 75 to 85 cents on the dollar and had now soared to 130 cents.

Duer: The "King of the Alley"

Needless to say, Duer was actively involved in the boom. Having left Hamilton's side in 1790, he played on his connections to his old boss, using this elegant and witty insider to maintain his ties to English and Dutch investors. Accordingly, Duer quickly emerged as one of the dominant forces in the market. One historian was to call him the "king of speculators, the man who called the tune. Should a stock dealer stand on good terms with Duer, his fortune was made; if not, he could count on eventual failure."[20] Less admiringly, Thomas Jefferson, watching with alarm from afar, called Duer "the King of the Alley."[21]

By late 1791, Duer took stock of his position. He was a major player in America's fledgling stock market. He also had his mills on the Hudson, commercial connections throughout Europe, and an organization for land speculation. Moreover, during the summer and fall of 1791 he received advances for an Army contract and had effectively relieved himself of most of the Scioto expenses.[22] Yet, he still lacked the necessary capital to satisfy all of his ambitions, which included the launching of a Pennsylvania turnpike, a Boston bridge company, and new banks in Providence, Boston, New Hampshire, and Albany. Money was tight and he needed more. So he concluded, apparently, that the best plan of attack was to either take control of a bank, or to corner the market in bank shares. Either approach required the same first steps: forming a group of speculators with the intention of buying up as many bank shares and other securities as possible.

At the time there was considerable debate about whether New York could support more than one bank. The Bank of New York was already in operation, but the BUS was seeking to open a branch in the city. The Bank of New York had been founded in 1784 by a group of New York merchants, including Alexander Hamilton, Alexander McDougall, and John Lamb, and its shareholders included wealthy and influential merchants, such as Rufus King, Isaac Roosevelt, and Nicolas Law. The problem was that for the BUS to open a branch in New York City it would need the support of the very same group of people.[23] Considering the situation, speculation about the state of banking in New York was rife.

The bank debate also had a political side. The BUS was a national bank, owned by men who shared Hamilton's desire for a strong federal government and national institutions. Yet, Hamilton was wary about allowing the BUS to open branches outside of Philadelphia, "fearing that rivalries between the national and local banks would politicize all banking, feed speculation and render the entire system unusable."[24] Despite Hamilton's concerns, local merchants in Boston, Providence, and Charleston were soon maneuvering to have their local banks absorbed by the BUS to become branches. This scheming by pro-federalists set off those on the other side who were loyal to local rather than national institutions, such as New York's Governor Clinton and his allies, the powerful Livingston clan. This meant that "scriptomania" (the selling of script, i.e., stock) had a strong political element to it (which would eventually have dire consequences for Duer).

But at the time, Duer had no uneasy inklings of his eventual fate. Quite the contrary: He observed these machinations in the banking industry and scented an opportunity. He formed a secret partnership with Alexander Macomb, a wealthy Irish land speculator, who he probably met during his brief tenure at the Treasury. Duer and Macomb got along well and soon the two were leading others into an investing cabal nicknamed the "Six Percent Club" because of a plan to monopolize 6 percent government bonds and other securities.[25] Other key players in the group were John Pintard, William Livingston, and Royal Flint, all well-known figures in New York society.

The group's plan was simple: Make large-scale secret purchases of government paper and bank stocks in order to manipulate the markets. Duer was already active in these markets, having bought over half a million dollars worth of such securities in the previous months. To keep the markets moving, the members of the group publicized the creation of a new bank with the initial capitalization of a million dollars. They then started a rumor that the "Million Bank" was considering a merger with both the Bank of New York and the BUS. As the rumor mills in the coffee houses, taverns, and dining rooms of the well-to-do picked up the tale, bank stocks soared. At some point, when the stock prices were deemed sufficiently high, the group around Duer and Macomb planned to sell its holdings, hopefully at the top of the market that they were manipulating.

Duer had his finger in other pies as well. He advised Macomb to purchase Bank of New York stock on the supposition that a branch bank, if established, would not last long, due to Treasury Secretary Hamilton's desire for a merger. Considering Duer's connections, Macomb believed that he had inside information on the banking scene and put his money down accordingly. But in fact, Duer had lied to his partner. Once Macomb had followed Duer's advice and bought the Bank of New York paper, Duer, who already held a considerable amount of the paper himself, was able to sell it at a higher price. Simply stated, Duer fed false information to Macomb so that Duer and others would win when Macomb's purchases sent the stock price sky-high. Duer was making a handsome profit. At the same time, Macomb and others within the Duer circle were plunging into debt in order to buy more shares.

The Million Bank sold shares in January 1792. Hungry investors, primed by rumors, moved in. Seeing the investor hunger for bank stocks, two other groups of speculators came into the market with two new banks. New York's stock market was in the grip of a mania. As one witness stated: "The merchant, the lawyer, the physician and the mechanic, appear to be equally striving to accumulate large fortunes through speculation."[26] (The comment could also be used to describe the Internet and technology stock boom that gripped Wall Street and the United States in the 1990s.)

The Boom Goes Bust

But by March 1792, Duer's luck ran out. A number of forces would now drag him down and, with him, the entire market and the local New York economy. First and foremost, Duer was hard-pressed financially. All of his schemes, including the double-dealing of Macomb and others in that group, required cash. According to his biographer, Robert J. Jones, Duer had just about exhausted all possible sources of credit by March 1792, borrowing heavily from friends and "as little as $500, from shopkeepers, widows, orphans, butchers, cartmen, gardeners, and market women at usurious rates of interest."[27] While this was fine in a market of upward moving share prices, it was a disaster when the market fell. As Duer was leading a bull raiding party into the market, Brockholst Livingston and others ran bear raiding parties into the stock market, betting that prices would fall. If the prices had remained high, Duer could have sold, made a profit, and repaid his debts. When prices began to slip, propelled by rumors that bank mergers were not going to happen, Duer lost money that he did not have. In a sense, he was losing other people's money. Although he was able to pay some of it back through his other enterprises, Duer was still critically short of funds.

The political dimension, centered around the Livingston family, also helped to bring Duer down. Although one of their family members (Walter) was with the Duer-Macomb group, another group of Livingstons had formed a bear raiding party set to manipulate the markets into a sudden price drop. These Livingstons were well-known opponents to Duer and Walter, having allied themselves instead with New York's Governor Clinton. As powerful short sellers in the market, Brockholst, John R., and Edward Livingston contracted to deliver most of the Bank of New York stock the Duer group had contracted to purchase. At the same time, the Livingstons pushed hard to keep alive the Million Bank proposal in order to keep the Bank of New York's stock price depressed. Governor Clinton, seeking reelection, obliged.

Word of Duer's financial difficulties spread quickly. The already nervous market rapidly transmitted the King of the Alley's distress throughout the taverns, offices, and other locations that formed the backbone of 1792's Wall Street. On March 8, the Bank of New York management, concerned about the growing number of loans (some to Duer and associates) that were being discounted by speculators, stopped all loans. Duer, seeing the risk of a snowball effect, scrambled about in a near-panic to salvage his credibility. He announced on March 9 that he had just discovered that his agents had borrowed money at usurious rates without his approval, and that he was halting payments until he could determine their true character.[28] The maneuver did not fool anyone. The King of the Alley was exposed—he was massively in debt, having gambled big and lost even bigger. The ripples soon spread across the entire stock market. The next day, twenty-five New York financiers went bust, including a number of well-known associates of Duer.[29]

What was to seal Duer's fate was unfinished business with the U.S. government. The Treasury had been pressing Duer for a number of years about several sets of accounts linked to war contracts and his service as secretary to the Board of the Treasury. Oliver Walcott, Jr., comptroller of the Treasury, was anxious to ensure that the government could collect its money before other creditors took everything. Consequently, the government notified the sinking financier of a $250,000 discrepancy in his accounts as assistant treasury secretary. Duer had no choice but to drop the rest of his securities into the market, only adding to the downward plunge. He also appealed to his old friend Hamilton "to use for once your influence to defer this [suit] until my arrival [in Philadelphia]… If a suit should be brought on the part of the public,—and in my present distressed circumstances—my ruin is complete."[30] Hamilton correctly refused to intervene in the government's proceedings against his old friend, though Duer's plight pained him. Within days, Duer's creditors had him arrested and thrown into debtors' prison.

Hamilton to the Rescue

The ensuing Panic of 1792 was devastating. As two historians of New York City noted: "New York appeared to have been struck by a disaster of staggering proportions. Duer alone owed more than $750,000. Judge Thomas Jones said that estimates of all losses ran as high as three million dollars—a huge sum, representing the savings of almost every person in the city, from the richest merchants to even the poorest woman and little shopkeepers."[31] Many leading merchants were ruined (having speculated or lent money to speculators), so trade slowed precipitously as buyers—the aforementioned merchants—lacked credit. The ripples spread to all those who were linked to New York's trade, such as the small artisans, workers, and farmers, who were faced with a sharp curtailment in business. While New Yorkers faced the unexpected snowball effect of a major financial crisis overflowing into the local economy, Duer was behind bars. However, the public was angry and demanded his blood. Indeed, on the night of April 18, a stone-throwing crowd of between three and five hundred persons descended on his jail, chanting angry epithets against Duer.

For Hamilton, the Duer-inspired Panic of 1792 was a disaster that threatened to overturn much of what he sought to create in terms of a sound and modern financial system. Hamilton believed that financial markets should be used prudently, not become a haven for crooks and speculators. The entire thrust of his financial program was to change the country's public creditors into a class of capitalists capable of lending to the government, hence providing stability and facilitating the production of tangible wealth. Certainly his reforms were not meant to enable foolish speculative binges that paralyzed the economy. The Treasury secretary fumed on March 2, 1792, "There should be a line of separation between honest men and knaves, between respectable shareholders and gamblers."[32] (At the time, he did not realize that his old friend William Duer was one of the leading knaves.) As Burrows and Wallace were to accurately note of Hamilton's statement: "Where, and how, to draw the line between respectable shareholders would remain a central dilemma of American capitalism for the next two centuries."[33]

Although Hamilton could not help Duer, he did act to end the crisis. In a very quiet, yet deliberate fashion he had the Treasury purchase large amounts of government securities. The government intervention had two results—it steadied prices, and it allowed the government to buy back debt at cheap prices. Hamilton's agent, William Seton, was given instructions to buy the bonds piecemeal at auctions held at the Merchant's Coffee House. For a market shell-shocked by Duer's double-dealing and implosion as well as the ripple effect of other investor failures, Hamilton's action indicated that there was a buyer—possibly the government, but a buyer nonetheless. Over a period of days, calm gradually returned to the market.

Aftermath

The Panic of 1792 left a strong impression on all involved. The country learned about the dangers of the stock market or, to be more precise, stock market manias. From the government's standpoint, the Panic of 1792 clearly demonstrated the risks inherent in a stock market. For Hamiltonians, however, it was important to draw a line between speculators/gamblers—bad—and investors—who were good. Hamilton, as a student of European bourses, clearly understood that the stock market could play a positive role in a country's economic development, especially if it was to move from an agrarian to an industrial economy. Yet, Hamilton was to leave government in 1795.

The Jeffersonians (Thomas Jefferson served as president from 1801-1809) moved to dismantle the system established by Hamilton, who himself died in 1804 in a tragic duel with Aaron Burr. While this ushered in a period of ongoing hostility to the development of a national banking system and central bank (evidenced by the government's decision to let the BUS charter lapse in 1811), it had a profound impact on the stock market. The Jeffersonians ultimately would leave the stock market alone, allowing Wall Street to emerge in a power vacuum. As historian John Steele Gordon noted: "For years to come, the Street would set its own rules, devise its own procedures. This made its financial market freer than any other in the world. But unregulated free markets are inherently unstable, likely to break down under stress."[34]

From Buttonwood to the NYSE

For market participants, the message of 1792 was clear: Clean up trading practices or risk greater volatility. A number of surviving brokers decided that self-regulation was the answer, so twenty-four brokers gathered on May 17, 1792 and signed what was to become known as the Buttonwood Agreement. Named after a popular buttonwood tree at

68 Wall Street, the agreement stipulated in writing that the assembled brokers would trade only with each other. In other words, brokers had to be mutually recognized.

This action did much to centralize the market and clarify the actors. The old practice of buying and selling securities in offices, coffee houses, and other locations in and around Wall Street ended. In the past, the lack of a set location and time for trading meant that buyers and sellers had been forced to search for each other, creating an inefficient market, easy to manipulate by the likes of Duer. Consequently, the Buttonwood Agreement began what would be a long history of self-regulation in the U.S. securities markets. With the market now limited to just the recognized market participants, the Buttonwood Group moved to a private room at the Tontine Coffee House on Wall Street to conduct business. From these beginnings, the Buttonwood Group would morph in 1817 into a more formal organization, known as the New York Stock and Exchange. In 1863 the name would finally be changed to the current name, the New York Stock Exchange.

Popular Reaction

Following the Panic of 1792, the American public came to fear that the stock market was nothing but an instrument for shady operators and speculators. But in fact the economic effects were limited. Some Connecticut investors took a loss because of Duer's operations, and speculators in Boston and Philadelphia felt the tremors, but for the most part the regional nature of the U.S. economy provided a buffer for other cities. This meant that New York City was hard hit, but the rest of the Eastern seaboard was relatively unaffected. However, the Panic and scandal did leave behind it a popular sense that unbridled greed was rampant on the stock market, and that trading securities was somehow an inappropriate activity.

Duer's Fate

William Duer never recovered from his fall from grace. Once deposed as the King of the Alley, he was unable to find the means to repay his many creditors. Yet, life in debtors' prison was not entirely grim. The debtors' wing of the prison did not hold those with criminal records. Moreover, Duer was treated reasonably well, being allotted two rooms—one for himself and one for two clerks who worked for him (in sorting out the various claims). Hamilton eventually sought to help his friend and obtained a brief reprieve for Duer from debtors' prison in 1797.

However, Duer was soon forced to return to prison, as his enemies held influence with the court. In 1797, he pleaded ill health. Through the good offices of friends (his conduct guaranteed by a $45,000 bond), Duer was released from prison in either late February or early March. He was not a well man, having problems urinating and being in extreme pain. His health quickly grew worse and on May 7, 1797, he passed away. His wife, Lady Kitty, and their eight children were helped by members of the family and managed to find what has been described as a nice home on Chambers Street. Her income came from two boarders and from payments on some remaining bank stock. Still an attractive woman, Kitty eventually married William Neilson, a successful yet quiet merchant, a major contrast to her days with the King of the Alley.[35]

Duer's Lasting Legacy

The Panic of 1792 was a landmark event in American financial history. William Duer, Revolutionary statesman, founding father, prominent New Yorker, and instigator of the Panic, was also to go down in history as one of America's first scoundrels and insider traders.

If Duer's schemes had succeeded, he would be remembered as something quite the opposite. As Robert Sobel noted: "Had he succeeded in all of these activities, he would have emerged as the most powerful businessman in America, and its most powerful until the days of J.P. Morgan."[36] Certainly, Duer would have been viewed as a much-lauded symbol of the new American economy, based more on industry and finance than on landholding and agriculture. The country's first millionaire, John Jacob Astor (1763-1848), was in fact a combination of the old and new economies, having first made his fortune in the fur trade and later investing his profits in real estate in New York. (Unlike Duer, Astor largely avoided the stock market.)

Looking back through the lengthy history of scandals on Wall Street, William Duer and the Panic of 1792 were like a passing storm on the landscape of U.S. financial history. The incident left a path of destruction in its wake, but New York, its merchants and brokers, even its speculators, were soon on the rebound. It triggered the first major U.S. government intervention in the stock market (courtesy of Treasury Secretary Alexander Hamilton), setting an important precedent for many years to come. It featured a sharp stock market buying mania, followed by an equally sharp bust accompanied by widespread public disillusionment with the markets—setting another, less fortunate, precedent. In the aftermath of Duer, the New York Stock Exchange was much better organized—largely thanks to the Buttonwood Agreement—and able to take business away from the Philadelphia Stock Exchange, which it soon overtook.

Moreover, New York was soon to benefit from a new boom in turnpike, canal, and manufacturing companies, all needy of the capital that was made available by an investing public. As the young American republic found its feet and its financial system matured, Duer would gradually fade in memory, though the greed and speculative intensity he helped generate—as well as the self-regulation his schemes helped to foster—would be lasting features of Wall Street throughout the centuries to come.

Notes

1. Forrest McDonald, Alexander Hamilton: A Biography (New York: W.W. Norton & Company, 1982), p. 4.
2. Ibid.
3. Robert Sobel, *Panic on Wall Street: A History of America's Financial Disasters* (Washington, D.C.: Beard Books, 1999), p. 10.
4. Ibid.
5. Quoted in Robert F. Jones, *"The King of the Alley" William Duer: Politician, Entrepreneur and Speculator 1768-1799* (Philadelphia: American Philosophical Society, 1992), p. 7.
6. For one example of "acceptable" speculation see Charles Royster, *The Fabulous History of the Dismal Swamp Company: A Story of George Washington's Time* (New York: Random House, 2000).
7. Thomas Jefferson to George Washington, 1792, ME 8: p. 244.
8. Jones, *"The King of the Alley"*, p. 25.
9. Ibid, p. 11.
10. See Merrill Jensen, *The New Nation: A History of the United States During Confederation 1781-1789* (New York: Northeastern University Press, 1981), p. 374.
11. Ibid.
12. For one aspect of the concerns about the early U.S. government and its strategic concerns see Charles A. Cerami, *Jefferson's Great Gamble: The Remarkable Story of Jefferson, Napoleon and the Men Behind the Louisiana Purchase* (New York: Source Books, 2003).
13. William Howard Adams, *Gouverneur Morris: An Independent Life* (New Haven: Yale University Press, 2003), p. 226.
14. For further information on the sad tale of the Scioto Company and French settlers in Ohio see Jocelyne Moreau-Zanelli, *Gallipolis: Histoire d'un mirage américain au XVIIIe siècle* (Paris: l'Harmatton, 2000).
15. Quoted from William Sterne Randall, *Alexander Hamilton: A Life* (New York: HarperCollins, 2003), pp. 229-230.
16. See David Cowen, *The Origins and Economic Impact of the First Bank of the United States, 1791-1797* (London: Garland, 2000).
17. Sobel, *Panic on Wall Street*, p. 16.
18. Ibid., p. 17.
19. McDonald, *Hamilton*, p. 223.
20. Sobel, *Panic on Wall Street*, p. 20.
21. Quoted from "Tench Coxe, Alexander Hamilton and the Encouragement of American Manufactures," *William & Mary Quarterly*, July 1978.

22.   Jones, *"The King of the Alley"*, p. 171.
23.   Edwin G. Burrows and Mike Wallace, *Gotham: A History of New York City to 1898* (New York: Oxford University Press, 1999), p. 308.
24.   McDonald, *Hamilton*, p. 224.
25.   Chernow, *Alexander Hamilton*, p. 380.
26.   Quoted from Burrows and Wallace, *Gotham*, p. 309.
27.   Jones, *"The King of the Alley"*, p. 176.
28.   Ibid, p. 177.
29.   Chernow, *Alexander Hamilton*, p. 381.
30.   Quoted from Jones, *"The King of the Alley"*, p. 177.
31.   Burrows and Wallace, *Gotham*, p. 309.
32.   Ibid.
33.   Ibid.
34.   John Gordon Steele, *The Great Game: The Emergence of Wall Street As a World Power 1653-2000* (New York: Scribner, 1999), p. 45.
35.   Jones, *"The King of the Alley"*, p. 203.
36.   Sobel, *Panic on Wall Street*, p. 21.

3

The Gilded Age Part I: All That Glitters

Delmonico's was the place to be seen. The restaurant had opened its doors in 1827 and was the first establishment in which diners could order whatever they wanted instead of what was prepared that day. It is also credited with inventing such popular dishes as Baked Alaska and Lobster Newberg, as well as offering the now famous Delmonico steak. Among those to dine at Delmonico's were Abraham Lincoln and his highly unpopular and hapless successor, Andrew Johnson. In 1876, the restaurant left its first home on Wall Street and moved to Fifth and Broadway "to provide a place for the cream of society to dine and dance."

Indeed, the cream of society did come to dine and dance, with one of the more memorable occasions being the 1884 Millionaires and Monopolists Banquet. At that function, the movers and shakers of the U.S. financial world were out in force. Among the ranks of bewhiskered grandees in attendance were Jay Gould, who made his fortune in rails; H. H. (nicknamed Hell Hound) Rogers, one of the founders of the Standard Oil Company; Cyrus Field, who laid the first transatlantic cable in 1856; Russell Sage, a former congressman and close ally to Gould in rails; and Philip Danforth Armour, one of the generation's toughest industrialists and a revolutionary in the area of meat-packing. While the Millionaires and Monopolists Banquet wined and dined the heavy-hitting industrial and financial movers and shakers, Delmonicos also was the stage for the Silver, Gold, and Diamond dinners. Matthew Josephson, who coined the term "robber barons," chronicled these extravagant social functions: "At one, each lady present, opening her napkin, found a gold bracelet with the monogram of the host. At another, cigarettes rolled in hundred-dollar-bills were passed around after the coffee and consumed with an authentic thrill... One man gave a dinner to his dog, and presented him with a diamond collar worth $15,000."[1]

For all the conspicuous consumption that took place at Delmonico's, there was another America, where hard times abounded. Throughout much of the second half of the nineteenth century, the hinterland was peopled by tenant farmers struggling to make a living; small storekeepers were hard-pressed by difficult business conditions and a lack of credit; and local bankers faced periodic crises, some being forced to close their doors. Survival of a family farm often hinged on whether or not it rained. As U.S. industry stretched across the country of a "new economy" in the form of iron works, coalmines, meatpacking plants, and railroads, a poorly paid working class arose. Living conditions in many cases were appalling, while wages were kept down. Alcohol abuse often went hand in hand with pollution, disease, and crime.

For the other America there would be no dining at Delmonico's. Indeed, this was one of side effects of the evolution of U.S. financial markets during the Gilded Age—the somewhat unstructured nature of the stock and bond markets made it relatively easy for strong-willed individuals to operate on their own or in small groups of like-minded allies and raid the market. It was clearly a case of speculation over investment; the raider over the empire builder. A few were enriched and many were impoverished, which over time was to have political consequences.

The Demon of Wall Street

It was lunchtime. As usual, on this April day in 1873, Delmonico's was busy. The small, somewhat frail-looking man, often described by his biographers as "saturnine," sat alone at a table. This was Jay Gould, the well-known speculator who had risen to head the Erie Railroad, a friend of William "Boss" Tweed of Tammany Hall, and the main perpetrator in the infamous gold corner of 1869 (more of this later). His seemingly endless stock market manipulations had left him a millionaire and ruined the fortunes of many. They also gave him an unfortunate nickname, the Mephistopheles of Wall Street—referring to the demon who figured prominently in the legend of Faustus, a man who sold his soul to the Devil. He appeared as a cold, calculating man, driven only by profit and speculation, lacking any moral compass. To put it mildly, Gould was not a popular figure.

As Gould sat, seeking to enjoy his meal, another customer walked over to his table. To his horror, the man proceeded to throttle him. The assailant, it turned out, was an attorney, who cursed Gould for bilking a client. Many Americans believed that Gould's public thrashing was justified, considering all of the misery that he and his ilk had caused by their exploits in the U.S. stock market. As one historian later commented: "Furtive and deadly as a spider...Jay Gould fed on the betrayal of friends, fattened on the ruin of stockholders, lied and bribed his way to a power that raised above the law."[2]

Yet, there was more to Gould. Although his early years on Wall Street were marked by his involvement in most major financial scandals, he was also a product of the times—hardnosed, willing to push the parameters of the game, and ruthless. If he had been anything less there would have been no Gould story, and certainly the ups and downs of the stock market during the Gilded Age would have been that much the less. Simply stated, Gould mirrored the rough and tumble nature of American capitalism at a formative stage. The business culture of the time rewarded those who played every trick they could to make money—even if it was of questionable legality. At the same time, it is important to recognize that without the excesses of scandal during the 1860s and 1870s, the shift away from speculation and toward investment and industrial consolidation that occurred in the 1880s and 1890s would have been less profound.

America's Transportation Revolution and Wall Street

A catalyst for this period of economic upheaval and financial scandal was the industrialization of the country, a process that commenced with the railroads. It was the birth of the railroads that bound the United States together via extended tracks running north-south and east-west, eventually across the nation linking the two coasts. Vast fortunes were made on the rails—and lost. Indeed, by the mid-nineteenth century, railroad company stocks and bonds were the most actively traded industry on the New York Stock Exchange. And with that flow of money and trading came some of the most egregious scandals of the nineteenth century.

In the first two decades of the nineteenth century, the key question for the young nation's leadership was how to maintain a westward expansion into the continent's interior and how to tap the region's productivity. Initially this was accomplished by the development of turnpikes. Over time, the focus shifted to canals, as the turnpikes were costly to build and were unable to handle a growing level of trade. Canals were also costly, but considering the importance of improving transportation, financial support was found from local and state government that issued bonds. Among the most famous of these canals was the Erie.

From Canals to Railroads

In 1825 excited crowds watched the first passage of a ship through the canal from Lake Erie to New York City. The new waterway was 363 miles in length and opened up new parts of the state and beyond to settlement and trade. The canal was to vastly increase New York's flow of trade, which in turn helped the city on the Hudson overtake Boston and Philadelphia as the nation's undisputed financial and commercial hub. Significantly, the Erie Canal's success worried other states, stimulating the construction of other canals.[3]

The canal boom was accompanied by rising debt—and, of course, speculation. By the mid-1830s state debt for canal construction and other projects reached unsupportable levels. In many cases, old debt obligations could not be met without issuing new debt. Canny investors had to wonder if they wanted to throw good money after bad. For a number of European investors, the answer was a simple no. Consequently, the combination of too much debt on the part of state governments, speculation on canal stocks, easy money followed by an abrupt monetary tightening, and a pullback by European investors resulted in a stock market crash—the Panic of 1837.[4] In a sense, the short-lived era of canal securities was over and the age of railroad securities loomed.[5]

Although the British had earlier been using steam engine-pulled locomotives, the U.S. rail age was not inaugurated until 1829 when Peter Cooper in New York built the Tom Thumb for the Baltimore and Ohio Railroad. (It hauled thirty-six passengers at 18 miles per hour in August 1830.) From those humble beginnings, there were 10,000 miles of track by 1850.

Railroads also offered new avenues of financial speculation. It is important to underscore that the railroad became a staple for Wall Street, much as bank and federal government bonds were in the 1790s and canal and state bonds were in the 1830s. As Wall Street historian John Steele Gordon noted: "In 1835 only three railroads were listed on the stock exchange; by 1840, ten were being regularly traded; and a decade later the number had swelled to thirty-eight. By the outbreak of the Civil War, railroad stocks and bonds accounted for one-third of all American securities."[6] Railroad construction did not stop during the war as President Abraham Lincoln was a firm supporter of extending the national rail system westward. By the end of the Civil War, dreams of a coast-to-coast railroad system were taking important steps forward.

The Scarlet Lady

On Wall Street, one of the most widely traded companies was the Erie Railroad Company, sometimes called the Scarlet Lady of Wall Street because she had lured so many men to their doom. The Erie was chartered in April 1832 to run from the Hudson to Lake Erie. Because of the very political nature of railway construction in New York, the Erie initially had to be built entirely within New York State, could not connect with any out-of-state railroads, and was allowed to raise only $10 million to pay for costs. The main trunk line was completed in 1851, while final construction costs were $23.5 million, well above what was originally forecast.

The Erie was a creature that required considerable capital, which brought it into the realm of Wall Street. Considering how quickly the Erie outpaced its original financing, management turned to Wall Street repeatedly. The result was a capital structure that was a prime example of how not to finance the building of a railroad, with issue after issue of debt and crushing interest payments.[7] In the 1830s, there was not enough local capital available to meet the Erie's needs, forcing management to raise capital from investors in London. Beyond London was continental Europe, which in the late 1840s and early 1850s was to witness considerable political upheaval, making U.S. investments more attractive, especially in the political calm that followed the U.S. Civil War. Thus by the end of the Civil War, the Erie had a wide range of securities, that is, a substantial array of stocks and bonds that were easy to manipulate.

Wall Street in the 1860s

As the United States economy changed, so did Wall Street. The combination of growing capital needs from a budding U.S. industrial sector, the need to finance U.S. government debt (something that increased considerably during the Civil War), and a wider pool of investors, all meant a deeper and broader national securities market. The fact that Wall Street survived the Panics of 1837 and 1857 and came back even stronger demonstrated an important resilience.[8] Also, the U.S. Civil War had an enormous positive impact on New York. Despite the claims by southerners that without their cotton, grass would grow on New York City's streets, the city on the Hudson thrived. Southern cotton was soon replaced by western grain that was in heavy demand in Europe, where harvests were poor. In addition, manufacturing benefited from higher northern demand for war material, while Wall Street's financial houses became the leading source of capital for Washington's war machine.

William Duer would not have recognized Wall Street in the 1860s. In 1836 trading was prohibited in the streets (though curb trading persisted) and in 1853, companies that were to be listed were required to provide complete statements of shares outstanding and capital resources. In 1863, the exchange became the New York Stock Exchange. In addition, there was the Open Board of Brokers, in which the more orderly traditional sit-down auctions were replaced by a continuous auction in which shares were traded at various posts around the trading floor. Eventually this system would become dominant as it allowed a far more accurate awareness of pricing and helped move along a higher volume of trading. Trading volume on Wall Street was estimated at $6 billion a year in 1865.[9]

Yet, not everything was far akin from Duer's freewheeling spirit. The New York Stock Exchange was still a poorly regulated institution, largely dependent on its members for self-regulation. Since that was not saying much, Wall Street enjoyed a poor image in the eyes of most Americans. Consequently, for the inventive and daring there was plenty of room to maneuver. Insider information was often available, as there was little stigma attached to trading on insider information. As John Steele Gordon noted: "At a time when there was no regulation of the securities industry, many men of the Street who called themselves brokers were little, if anything, more than con men. The real business of these men was not brokerage but separating fools—then as now an endangered species—them and their money."[10] As the Erie was to show, there were always some fools.

The Usual Suspects

What made the Erie memorable was its ability to attract some of Wall Street's most well-known players. The cast of characters included Cornelius "Commodore" Vanderbilt, Jim Fisk, Jay Gould, and Daniel Drew (who some called the first robber baron). In a very clear sense, the group came to encompass some of Wall Street's prime movers and shakers, men who cast a long shadow over America's financial and industrial development.

The Stock Market Sphinx

Daniel Drew was born in 1797 in Carmel, New York and his career was a hallmark for unscrupulous business practices. Coming from a poor background and with little schooling, his first job was herding cattle. He became known for watering stock: Prior to reaching the sales point, Drew would give the cattle salt, then walk them. Then, just before weighing the cattle for sale, he would provide the thirsty animals with all the water they could drink. This meant that whoever purchased such cattle was actually paying a higher price based on water weight. Drew made a considerable fortune watering up his cattle. From cattle, Drew went into the steamboat business, where he unsuccessfully collided with Vanderbilt. Drew subsequently turned to Wall Street, where in 1844 he founded his own brokerage firm and bank, Drew, Robinson & Company. Through that venture, he came to loan money to the Erie in 1854. After the Panic of 1857, he became the Erie's treasurer and a director. From that position, Drew was able to conduct a number of transactions, based on insider information and often using the company's money to increase short-selling on his own company.

By the early 1860s Drew was known as the "Sphinx of the Stock Market," a mistrustful, ruthless, and energetic player. Drew's manipulation of Erie stock and the poor condition of the actual railroad became well-known and were a standard of the shady side of Wall Street. The Erie's assets, however, were attractive and eventually drew the attention of Drew's old steamboat rival Vanderbilt.

The Commodore

Described as "handsome, sandy-haired, yet profane, illiterate, a man of coarse habits and a fiery temperament," Vanderbilt, according to one British observer, was a "favorite type of the kind of (New York) success which the average American has constantly before his eyes."[11] Like Drew, Vanderbilt came from a poor background. Born in 1794 on Staten Island, Vanderbilt's family struggled to make a living. By the age of eleven, Vanderbilt left school to work with his father in boating, hence beginning a lifelong association with the development of U.S. transportation. Over time he came to dominate the shipping business in New York City, an association that eventually earned him the nickname "Commodore." He also gained a reputation as a ruthless competitor, able and willing to undercut his rivals' rates. His shipping empire eventually encompassed a New York-to-California steamship line and a transatlantic shipping line. Vanderbilt's efforts were profitable and he amassed a large fortune.

As the U.S. economy shifted gears with the development of railroads, Vanderbilt sensed opportunity. In 1862 he sold his steamship businesses and commenced buying railroad company stocks. Within a short period of time, Vanderbilt came to own the Hudson River Railroad, which he eventually consolidated with the New York Central and Harlem Railroad. The Erie loomed large as the next takeover candidate. At roughly the same time, Drew developed an interest for the Harlem. Hence, in 1864 the stage was set for a battle of the titans over the fate of two railroads (the Harlem and Erie), involving the fortunes of Drew and Vanderbilt and two newcomers, Jay Gould and Jim Fisk.

Gould and Fisk would emerge as two of the most memorable figures in U.S. financial history. Fisk was born in 1834; Gould in 1836. Both were born to very modest families, worked hard to rise up in society, and were strongly motivated by personal gain. They were also willing to use everything in their financial, legal, and political arsenals to master the market and get the best of all other players, including the young and foolish. Although Fisk would die at a young age, Gould would survive several more decades and gradually morph from a despised speculator into an important investor and railroad baron, leaving a considerable fortune to his family while donating some of his wealth for society. Within the context of the Erie wars, this strange duo would emerge to triumph over older and seemingly more seasoned players.

Jay Gould: Surveyor, Tanner, and Robber Baron

Gould came from humble beginnings, the son of a small farmer in the hardscrabble soil of upper New York State. He lost his mother at a very early age and was largely brought up by his elder sisters. Intelligent and hard-driven, Gould attended school, helped his father run a country store, and for a period struck out on his own as a surveyor. In the last mentioned position, he demonstrated a life-long ability to be a very rapid learner, mastering new skills through sheer drive, energy, and intelligence. After a number of different ventures, including managing a tannery in New York, Gould turned to railroads in 1863, when he married Helen Day Miller, the daughter of Daniel S. Miller, who lent him money to buy the Rensselaer & Saratoga (R&S) Railroad. Unlike Fisk, who had a strong appreciation for attractive women and dallied with many, Gould was loyal to his wife throughout their long marriage.

Gould become the manager of the R&S, an act that would have long-standing repercussions. Under his hand, the R&S was brought back to life. From the R&S, Gould moved to overhaul the Rutland & Washington Railroad, which was then sold at a handsome profit. Following the Panic of 1857, Gould made a modest and profitable investment in shorting rail stocks. By the time that Drew and Vanderbilt were ready for war, Gould had quietly built up a reputation for his market acumen. He had become a millionaire, a remarkable achievement for a boy from upper New York State. Gould was also ruthless and appeared to function without a moral compass. As the intellectual Henry Adams noted: "It is scarcely necessary to say that he had not a conception of a moral principle."[12] For someone like Drew, the soft-spoken, yet brilliant Gould was an excellent ally.

Diamond Jim Fisk

Where Gould was soft-spoken and happy to be out of the limelight, Fisk was loud, brash, and completely enjoyed being the center of attention. The son of a country peddler, young Fisk was intelligent, but clearly had a wild streak. At the age of fifteen he ran off to join the circus. He spent the next couple of years doing odd jobs and working with the showmen. The circus experience was important. As one historian observed: "Somewhere along the way, the transformation of Fisk into a full-borne huckster was complete. He had always had the raw ability, but the circus polished it into a diamond-hard smoothness."[13]

Upon leaving the circus, Fisk joined his father as a traveling salesman, using garishly decorated wagons to draw the public's attention. He was exceedingly successful in doing this—despite his father's doubts. Although highly successful as a traveling salesman in Vermont, Fisk hungered for more. This brought him to Boston, where he joined the retail firm of Jordan & Marsh. Initially this was not a successful venture, but the outbreak of the Civil War provided an opening for someone with his talents as he soon headed down to Washington, D.C., where he wined and dined and obtained lucrative contracts for Jordan & Marsh with the U.S. military.

Not everything went well for Fisk. After his well-paid departure from Jordan & Marsh at the end of the war, his first effort to establish a brokerage in New York failed. However, Fisk met with Drew, with whom he shared a past experience of working at a circus. Fisk and Drew got along well, with the latter helping in the creation of the brokerage firm of Fisk & Belden in 1866. And Fisk certainly made an impression. As one contemporary noted: "The blonde, bustling and rollicking James Fisk, Jr. came bounding into the Wall Street circus like a star-acrobat, fresh, exuberant, glittering with spangles, and turning double summersets…He is first, last and always a man of theatrical effects, of grand transformations, and blue fire."[14]

The Erie Wars

With this colorful cast of characters in place, the first round of the Erie war began in 1866, when Vanderbilt started purchasing large amounts of Erie stock. As a director for more than seven years and with his own railway company, Vanderbilt knew exactly what he was doing. And so did Drew, who patiently bided his time. Drew struck back after loaning the Erie $3.5 million for which he received 28,000 shares of un-issued and un-registered stock. He also had $3 million in convertible bonds. Drew quietly and gradually sold his stock, which Vanderbilt quickly bought, helping push the price to $95 a share. Drew then executed a bear market raid, taking out several large short contracts and simultaneously dumping 58,000 shares on the market. By this action, Drew killed the run-up in Erie stock, dropping it to $50 a share. While Drew earned millions, Vanderbilt lost millions.

Vanderbilt had no intention to let the matter rest there. Considering the manner in which business was conducted, the next stage was to use the legal system—such as it was. Big financial players had enough influence and cash to buy what they needed from the legal system, including judges. That was, after all, the New York of Tammany Hall, run by the colorful Boss Tweed. Political favors were available—for a price. Vanderbilt soon had injunctions brought against Drew. He also approached the directors of the Boston, Hartford & Erie (BH&E) Railroad, a line that was close to bankruptcy, but owned a sizeable block of Erie stock. Vanderbilt struck a deal with the BH&E directors that he would merge the Erie with their railroad if they supported his bid to oust Drew as Erie's treasurer. With the backing of the BH&E gang, Vanderbilt then used the courts to prohibit Drew from using the voting rights of the converted stock.

Drew panicked, realizing that he could be ousted at the upcoming director's meeting. Swallowing his pride, Drew went to Vanderbilt, asking for leniency. Considering that he had cost Vanderbilt millions of dollars, this was a bold (and desperate) move on Drew's part. One is left wondering at what actually transpired between the two rivals. Surprisingly, Vanderbilt was cordial and open to a tactical alliance of sorts vis-à-vis the BH&E bloc, who were expecting big things for their support. Consequently, at the next board meeting, the Vanderbilt forces were triumphant, but Drew was soon brought back as treasurer—with the Commodore's blessings. Thus far, the Erie war involved poor corporate behavior, with the main legal transgression being the bribery of public officials. A scandal, yes, but hardly a major event.

Vanderbilt had won the first round, but a second round was looming. In November 1867 Vanderbilt sought to raise the company's stock price by buying more. The price, however, only nudged up, indicating that as he accumulated shares, someone else was pumping in a new supply. The Commodore quickly suspected Drew, who in the meantime had joined forces with Fisk and Gould, who had been made board members in October. The Drew group also made inroads into the BH&E group, who soon voted with them against a Vanderbilt proposal to merge the Erie with his own Central line. Furious with such opposition, Vanderbilt changed track by deciding to buy every bit of Erie stock that his brokers could obtain.

For their part, Drew, Fisk, and Gould were not to be ousted so easily. Armed with the ability to print more stock (having control of a stock printing machine), they did so. Soon the market was flooded with the new Erie stock. Vanderbilt turned to Judge George Barnard to issue an injunction halting the issue of any more new stock. Drew, Fisk, and Gould responded by gaining the support of William Tweed, who was hired as a "consultant" to Erie. Through the Tweed connection, they won over their own judge, who signed an injunction against Vanderbilt. Vanderbilt, however, was able to wield greater legal clout in New York. Fearing arrest, Drew, Gould, and Fisk made a hurried retreat with the company's books from Erie headquarters in March 1868 to the safety of Jersey City.

While Jersey City offered relative safety, it was not New York. Soon the exiled Erie gang grew restless. While Gould waged a war of influence in Albany by handing out a considerable amount of the Scarlet Lady's cash to state politicians, Jersey City's smaller world contributed to a growing split between Drew, who openly longed for his home in Manhattan, and his two younger partners, Fisk and Gould, who, in turn, were growing suspicious of the older speculator. Indeed their suspicions were right: Drew was willing to talk to Vanderbilt.

After a considerable maneuvering via the courts and the wallets of New York politicians, the warring sides settled their differences. Vanderbilt was paid for his stock losses and Drew was forced to resign from the board and relinquish his position as treasurer. In return, Drew was allowed to return from Jersey City and was not charged with offering bribes. This effectively cleared the way for Gould to become president of the Erie in July 1868, with Fisk elected to be his treasurer and chief operating officer.

Although the company had little in its treasury, Fisk and Gould moved the Erie's headquarters to Pike's Opera House on West 23rd. This move took the railroad's headquarters into a garish urban palace, more suited to the theater than to business. It also fit Fisk's brash personality—he was able to attend to railway work, while overseeing the production of a number of musicals. The new headquarters were also close to the apartment in which he set up his mistress, Josie Mansfield. In many regards, the circus had come to town and Fisk was overseeing it at the Erie headquarters in a lavish, expensive style.

While Fisk and Gould presided over the circus, the company was in poor shape. The company's tracks were in need of repair, service was poor, and labor was badly paid. Considering the above, there were a number of accidents. In 1868 alone, twenty-six passengers died in accidents on the railway. Yet, the Erie's stock sat in the market, a lure to speculators. One of those speculators was Drew, now back in action against his former comrades. In November 1868, Drew and a number of other bears, such as August Belmont, Rothschild's representative in the United States, sold Erie short.

Gould and Fisk, however, outsmarted the bears by buying up the stock and driving prices higher in Erie stock the day before delivery of shorted stock. While many shareholders were angry over the ongoing manipulation of the company's stock, Drew was financially ruined. Once a dominant force on Wall Street, his power was eclipsed and he was forced to go live with his son. As for Gould and Fisk, they had won the Erie wars, beating Vanderbilt and Drew. But there was a cost. As historian Thomas Kessner noted: "While Gould, Fisk, et al. were no doubt astonished by what they had managed to pull off, no one stopped them from wasting millions of other people's money on a personal power struggle. Corporate officers had mocked their fiduciary responsibilities, printed reams of depreciated stock, undermined equity values, and frittered away the company treasure on personal caprice. And along the way, they had managed to tempt even respected judges into rascality, while laying waste to any notions of legislative integrity."[15]

The Gold Corner

Although he had secured his control over the Erie, Gould was not done with speculation. In 1869, he launched one of the more audacious speculations ever: cornering the U.S. gold market. New York City was the key market for gold: The total gold market had a value of between $15 and $20 million. Moreover, gold could be purchased on credit with a modest investment and then loaned to merchants who were short. In other words, a focused speculator with a relatively small amount of credit could corner the nation's gold supply, with the only remaining supply being U.S. government gold reserves. What if those gold reserves could also be manipulated?

During the Erie wars Gould had learned that he could bribe local and state officials with considerable ease. Now he looked higher—to the presidency. If he could get the U.S. government to remain on the sidelines, his bet on gold would work. Consequently, Gould sought to gain access to President Grant through his brother-in-law, Abel Corbin, who lived in New York. Corbin was not a particularly distinguished man, having had a lackluster career as a lawyer, lobbyist, and speculator. Nonetheless, he was greedy. More importantly, thought Gould, he had access to the U.S. president.

If Gould could convince Grant that releasing the U.S. gold supply would be bad for the economy, his gambit would pay off. During the Civil War the U.S. government had issued a large amount of money (greenbacks), backed by nothing but credit. At the end of the war, it was believed that Washington would buy back the greenbacks with gold. Consequently, a higher price of gold would help the country's monetary policy. Corbin set up a meeting between Gould and Grant in June 1869. At the time Gould was unable to persuade the president, though at a later meeting he felt he had a more sympathetic hearing.

More significantly, Corbin was able to convince Grant to appoint General Daniel Butterfield as assistant treasurer of the United States. Butterfield agreed to notify Corbin and Gould when the government was planning to sell gold. Armed with such insider information, Corbin, Gould, and their allies could sell at the height of the market, making a fortune.

Gould also persuaded his erstwhile cohort Fisk into getting involved. By late summer Erie money went into the gold market and the scheme gained momentum. Adding to the excitement, Fisk hired a small army of brokers to mask his activities.

By mid-September bulls and bears were locked into a fierce fight over gold. Although Gould still counted Grant in his corner, the president was becoming suspicious of his brother-in-law and worried about the level of speculation. As the gold market continued its frantic gyrations, Grant wrote a scalding letter to his sister, demanding that her husband stop his speculation. Corbin panicked, quickly notifying Gould.

Gould was able to calm Corbin—and swear him to silence about the president's warning. The game had changed. Gould understood that the gold corner was going to fail, and soon. Using other brokers, he quietly unloaded as much gold as he could. Meanwhile, his ally Fisk was still on the gold trading floor, furiously seeking to push gold prices higher. Gould did not tell Fisk of the change in events—he thought there was no sense in both of them losing their fortunes.[16]

On what was to become known as Black Friday (September 20, 1869), Grant decided that with gold hovering above $160, it was time for intervention, releasing $4 million in U.S. gold reserves into the market. The bubble quickly burst, taking a number of brokers and bankers with it. Fisk lost a small fortune, but was able to survive, though he must have wondered about his close "ally."

Black Friday in 1869 soon rippled throughout the U.S. economy, reflecting the negative nature of unchecked speculation. Gould, however, was hardly alone as the source of speculation and scandal. Indeed, the lure of the railroads proved strong to many other individuals, including many among the political elite in Washington, D.C.

The Credit Mobilier Saga

The Credit Mobilier story begins in the frantic days prior to the U.S. Civil War and spans two decades, until it finally erupted in 1872. As rail fever infected the United States in the 1840s, most of the new lines were in the East, mainly in the industrialized Northeast. The U.S. frontier, however, was opening up the country's hinterland. Following the 1846 U.S.-Mexican War and the Bear Flag Revolt, California became part of the United States.[17] In January 1848, gold was discovered in California, setting the stage for a gold rush. Getting to California, however, was not easy. A voyage from the East Coast to California around South America's Cape Horn was 17,000 miles long and could take up to five months. An alternative route (available in 1850) was by steamship to Central America, then by train across the narrow belt of the Americas and finally by ship to California—lengthy, disease-ridden, and exceedingly uncomfortable.

The California Gold Rush, the poor nature of coast-to-coast communications, and the railway boom combined to thrust one Theodore Judah (1826-1863) onto the historical stage. Referred to as "Crazy Judah," he was a qualified railway engineer, who had a vision of a transcontinental railroad. Having gained his experience in the East, Judah was asked in 1854 to survey from Sacramento to Fulsom, California for a new line. During this period, he became convinced of the pressing need for a transcontinental railroad system, a view he was soon thereafter to advocate strongly in Washington, D.C.

Although Judah tracked down many a congressman and senator, his ideas failed to sway the Washington establishment. In fact, in some parts of the nation's capital, his sanity was questioned. However, back in California a group of entrepreneurial individuals found the idea intriguing. The group that would come to be known as the "Big Four" was supportive. This group included Colis Huntington, Mark Hopkins, Leland Stanford, and Charles Crocker—all successful men who had come to California from the East, seeking to make their fortunes. As a group they were also politically well-connected, with ties to Abraham Lincoln and the fledgling Republican Party. In 1861, Judah was hired by the Big Four, who supported the need for a transcontinental railway.

The outbreak of the Civil War changed the consensus over the establishment of a rail going coast to coast. Suddenly Crazy Judah did not seem so crazy. Indeed, Lincoln, who had worked as a lawyer with railroad companies in the Midwest, approved the idea of a transcontinental railroad. In his view, this would help provide a line of communication to California and consolidate that state to the Union. This would be done through the movement of troops and settlers. In July 1862 Congress passed the Pacific Railroad Act, paving the way for the creation of the Union Pacific Railroad, the first corporation chartered by the U.S. government since the Second Bank of the United States in 1816.

The passage of the Pacific Railroad Act, however, did not bring about action. One problem was how to pay for such a company. In 1862, the federal government was at war and the idea of any additional expenditure beyond the immediate task of subduing the South was a nonstarter. This meant that creative financing was required.

Building the Union Pacific

After considerable debate, it was agreed that the federal government would issue to the Union Pacific thirty-year bonds with an interest coupon of 6 percent upon the certified completion of each 40 miles of track. The company obtained the bonds, which as government obligations, could be sold for cash. The attraction of such an instrument was that the buyer would own a bond supported by the full faith and credit of the U.S. government as opposed to a private sector rail company. At the same time, Union Pacific would have an obligation to pay the government the face value of the bonds. If the bonds traded above the face value, which was a possibility, Union Pacific could actually make money on the bonds—which had little to do with the actual construction of rail lines. There was one other stipulation worth noting: If the Union

Pacific did not repay its debt, the government could foreclose on the company's assets.

The Union Pacific was created with an organizing board of 163 members, dominated by one Thomas C. "Doc" Durant (1820-1885), one of the more nefarious yet resourceful characters in American financial history. Described as mercurial and autocratic, Durant started in medicine, but was soon lured to law, in particular, issues surrounding the U.S. prairie wheat trade and railroads. By 1853, he had become the dominant player in the Missouri and Mississippi Railroad (M&M). Although the M&M, like many railroads at the time, was not profitable, Durant benefited from the rail's strategic location bordering the south: He dipped into the contraband trade of southern cotton during the Civil War. At the same time, he was able to project himself as a mover and shaker in a rail world that increasingly revolved around the debate over a transcontinental railway.

Durant emerged from the lobbying game in Washington as the dominant player in the newly formed Union Pacific. Managing to take the vice president's seat, Durant was able to place his willing ally, John Dix, as president. Although Dix sat in the president's office at the Union Pacific, it was Durant who called the shots.

The Credit Mobilier ultimately was a phantom construction company, connected with the building of the Union Pacific. The name of the company was taken from a company by the same name in France, formed to help fund public utilities. (Ironically, the French company would fail—the victim of a major financial scandal!) Durant's crony, Herbert Hoxie, was put in charge. Durant and Oakes Ames, a member of Congress from Massachusetts, and a handful of other influential stockholders of the Union Pacific organized the Credit Mobilier under an existing Pennsylvania charter. Acting for both the Union Pacific and for their newly created construction company, they made contracts with themselves. This practice ultimately depleted generous congressional grants to the Union Pacific and left it under a heavy debt by the time of its completion in 1869.

The creation of the transcontinental railroad was not left to one company. While the Union Pacific moved from the East, the Central Pacific moved from California. The Big Four had foreseen that the passage of the Pacific Railroad Act of 1862 and its amendment in 1864 meant that government support could also be extended to another railroad. Indeed, the Big Four were active in lobbying Washington. While Crocker, Huntington, Stanford, and Hopkins were visionary in the idea of a transcontinental rail and seized the opportunity, they were also ruthless and egotistical. Unfortunately Theodore Judah, who had returned from Washington excited about the railroad, fell afoul of the Big Four and left their company. In 1863, Judah decided to return to the East, but fell ill in Panama. He was to make it to New York City, but died there in the arms of his wife.

By 1864, the United States was witnessing a major restructuring of its national communications. Two railroads were competing to complete the task of uniting East and West coasts with a belt of steel over which trains with passengers and goods would flow.

Black Holes and Time Bombs

Yet, the pace was glacier-like. Lincoln became concerned about the slowness of the project and, increasingly, the costs. Beyond the arrogant nature of Durant, Union Pacific offered no financial statements or audits. To those watching from the outside, the Union Pacific was a financial black hole. Money went in and nothing came out. From the inside, the flow of government bonds helped generate a nice cash stream into the coffers of the Credit Mobilier. Lincoln managed to sideline Durant, by giving Oakes Ames more authority to run Union Pacific, but Lincoln's interest in cleaning up the Union Pacific came to an abrupt end when he was assassinated in April 1865. Lincoln's immediate successor Andrew Johnson soon became embroiled with the Republican dominated Congress over the shape and form of Reconstruction in the South, and had little time for the goings-on at Union Pacific.

Although federal government pressure eased during the Johnson administration, Credit Mobilier remained a time bomb. The whiff of corruption was picked up in the U.S. Congress, but a liberal spreading around of Credit Mobilier stock to key members of Congress forestalled any action. Among those to receive shares were future President James Garfield, James Blaine (speaker of the House), and Vice President Schuyler Colfax, who had come to office with the Grant administration (which followed the Johnson administration).

Although President Grant was not thrilled with Durant and had his suspicions, Union Pacific and Credit Mobilier were allowed to carry on for a little while longer. Indeed, Credit Mobilier announced in 1866 and 1867 a dividend of 12 percent, payable in Union Pacific stock and bonds. This news caused a run on the company's stock, pushing it up from $30 a share to over $300 a share. In 1868, some $15 million went back to shareholders.

In 1868 and early 1869 the nation was transfixed as the Union Pacific and Central Pacific raced to completion. On May 10, 1869, the two railroads finally connected, resulting in a nationwide celebration. The United States was finally linked coast-to-coast by a railway system, a remarkable achievement.

But, the Credit Mobilier story would not go away. Turmoil continued between the abrasive Durant and other members of the board. Finally, after the linking of the two lines, he was thrown off the Union Pacific board. Without his dominant personality, leaks about the state of the company's finances and the nefarious nature of the Credit Mobilier connection could not be hidden. The story gradually gained the attention of the U.S. press, in particular the New York *Sun*. In 1872, the newspaper broke the story, headlining that the Credit Mobilier was "the most damaging exhibition of official and private villainy and corruption ever laid base in the gaze of the world."[18] Along with the tale of kickbacks to members of Congress came a list of Credit Mobilier's major stockholders. As Charles Francis Adams, Jr., grandson of John Quincy Adams and a historian of railroads, noted:

> Something called the Credit Mobilier… It is but another name for the Pacific Railroad ring. The members of it are in Congress; they are trustees for the bondholders, they are recontracters; in Washington they vote subsidies, in New York they receive them, upon the plains they expend them, and in the Credit Mobilier they divide them… As stockholders they own the read, as mortgages they have a lien upon it, as directors they contract for its construction, and as members of the Credit Mobiler they build it. Here is every vicious element of railroad construction and management; here is every element of cost recklessly exaggerated…[19]

In the aftermath of the New York *Sun*'s exposure, Congress acted. A commission was formed, headed by the respected Judge Luke Poland from Vermont. The Poland Commission was soon investigating congressional behavior. Although many were implicated in the Credit Mobilier scandal, ultimately only one congressman (Ames) took the fall. The Central Pacific was also called to testify before the Poland Commission, but the company claimed that its books were burned in an office fire.

The Credit Mobilier was but one of a series of financial scandals that broke out during the 1870s, tainting the Grant administration. Despite the nefarious nature of the scandal, some good did emerge. As financial historian Sanford J. Mock noted: "Out of the plunder and corruption by some, along with the honest hard work and integrity of others, emerged America's transcontinental railroad, the major engineering achievement of the century, which made possible the nation's great westward expansion."[20]

1873: A Reckoning

By 1873, the U.S. financial system appeared well-established and able to survive an almost bewildering series of scandals. Most of the major players were still active, including Gould and a now aging Vanderbilt. Following the failed gold market corner in 1869, Fisk and Gould had drawn apart. Though both men remained tied to the Erie, the brash Vermonter gave more attention to his opera house, steamships (he now owned several), and mistress problem. The last was to do him in.

Josie Mansfield was a hard woman to keep. Young and attractive, Mansfield eventually tired of Fisk, who was often busy with other ventures (some of which might have included other mistresses). Indeed, Fisk probably exacerbated the problem by introducing Josie to a steady stream of high-ranking and socially prominent men with whom he conducted business. One such man was the handsome and socially well-placed Edward "Ned" Stokes. Ned and Josie clearly got along well, certainly enough to raise eyebrows among New York high society. Fisk, however, refused to surrender. As for Josie, it appeared that she enjoyed her role in the love triangle and thought little of taking Stokes as a lover while still living off Fisk's largesse.

Fisk was not above using his legal connections to have Stokes thrown into jail overnight at least once. The upshot of this was that after a lengthy period of squabbling between Fisk and Stokes, the New York court system decided in favor of the former. Stokes, a man of delicate mental health and limited means (for the lifestyle he wanted), took matters into his own hands and on January 6, 1872 shot and killed Fisk as he climbed the stairs to visit friends at the Grand Central Hotel. While Fisk's death shook up the close-knit world of speculators, it was an omen that bad times were coming. The American financial community, based on strong-willed individuals with raiding mentalities, was on the edge of a reckoning.

Gould was to face the consequences of a changing environment before many others. He managed to maintain control over the Erie in the board of directors meeting in October 1869. But though he dominated the board, all was not well. Close to $45 million of the $78 million in Erie stock belonged to English investors and they were not pleased by the antics of Gould and Fisk.[21]

More dangerous was another group of disgruntled American investors, such as James McHenry of the Atlantic Company. The combination of Fisk's public airing of dirty laundry and death, as well as the downfall of Tweed during 1871 and early 1872, served to erode Gould's dominant position. By March 1872, the plotting to oust Gould was well-advanced. Despite the drama of a last-minute physical battle for Erie headquarters between rebel directors and Gould thugs, the president was forced to resign. Gould, however, did not suffer financially—a major shareholder, he benefited from a substantial rise in the company's stock caused by the positive market reaction to his ouster. All the same, Gould would never again hold court at the Erie.

The reckoning for the rest of Wall Street was to come in the form of a severe depression that devastated American financial markets. From the surface in 1873, the U.S. economy was moving in the right direction. Yet, there were problems lurking not far from the surface. Grain prices had fallen since the end of the Civil War, squeezing farmers between the pressure of oversupply and the need to produce more to make debt repayments. This situation ultimately pushed prices one way: down. At the same time, U.S. economic development was still dependent on foreign capital. This was certainly the case of railroad financing. As the U.S. emerged from the Civil War intact and political tensions mounted in Europe (much of it related to German unification), foreign capital poured into the American railroad sector. In 1853 foreign investors owned $51.9 million in railroad securities; by 1869 the figure was $243 million and climbing.[22] As Robert Sobel noted: "Clearly, America's economic boom had its motor in London and other European capitals. Undercapitalized American railroads with large debts could easily collapse should this flow of funds cease. A momentary shudder in London or another important capital could lead to panic, not only in America but throughout the world."[23]

That shudder came in May 1873, when a financial panic hit Vienna and Berlin. The ripples continued outward, eventually rolling into the United States, with considerable devastation. The key prop of European investment was pulled, revealing a far weaker financial system than had been supposed.

Adding to the weakness of the American economy was the scandalous nature of its financial markets. This was amply demonstrated by the antics surrounding the Erie, the attempted gold corner of 1869, and Credit Mobilier, which broke as a news story in 1872. The seedy underbelly of railroad financing was a major Achilles heel for the U.S. economy. Revelations of wrongdoing at the Erie, Credit Mobilier, and others fit the pattern that again emerged with the market meltdown in 1873, which sank the once august banking house of Jay Cooke & Company. For Jay Cooke, 1873 was a reckoning—as it was for so many other brokers and investors who had thrown considerable capital into the railroad sector. Unknown to the public, Cooke's financial position, so closely tied into the Northern Pacific Railroad, was weak. The bank needed capital to stay afloat. When the ripples of financial turmoil started to come out of European markets in May 1873, they found Jay Cooke & Company in a very vulnerable position. Cooke & Company were not the first to fall nor did U.S. markets immediately falter. But a dangerous undercurrent had started to flow, a situation not helped by the Grant administration's shift to a tight monetary policy. During the summer, liquidity dried up. By late August, Cooke was in deep trouble. In early September, the reckoning was at hand.

One of the first companies to fall on September 8 was the New York Warehouse & Security Company—hit by a default of the Missouri, Kansas & Texas Railroad. Another casualty was Daniel Drew's old firm, Kenyon, Cox & Company, done in by a default by the Canada Southern. A number of smaller railroad companies followed, declaring bankruptcy. By the evening of September 17, panic was in the air. At the offices of Cooke & Company, in both its headquarters in Philadelphia and its branch in New York, there was a frantic effort to borrow the finds to remain open. Cooke, however, realized that the game was up. The misadventure in rails, something beyond the bank's core experience, had pulled down one of the nation's most august banking houses. On September 18, Cooke & Company announced their closure and a massive financial panic followed.

The devastation of the financial panic of 1873 was to result in what was then called the Great Depression, lasting until 1879. The rail bubble had finally burst, shutting down the New York Stock Exchange for ten days. Some eighty-nine of 364 listed railroad companies crashed into bankruptcy, a total of 18,000 businesses failed in two years, and business activity contracted by 32 percent in the 1873-1879 period. Hard times had come to Wall Street.

Conclusion

As the major drivers in the U.S. stock market, railroad securities had offered an almost irresistible lure for investors, much like tech stocks would have during the 1990s. The rail scandals showed, above all, that the existing constraints of anti-monopoly law, social legislation, taxation, editorial freedom, and judicial independence were weak or non-existent. As Vanderbilt tellingly stated: "What do I care about the law? Hain't I got the power?" Historian Kessner noted: "With few rules and little precedent, they kept pushing back the margins of restraint, and the barriers kept falling."[24]

At the same time, the men involved in much of the stock market drama of this era reflected some of the myths of the American dream of hard work resulting in wealth and upward social mobility. Jay Gould, for example, was vilified for his stock market exploits, but respected for his rise to great wealth from humble beginnings. In addition, without men such as Gould, Vanderbilt, and others, the capital for much of the rail revolution would not have been forthcoming.

In another legacy from the Gilded Age, the major financial scandals involving railroads, in particular the Erie Railroad and Credit Mobilier scandals, helped set the stage for the Panic of 1873 and the Great Depression that began that year and continued for the better part of the next two decades. Scandals in the rail sector were hardly alone, but were part of a larger economic movement, involving coal, steel, oil, and food processing, as the industrial captains of the new economy tested the parameters of business power vis-à-vis the state and society (much as Enron and its enablers would "push the envelope" in the 1990s). While railroads played an important role in the industrial revolution, the testing process would continue through the Great Depression of 1873, eventually provoking a reaction during the presidencies of Roosevelt and Taft. Despite the very tainted nature of railroad financing, Wall Street helped provide capital for the creation of a national railroad system, a critical step in making the United States into a modern industrial economy.

Notes

1. Matthew Josephson, *The Robber Barons* (New York: Harcourts, 1962, reprint of the 1934 edition), p. 338.
2. Robert V. Bruce, *1877: Year of Violence* (Indianapolis: Bobbs-Merrill, 1959), p. 25.
3. Other canals to be built included the Pennsylvania Canal, opened in 1834, linking Pittsburgh and Philadelphia, and the Ohio and Erie Canal, stretching from Portsmouth on the Ohio River up to Cleveland on Lake Erie (opened in 1832). Even Connecticut was to have the ill-fated Farmington Canal, a waterway destined to be a black hole for its investors.
4. Complicating matters, the U.S. banking system was volatile and not on firm ground. President Andrew Jackson in 1832 had gleefully vetoed the re-charter bill for the Second Bank of the United States, thwarting the ambitions of Nicholas Biddle, the bank's head, and removing the country's sole national bank from the scene. In many regards, the Second National Bank had functioned as a de facto central bank and as such instilled some discipline into the banking system. With the Second National Bank's removal, discipline eroded and credit was much more easily extended into the economy and the stock market by a myriad

of small regional banks. Jackson inherited Jefferson's strong distaste of securities speculation and as the stock market bubble deflated decided that it was time to bring the stock market (flush with canal securities) under control. Instead of an orderly deflation of the stock market bubble, what occurred was the Panic of 1837.

5.   John Steel Gordon, *The Great Game*, p. 76.

6.   It did not take the railroad long to eclipse the canal. The reasons were multiple. First and foremost, railroads could be built almost anywhere and were usable year-round. In contrast, canals were limited to areas with ample water supplies and in the north were lost for several months during winter due to freezing. In addition, rail ultimately was to prove faster and able to haul more freight and people. Rail was to become a major force in transforming the economy, society, spatial relations, and the environment.

7.   John Steel Gordon, *The Great Game: The Emergence of Wall Street As a World Power 1653-2000* (New York: Scribner, 1999), p. 76.

8.   The Panic of 1857 followed the boom that came in the wake of the Mexican War. The initial spark for the panic was the failure of the New York branch of the Ohio Life Insurance and Trust Company. That institution was the focus of a major scandal involving large-scale embezzlement. While the failure of Ohio Life was devastating, a series of other blows made certain that the panic gained momentum. These blows included the decision by British investors to remove funds from American banks due to concerns over safety and soundness; a steep decline in international grain prices (which hurt Midwestern farmers); a large build-up in manufacturing inventories that eventually caused layoffs; a number of failures of U.S. railroad companies; and the sinking of the USS *Central America*, carrying 30,000 pounds of gold going from California to eastern banks.

9.   Wall Street was also benefiting from improvements in technology. In 1844 the telegraph had been invented, which served to broaden market participation by enhancing communications with brokers and investors outside of New York City. In 1866, the first transatlantic cable was completed, establishing instantaneous communication between London and New York. Equally important, in 1867 the first stock ticker was invented, bringing current prices to investors everywhere— something that would have put a rapid halt to the activities of a William Duer.

10.   Gordon, *The Great Game*, p. 76.

11.   Quote from Robert Greenhalgh Albion, *Rise of New York Port, 1815-1860* (New York: Charles Scriber & Sons, 1939), pp. 241-242.

12.   Quoted in Thomas Kessner, *Capital City: New York City and the Men Behind America's Rise to Economic Dominance, 1860-1900* (New York: Simon & Schuster, 2003), p. 107.

13.   Russell Roberts, "Jim Fisk, Wall Street Scoundrel, Con Artist and Schemer," *Financial History* (Winter 2002), p. 4.

14.   Quoted from Roberts, p. 2.

15.   Thomas Kessner, *Capital City: New York City and the Men Behind America's Rise to Economic Dominance, 1860-1900* (New York: Simon & Schuster, 2003), p. 113.

16.   Kenneth D. Ackerman, *The Gold Ring: Jim Fisk, Jay Gould, and Black Friday, 1869* (New York: Carroll and Graf Publishers, 1988, 2005), pp. 157-158.

17.   The Bear Flag Revolt was a short-lived independence revolt (June-July 1846) that ousted Mexican forces from California and opened the territory to become part of the United States. The revolt was named after the flag used by the rebels—it featured a star and a grizzly bear on a white background.

18.   Quoted from David Howard Bain, *Empire Express: Building the First Transcontinental Railroad* (New York: Penguin Books, 1999), p. 677.

19.   Quoted from Robert W. Johannsen, "Credit Mobilier of America," *Encyclopedia Americana*, http://ap.grolier.com/article?assetid=011280-008templatenome=/article/article/html. Adams (1835-1915) was a railroad expert, writing *Chapters of the Erie* (1857), which exposed the corruption surrounding that company. He was also to serve as the chairman of the Massachusetts Board of Railroad Commissions and chairman and president of the Union Pacific—after the scandal.

20.   Sanford J. Mock, "The Credit Mobilier: Financial Scandal of the 1860s," *Financial History* (Winter 2004), p. 33.

21.   Maury Klein, *The Life and Legend of Jay Gould* (Baltimore: The Johns Hopkins University Press, 1986), p. 117.

22.   Robert Sobel, *Panic on Wall Street* (New York: Truman Talley Books, 1988), p. 161.

23.   Ibid., pp. 161-162.

24.   Kessner, *Capital City*, p. 124.

4

The Gilded Age Part II:
Of Presidents and Bankers

In 1884 Ulysses S. Grant was diagnosed with terminal throat cancer. He had discovered his illness when his throat registered a sharp pain as he tried to eat a peach. Grant's last days were spent in a macabre race against time. Encouraged by his long-time friend Mark Twain, Grant struggled to finish his *Personal Memoirs*. Using a cottage located at Mount McGregor, near Saratoga, New York that was owned by financier Joseph W. Drexel, Grant spent his final days writing. There is a memorable and haunting photo of him on the cottage's porch, near death, yet scribbling away. By then he had lost his voice, communicating only in whispers and in penciled notes. On July 23, 1885, only four days after the manuscript was completed, the ex-president died. He was sixty-three years of age.

The cottage and the clock are still there in mute testimony. Twain published Grant's book, which became a national bestseller—allowing his widow Julia to pay off the family's debt and live in comfort for the rest of her life. Upon his death, Grant achieved a major victory in his life-long quest to secure the family fortune.

This was important because other than the book, Grant left very little to his widow. What had been accumulated through the years was lost because of Grant's unintentional involvement in yet another of Wall Street's financial scandals. The machinations of Ferdinand Ward had enmeshed the elder Grant and his son, Buck, into a Ponzi scheme that ultimately crashed, setting off the Panic of 1884.

Although the Panic of 1884 did not result in a substantial economic downturn, it captured the public's attention because of the involvement of the former president and war hero. It also reinforced a view among the nation's financial elite, in particular with bankers such as J. P. Morgan, that it was time to bring under control the Darwinian tooth and nail struggle among the nation's major industrialists, especially their use of Wall Street as a major arena. The simple truth was that Wall Street's many scandals reduced the value of industrial securities for the banks, their customers (both in the United States and Europe), and insurance companies.

Indeed, the machinations of unseen speculators and brawling corporate chiefs created a strong desire for change among many sectors of the country. Urban workers, farmers, and small town professionals found the ways of Corporate America incomprehensible, and the frequency of scandals alarming. At question was not the idea of capitalism verses some other kind of economic system (as favored by fringe groups of socialists and communists), but how to make capitalism work for a broader range of players. The myth of upward social mobility and the United States as a land of opportunity was still very attractive to the waves of immigrants that came to the country during this period. What was needed was a more level playing field.

In the Midwest and South discontent with the direction of the national economy and those who guided it was mirrored in the rise of labor unions, populism, anarchists, and the ill-fated presidential candidacy of William Jennings Bryan. Between the rise of the financial capitalists around Morgan and populists like Bryan, Wall Street was pushed into a more structured and—for a while—less volatile era. The long string of Wall Street scandals was a major factor (among many) in the shaping of U.S. economic development in the late nineteenth century. And in the Wall Street drama of the last decades of the century, the main actors shifted from the bear raiders and former circus workers (like Drew and Fisk) to bankers and presidents.

President Ulysses S. Grant and the Panic of 1884

In May 1884, the American public was once again transfixed by a major financial scandal. Although speculation on Wall Street had cooled following the Panic of 1873 and the ensuing depression, eventually financial manipulators made a comeback. What caught the public's attention was that the new scandal entangled no less august a figure than Ulysses S. Grant, former president (1869-1877), national war hero, and ill-fated partner in a New York City brokerage and bank, Grant & Ward.

As president, Grant presided over what was arguably one of the most corrupt periods in United States history, with one scandal after another rocking the government or Wall Street.[1] Grant, however, was regarded as honest. Despite all of the corruption surrounding his administration, he made little money throughout his two terms as president of the United States as he diligently trooped on, paid by the small government salary.

Grant suffered from two things: He was loyal to members of his government (even though many of them were corrupt) and sometimes exhibited poor judgment in selecting people to serve under him in Washington. As biographer Michael Korda noted: "Grant's presidency was to end in a welter of scandals, none of them directly connected to Grant, but most of them the result of his engaging, but mistaken loyalty to people who had served in the Grand Army of the Republic during the war, or fast-talking, high-living rogues, or friends, or members of his own official or Julia's family."[2]

His second weakness was that he was easily impressed by confident and successful businessmen, a reflection of his own lackluster business record. Prior to the Civil War, Grant had been among the many that were negatively affected by the Panic of 1857. The Civil War had been a godsend for Grant as it gave him the opportunity to lead troops, something at which he was highly successful.

Following his presidency Grant still could not achieve his dream of great wealth. His bid to become president of the Mexican Southern Railroad did not lead to riches, and his attempt to reenter the political arena to serve a third term in the White House failed in 1880. Surrounded by the wealthy and famous, Grant was famous, but relatively poor. Indeed, the ex-president relied on the kindness and pocketbooks of others to establish a trust to provide him and his family with a small yearly income. Even the financing for a modest home in New York City on East 66th Street came from the funds raised by George W. Childs, the publisher, and Anthony Drexel, the financier. The simple truth was that Grant was a great general, but a failure as a businessman.

The Napoleon of Wall Street

The last point is underscored by the events of the early 1880s. Grant's son Ulysses, Jr., or "Buck," had gone into business with one Ferdinand Ward, a well-connected New York native who was also known as "the Napoleon of Wall Street" (as were dubbed a number of young and successful financiers by the press). The easygoing, younger Grant had gone to the best schools, finishing at Columbia Law School. Although not considered a man of great talent, he married well (to the daughter of the influential former New York senator Jerome Chaffee), which gave him the capital to get into the stock business. In 1881, he had made the acquaintance of Ward, and the two discussed the idea of going into business together.

When President Grant returned to New York in 1881, Buck brought young Ward with him. A good showman with a reputation for financial smarts, Ward impressed the Grants. Soon both father and son Grant put up $100,000, a considerable sum at the time, to start the firm of Grant & Ward, Bankers and Brokers, which was to manage the money of veterans and millionaires. Although the former president was a silent partner, knowing little about the investment business, his involvement was clearly an attraction for the ambitious Ward.

Who was Ward? Like many of the individuals to become entangled in American financial scandals up to the present, Ward was from a relatively humble background, hardworking and filled with energy. In many regards, he epitomized the idea of the American dream of upward social mobility. The son of a Baptist minister in Geneseo, New York, Ward arrived in New York City in 1872. He initially was involved in the stock market, but apparently did not do well. His brother helped him to get a job in the New York Produce Exchange, which probably saved him from the Panic of 1873. The impact of the panic was devastating, as it almost wiped out an entire generation of Wall Street firms and suspended the activities of speculators for several years.

Ward observed of the Panic of 1873 and certainly must have felt the impact of the economic chill that followed. However, from his position at the New York Produce Exchange, he was able to climb the ranks, eventually buying a seat on the exchange. In 1878 he married Henriette Green, the daughter of one of the directors at the Marine National Bank. Eventually, Ward moved away from the produce exchange into the stocks of mining and elevated trains firms (of which New York City got its first in 1881). Indeed, Ward's timing was impeccable: As he moved into trading stocks and bonds, the stock market hit the bottom in 1879 and by 1880 was bouncing back. Ward rode the market upwards. Before the age of thirty, Ward was seen as an up-and-coming force on Wall Street, with an office on Broadway, a lavish home in Brooklyn, and a country home in Stamford, Connecticut.

Ward was well aware that the Grants were innocent in the ways of Wall Street and that he would have a free hand in their joint ventures. In addition, Ward very much wanted to cash in on President Grant's fame, especially as it suggested that his new firm had access and influence in Washington, D.C.

Armed with an ex-president as a partner and Ward's well-placed (and false) rumors that government business was going to the companies into which the firm was invested, the investing public, including friends of the former president, poured money into the firm. The company became a high-flying star on Wall Street. Grant Senior's role was largely confined to meeting and greeting potential investors, who were thrilled with meeting a Civil War hero and former president. The ex-president's office was often filled with some of the well-known personalities of the time, including Mark Twain, General Philip Sherman, and Russell Sage. For three years, Grant & Ward did well, with all of its investors earning healthy dividends—or at least it appeared to be that way.

The Ponzi Scheme

The problem at Grant & Ward was that the real core business was a Ponzi scheme. The Napoleon of Wall Street was actively borrowing money from banks and investors and using the proceeds to buy stocks. The scheme worked as follows: Investors bought securities through Grant & Ward, leaving them with the firm as collateral on loans with which they could purchase still more securities. This practice was called hypothecation.[3] Grant & Ward, in turn, and in accordance with what then was legal, borrowed against the securities in order to invest for the firm's own account. So far all of this was legal. What was not legal was that Ward pledged the same securities to support more than one bank loan (needed to speculate in the market). This might have been a problem if the bank's management disapproved of such practices. However, in this case, the financial institution was the Marine National Bank, whose president James D. Fish was very impressed with Ward.

To be more precise, Fish was impressed by the ability of the young speculator to get Grant to join as a partner. The bank president was also influenced by a letter sent by Grant on July 6, 1882, in which the former president clarified that "Mr. Ward should derive what profit he can for the firm that the use of my name and influence may bring."[4] Although Grant's intention was simply to support Ward in his business at the bank, this conveyed the view that Grant was allowing his name to be used to unfairly gain business with the U.S. government for favored companies. Ironically, just the opposite was true, as Grant was strongly opposed to such behavior and told Ward just that. Indeed, Grant was to later state: "I had been President of the United States, and I did not think that it was suitable for me to have my name connected with government contracts, and I know that there was no large profit in them except by dishonest measures."[5]

Nonetheless, Ward had Grant as a partner, and even if the older man was opposed to using his name to gain influence, the younger man had no such qualms. It certainly worked on Fish, who was more than willing to overlook Ward's questionable practices with loans. Over time Fish was pulled into some of Ward's investment schemes as well, using the bank's capital (i.e., deposits from the bank's customers).

To keep investors happy, Grant & Ward showed large profits—on paper, that is. Questions raised by the Grants were blocked by Ward's insistence on secrecy and paranoia about the unscrupulous nature of others on Wall Street who could be listening. As long as the money kept coming in and Ward was able to convey the impression that he was making sound investments, the questions were not pressed. At the same time, Ward was constantly seeking new investor funds to reimburse the earlier investors. When attracting new funds became difficult, he borrowed heavily from Marine National Bank. As is the way with such schemes, everything went well as long as the stock market moved upwards.

The stock market began to slide in 1883. A short-lived panic gripped the market in August when the high-flying firm of E.C. Stedman & Co. collapsed, due to bad investments, compounded by financial irregularities. Although that panic was overcome, market conditions were deteriorating. In particular, the government's repayment of debt was tightening the nation's money supply, which of course meant less capital for investment on Wall Street. Despite mounting losses during 1883, Ward managed to extract more money from Grant's family, his friends, and acquaintances. The new money allowed Ward to funnel the money back to earlier investors, giving the appearance of successful investing.

Both Grants were unaware of the looming disaster and shady practices. For Grant Senior and Buck, 1883 was a great year. Family fortunes soared. The ex-president's deep concerns about the family financial situation appeared to have been finally resolved. He was convinced that Grant & Ward had made him a millionaire. The year, however, did not end on a good note, as Grant, now sixty-one, slipped and injured himself badly on Christmas Eve. Shortly thereafter he came down with a case of pleurisy. The combination of health issues kept Grant from returning to his office in the financial district until April, relying on the clueless Buck and the deceptive Ward for information as to the firm's performance.

In early 1884 there were a number of events that eroded confidence in the market—a decline in European demand for U.S. agricultural goods, the failure of the New York and New England Railroad, and an ongoing outflow of gold to Europe. In addition, poisonous wars for control over the nation's railroads were undercutting European investor confidence. By April, the stock market had settled into a period of little activity, no direction, and poor liquidity. This was a disaster for Ward, for he needed the market to move up, in order to continue his game. At this juncture, only more money would have allowed the charade to continue and this was no longer available.

Grant & Ward's Waterloo

By the first days of May, Ward's scheme started to unravel. Rumors arose that Grant & Ward was in financial difficulty; other rumors surfaced that Marine National Bank was in danger of failing. The City of New York, concerned about the rumors, withdrew funds from Marine National Bank at the end of the week. This naturally raised real concerns as to whether the bank could meet demands from other depositors the following week. Short of relying on the support of other banks or the deep pockets of wealthy individuals, a run on a bank in the late nineteenth century was usually fatal.

Seeking to save his firm and fortune, Ward went to the Grant residence on Sunday night, May 4 and met with the former president. He pleaded with Grant Senior to request help (in the form of $150,000) from the former president's friend William Vanderbilt, the son of Cornelius Vanderbilt, long a major player on Wall Street. William was a player in his own right on Wall Street and was one of the wealthiest men in the United States. He also liked the former president.

Ward was aware of Vanderbilt's friendship with Grant. Ward indicated that while Grant & Ward was solid, the Marine National Bank was shaky. The problem was that the City of New York, one of the largest depositors, had taken $300,000 out of the bank. This meant, according to Ward, that Marine National Bank could be short of funds when it opened for business on Monday morning. If that were to happen and a run developed on the bank, Fish would have no choice but to close the bank's doors. As Grant was well aware, such an event could cause a major panic on Wall Street. This was something that Grant was sensitive to, considering that during his two administrations a number of panics had rippled through the U.S. financial system, the most damaging coming in 1873, which precipitated a major economic depression.

Ward then also let Grant know that he had deposited their firm's money at Marine National Bank. Along these lines, Ward made his case for

Grant to raise money from his friends (i.e., Vanderbilt) with the intention of providing Fish at Marine National Bank with a temporary loan to deal with what was really a short-term liquidity problem. Of course, Ward himself would also be seeking to raise the same amount from other friends to help save the day.

A somewhat shocked Grant made his way that evening to the home of Vanderbilt. Vanderbilt had a keen understanding of the ways of Wall Street and was aware of the various rumors surrounding Grant & Ward. He wrote the check, but allegedly groused: "I don't care anything about the Marine National Bank. It can fail without disturbing me; and as for Grant & Ward—what I've heard about that firm would not justify me in lending it a dime. But I'll lend you a hundred and fifty thousand dollars personally. To you—to General Grant—I'm making this loan, and not to the firm."[6] A somewhat startled Grant accepted the check.

The former president returned home. Ward was waiting. The young man had failed to raise any money, but willingly took Vanderbilt's check. Ward quickly excused himself and soon cashed the check.

Pressure on the firm and Marine National Bank did not go away. Although Marine National Bank survived Monday, the rumors of problems refused to evaporate. On Tuesday, May 6, Grant & Ward, along with Marine National Bank, failed. A couple of other firms failed and there was a considerable nervousness in the stock market, but a full-fledged panic was averted. The damage was quickly contained, partially through the quick and forceful action of the clearing house banks that provided liquidity to a number of banks, and partially due to J. P. Morgan, who purchased many of the stocks being sold by nervous American speculators. The Napoleon of Wall Street had met his Waterloo and was nowhere to be found, while Grant & Ward was revealed to have $67,000 in assets and liabilities of $16 million. Grant had arrived late on Tuesday morning at the office and heard the news from Buck. After sitting for a long period, Grant rose and went home, never again to return to the financial district.

Aftermath

Ward was soon caught trying to flee the country. After a well-attended trial, he was sent to the state penitentiary of Sing Sing, where he served seven years of a ten-year sentence. He was released early on good behavior. He then moved to upper New York State, living in relative poverty. He had lost everything—his offices, the Brooklyn home, and the Stamford country house—all to pay the firm's angry creditors. In a series of articles in the New York *Herald* in 1909, Ward expressed his friendship to Grant, but tellingly admitted that the ex-president was "so much the child in business matters." Ward was not alone in being sent to jail. The former president of Marine National Bank, Fish, was put on trial and sent to prison, his career ruined.

As for Grant, the scandal was a major blow. To say that he was devastated was an understatement. Grant's long battle to attain financial security was once again at a critical stage. Grant & Ward bankrupted the family and put a stain on the aging ex-president's reputation. The family soon liquidated their holdings and made a sustained effort to repay their creditors, in particular Vanderbilt. The sale of the Grant holdings, however, did not reach the amount of $150,000 that Vanderbilt had lent the ex-president. In addition to the cash raised by selling their assets, the Grants transferred to Vanderbilt a number of household and personal items, including the memorabilia and awards Grant had received for his Civil War accomplishments. Vanderbilt had earlier indicated that he would forgive the loan, but Grant's pride would not let the matter rest. Vanderbilt did seek to return everything to the Grants, but the former president was adamant. Consequently, Vanderbilt gave the historical items to the U.S. government.

Grant's services to the country were not forgotten and friends quickly rallied sufficient funds to keep the financial wolf of insolvency from the door. More tellingly, Mark Twain managed to get Grant to write his memoirs. Although Grant's health rapidly deteriorated because of inoperable throat cancer (a result of years of chain-smoking cigars), the ex-president demonstrated his strong will in writing what was to become a national bestseller. It also guaranteed that even though he was to die shortly after completing the book, his family would be in good financial shape. Grant's memoirs were to result in the largest royalty check ever to be awarded by Mark Twain's publishing company, to Mrs. Grant, eventually netting the family $450,000.

In the aftermath of the Grant & Ward scandal, Americans were left to ponder a number of difficult questions. How much did Grant Senior know? Should he have been put on trial (after all, Fish and Ward were)? Should Grant Junior, a lawyer, have been more aware of what was going on under his nose? For many Americans, the sentiment was to leave Grant alone, especially once it became evident that his health was in decline. Why sully the name of the Civil War hero? At the same time, the scandal reinforced a widespread perception in which Ward and Fish were villains that fit part of a long tradition surrounding Wall Street. And villains pay.

Among the nation's financial elite, the Panic of 1884 reinforced a growing view that the ongoing struggles between the major figures in U.S. industry over railways, steel mills, meatpacking plants, petroleum, and coal were bad for Wall Street. The wars over ownership of various railroads, in which companies were bankrupted and operationally gutted of anything valuable, were bad business for shareholders. One banker in particular stood out in wanting to rationalize U.S. industry and that was J. P. Morgan. Having been in England during the Panic of 1884, he was exposed to the considerable European frustration over the chaos in U.S. securities markets. When he returned to the United States in 1885, he was determined to make changes.

Why J. P. Morgan?

Why was it that the resolution of market upheaval was left to the private sector and not the federal government? Why was it J. P. Morgan who would emerge as guiding hand, and not the U.S. government?

While the Grant administration was riddled with corruption, the following administrations of Rutherford Hayes (1877-1881), James Garfield (1881), Chester Arthur (1881-1885), and Benjamin Harrison (1881-1885) largely blended together as being generally pro-business and non-interventionist.[7] Even Grover Cleveland, the only Democrat in the group, was also a friend of big business and Wall Street during his first term (1885-1889), though he did sign the Interstate Commerce Act, the first law seeking federal regulation of railroads. Prior to the presidency, Cleveland had worked at the Wall Street firm of Bangs, Stetson, Tracy and MacVeigh, "where he handled few cases and hobnobbed with the most powerful financiers in the nation."[8]

While Lincoln had been a strong president, his successors were less powerful and forced to work through influential figures on Capitol Hill. As Geoffrey Perret, a biographer of Grant, noted: "However much he liked to think he was President by the will of the people and therefore free to ignore the selfish, blinkered wishes of the Republican party leadership, the reality was that when he pulled on the levers of power what he seemed to get in return was the sound of wheels spinning and gears clashing somewhere in the direction of Capitol Hill."[9] In a sense, the presidents were heads of factions and to pass any meaningful legislation were required to horse trade with other factions.[10]

At the same time, presidents, congressmen, and locally elected officials depended on support from members of the business world. To gain the presidency during much of the Gilded Age, each candidate needed wealthy patrons to finance the campaign and help steer their man through the convention. This clearly was the role played by Amasa Stone (industrialist) for James Garfield and by Mark Hanna (a rich Pennsylvanian businessman) for William McKinley. Along these lines, the single most important act of the new national chief executive was the appointment of his cabinet, as this was where he paid back favors and gained leverage on Congress. This left the president, as a leader, presiding over various factions, not the dominant player.[11]

Below the presidents, the tangle of politician and businessman interest often meshed. Businessmen were not above offering long-term guarantees of campaign funds, lucrative tips, and jobs, and frequently a promise of employment upon retirement from politics.[12] This was the time when, as American reformer Henry Demarest Lloyd caustically remarked, "Standard Oil did everything to the Pennsylvania legislature except refine it." Throughout much of the country, lawmakers came to expect cash and whiskey, a practice that was known to all.

The blandness of U.S. political leadership, at least in terms of its dealings with big business and Wall Street, stemmed from a change in the American mood following the Civil War. Novelist Zachary Karabell noted: "The years before, during, and immediately after the Civil War had been characterized by an excess of ideology. The politicians of the Gilded Age, perhaps mirroring the mood of the public, turned away from troubling intractables like freedom, democracy, equality, and attended instead to order, stability, and prosperity."[13] Consequently, the better management of American industry and its extensions into the realm of Wall Street was defaulted to the private sector, in this case, the masters of finance.

Who was J. P. Morgan?

While a financial elite had emerged on Wall Street, the figure who towered over all others was John Pierpont Morgan. He was born on April 17, 1837, in Hartford, Connecticut, the son of Junius Morgan. Pierpont, as he was known, was the oldest of five children: three sisters, Sarah, Mary, and Juliet, and a brother, Junius Jr., who died at the age of twelve. As a youth, Pierpont was known to be a high-strung, yet shy child given to mood swings. Despite these issues, he excelled in his studies and was competitive at sports.

Pierpont's involvement in finance came from his father, who in 1854 had formed a partnership with the American banker George Peabody and moved to London, where the headquarters of George Peabody and Co.

were located. London was still the center of the financial world. Peabody was a major actor in matching the British surplus of investment capital with the Americans who needed the capital for industrial development. While Junius would soon emerge as one of Europe's prominent investment bankers, the younger Morgan graduated from high school in Boston and was sent to the Institut Sillig on Lake Geneva, Switzerland, where he mastered German and French. From there he attended university at Gottingen, Germany, excelling in math. Morgan apparently enjoyed his stay in Germany, becoming a well-dressed and beer-drinking dandy—not exactly what his father had in mind. Junius soon sent Morgan to work at Duncan, Sherman, a merchant banking firm in New York City. From this beginning, Pierpont was never to look back.

By the early 1880s, J. P. Morgan had eclipsed many of his rivals as the dominant banker. From his apprenticeship at Duncan, Sherman, Pierpont opened (with his father's support) his own firm, J. P. Morgan and Co. Despite a bout of depression (at the age of twenty-four) following the death of his first wife, Amelia Sturges, Morgan's business continued to expand and survived the periodic upheaval of Wall Street's many scandals.[14] In the years that followed, Morgan was to remarry, have several children, and enjoy success as a major banking figure on both sides of the Atlantic. By the time of the Grant and Ward scandal, Morgan was well-established, regarded as a force to be reckoned with. As his biographer, Ron Chernow, noted: "The early 1880s saw Pierpont's metamorphosis from a dashing, muscular young man into the portly tycoon with fierce visage and blown-up nose."[15]

Morgan's rise to prominence also came at a period there was a lack of clear-cut leadership on the American business scene. Jay Cooke was gone, Jay Gould was often ill, and William Vanderbilt would die in 1885. The stage was ready for a new star.

Morganization

Now in his forties, Pierpont found the ongoing turmoil in American industry and its echoes on Wall Street problematic. The rail barons were once again actively engaged in fighting each other, this time New York Central's Chauncey Depew and George Roberts of the Pennsylvania Railroad. Watching the Grant & Ward scandal and ensuing panic, and the battle between the two railroads from London, where he had gone to consult Junius, Pierpont fumed over the "absurd struggle for preeminence" plunging America's railroads into internecine warfare.[16] He returned to New York determined to change things.

In July 1885, Morgan invited New York Central's Depew and Pennsylvania's Roberts to a meeting on his yacht, the *Corsair*. With his imposing personality and a captive audience (as they could not leave the boat for several hours), the banker managed to begin the process by which the devastating rail wars were brought to an end. As Matthew Josephson in his 1934 classic, *The Robber Barons*, noted: "Here were the profound symptoms of a new phase of industrial or capitalist revolution; the great monopoly or Trust can make unlimited profits when confronted with unorganized, divided sections of consumers and vassals; on such ground it is irresistible."[17] Morgan clearly understood this and was to reconstruct American industry, beginning with the railroads, into something that was more predictable, stable, and profitable, especially for bankers and shareholders.

Following the meeting on the *Corsair*, Morgan was to follow through with the same approach. As Chernow noted: "Over the years, Pierpont would employ the sharpest lawyers, yet his preferred style was more British—informal deals, handshakes over brandy and cigars, cordial clubroom chats among bankers as they stood in frock coat and stiff collars."[18]

Morgan's interest in consolidation of U.S. industry dovetailed nicely with what some of the surviving industrial barons wanted. Indeed, one of the most notorious of all the speculators, Gould, was to settle down, raise a family, and become a member of the establishment. After angry shareholders at the Erie finally rebelled and threw him out in 1872 and the Great Depression of 1873 hit, Gould's fortune came under considerable pressure. Gould rose to the occasion, making a remarkable shift from speculator into empire builder. In the following years, he assumed control over the scandal-ridden Union Pacific Railroad and cleaned up its books. Gould worked to improve operational efficiency and sought to meet local demands as opposed to the traditional long-distance manipulation by Wall Street speculators. The company soon saw its stock value increase and in 1874 it offered its first dividend. Gould also went on to construct an empire in the telegraph industry, actually hiring Thomas Edison for a brief period. Not satisfied with that, Gould in 1881 undertook the development of New York City's rapid transit system, a venture that had floundered for years due to political infighting.

By the mid-1880s, other survivors also leaned in the direction of consolidation as opposed to speculation and scandals. Consolidation, however, required money—something that Wall Street had and many of the industrialists lacked (at least in the amounts needed). People like Gould and steel king Andrew Carnegie saw the value in finding a more stable path to profits than the destructive option of speculation. Morgan, with other powerful bankers such as Jacob Schiff of Kuhn, Loeb, was willing to provide capital, but in return he demanded that the industrial leaders turn over some managerial control.

The bankers also paved the legal path, underwrote the securities, appointed the managers, and framed the policies.[19] This concentration of power should not be understated. As historian Thomas Kessner wrote: "Unregulated, working behind closed doors, often in collusion with other bankers, they set the initial stock values for new issues that they then marketed to a gilt-edged international clientele. Companies that failed to get their approval did not make it to market."[20] The clout of the bankers and their push for greater consolidation was only to accelerate in the aftermath of the 1893 depression, when a large number of rail companies failed. Morgan and allied bankers reorganized and consolidated many of these failing companies.

By the end of his career, Morgan had "morganized" 33,000 miles of railroad track—about one-sixth of all the tracks in the nation. Such railroads as the Erie, Chesapeake & Ohio, Philadelphia & Reading, Northern Pacific, Great Northern, and New York Central came under his control.

Morgan also was to have an influence on other industrial sectors in the U.S. economy. Recognizing the benefits from increasing market share through mergers, other corporations followed Morgan's morganization techniques, with business-friendly states such as New Jersey offering liberal rules for forming trusts. Such changes enabled Morgan to further consolidate his power. The trust soon became a weapon of mass consolidation.

One such case was the steel industry. Morgan already controlled the nation's second largest steel operation; Andrew Carnegie owned the largest. After a meeting in 1900 with Carnegie's chief assistant, Charles M. Schwab, Morgan learned of Carnegie's potential interest in selling Carnegie Steel. Morgan, however, suggested that Carnegie put a price on his holdings. After considering the matter during a round of golf, Carnegie penciled a figure of $480 million on a scrap of paper. When the price was presented to Morgan, he accepted it without hesitation. Later realizing that he could have held out for more, Carnegie mentioned the thought to Morgan. Morgan showed no emotion as he responded: "Very likely, Andrew."

To finance the creation of the new company, Morgan organized a syndicate of more than 300 firms. The deal was unprecedented, valuing the company, to be called U.S. Steel, at a market capitalization of more than $1 billion in 1901 dollars, the first billion-dollar corporation in history. By comparison, the rest of corporate America had a combined market value of $9 billion.

Morgan's rise to prominence and the collection of financial power-houses on Wall Street induced deep suspicion in other parts of America. While industrial America grudgingly accepted the process of consolidation, the emergence of trusts and the massive concentration of economic power represented by those bodies raised serious questions over the state of the "free market." It also raised a question over the relative power between Wall Street and Washington. Along these lines, J. P. Morgan and other bankers were reviled by the rising Populist movement. Nevertheless, Morgan's legacy was a more mature, less scandal-ridden and rationalized approach to industrialization.

Two Americas

While Wall Street was the domain of a relatively small number of Americans, its activities had an impact well beyond the confines of Manhattan. Bank failures in New York (which dried up the nation's monetary supply), poor attention to the maintenance of company assets (railroads had a high number of accidents), no concept of customer service (the companies were there for the benefit of the owners), and a lack of social consciousness (big business had very little regard for local communities), left the vast majority of Americans with a very low opinion of the nation's business elite, often referred to as the robber barons.

The ongoing battles over corporate domination that controlled the energies of individuals such as Gould, Henry Villard, and James Hill translated into few benefits for workers and farmers. Battles over railroads often meant lower wages for workers and higher transportation costs for farmers. Simply stated, as the wealthy captains of industry and their allies in the financial markets got rich by financial manipulation, the vast majority of Americans did not share in the wealth.

Indeed, the advent of the new economy, powered by locomotives and steel, had a distinctively brutal and uprooting side effect. This was captured in Upton Sinclair's *The Jungle*, a polemical tale of the evils of big capitalism. The family of immigrant Jurgis Rudkus is followed as it enters Packingtown, the apex of the new economy in the meat processing industry. One by one the family is destroyed by the greed of Packingtown, leaving only Jurgis, now a common thief, and his wife's cousin, now a prostitute. In Sinclair's view, the new economy used all the parts of the animal for profit, much like the people that worked there. There were no

Delmonico's or invitations to balls in Newport. Rather we are left with the following depiction of the raw nature of the new economy: "It was a sweltering day in July, and the place ran with steaming red blood—one waded in it on the floor. The stench was almost overpowering…"

Sinclair was not alone in bringing forth the disequilibrium in America caused by industrialization and urbanization. Frank Norris wrote *The Octopus*, which described the struggle between farming and railroad interests in California, and Stephen Crane wrote *Maggie, Girl of the Streets*, the tale of a pretty young slum girl driven into brutal excesses by poverty and loneliness.

Far removed from the grit and harsh conditions of Packingtown, the wealthy of the Gilded Age lived in an age of excesses. The newly rich embarked upon art buying sprees in Europe, while entire families vacationed in the Old World to suck in the culture and to gain sophistication. Mrs. Astor became the doyenne of New York's high society, with her list of "the Four Hundred," the most elite of the elite of the wealthy and famous. There was also the Millionaires and Monopolists' Banquet, held in 1884 at Delmonicos in New York City, which was attended by the likes of Jay Gould, H. H. Rogers, Cyrus Field, Russell Sage, and Armour (one of the dominant figures in the U.S. meat industry depicted by Sinclair's *The Jungle*).

And then there was Newport.

During the Gilded Age Newport, Rhode Island became the social playground of New York's finest—and the place where they brought their game of social one-upmanship to new highs. In 1888-92 William K. Vanderbilt built a "summer cottage" in Newport for his wife, Alva. This home was designed by architect Richard Morris Hunt to sit on the beautiful Atlantic coastline, and it was called the Marble House, in honor of its 500,000 cubic feet of imported Italian marble. William presented it to Alva for her thirty-ninth birthday. (Presumably she liked the gift, but she still divorced William three years later amid considerable society scandal to marry equally wealthy neighbor and William's best friend, Oliver Hazard Belmont, son of August Belmont, the Rothschilds' agent in the United States.)

In an attempt to outdo the neighbors, Alva wanted the Marble House to be modeled after Marie Antoinette's Grand Trianon at Versailles. While the Vanderbilts only spent six weeks in Newport each year, they employed a staff of thirty-six to run the house. The house cost $11 million to build, $7 million of which was spent on the marble. All of the stone was hand carved by European stone masons. The entrance refers to that of the White House in Washington, D.C., and the central grand staircase ushered guests into rooms such as a pink marble dining room and a gold ballroom decorated in the style of the Palace of Versailles.

Daughter Consuelo Vanderbilt (who was later to become the ninth Duchess of Marlborough) wrote about the house in her memoirs:

> Our new and magnificent home…was inspired by the Grand Trianon in the park of Versailles. Unlike Louis XIV's creation, it stood in restricted grounds, and, like a prison, was surrounded by high walls. Even the gates were lined with sheet iron. But it cannot be gainsaid that Marble House both within and without impressed one with its splendour and grandeur. The halls and staircase were built of yellow marble, and there were fine tapestries flanking the entrance, depicting the Death of Coligny and the Massacre of St Bartholomew's Eve, which always gave me a momentary chill. The beautiful dining-room, built of red marble, gleamed like fire.[21]

Not to be outdone, social rival Caroline Astor entertained royally at her new marble palace in Newport, known as Beechwood. Some of her grand Newport balls cost as much as $200,000 each. At one dinner party in particular, Caroline covered her dining table with a depth of several inches of sand and buried in it diamonds, sapphires, rubies, and emeralds to serve as party favors for her guests. By each plate setting there was a small sterling silver bucket and spade that guests used to "dig for their buried treasures."

And then there was Mrs. Stuyvesant Fish, who held a dinner party in New York City in honor of her dog, who arrived at the party wearing a $15,000 diamond collar.

Probably the apex of the Gilded Age was when Ward McAllister, described as New York's self-appointed social arbiter and devoted to more than one glass of Madeira, decided to reveal who was on the list of Mrs. Astor's Four Hundred. On February 2, 1892, the *New York Times* ran the list of who constituted New York "society." As a multitude of other New York newspapers followed suit, the list of Astors, Vanderbilts, Livingstons, and Whitneys was greeted by the public as would an announcement about rock stars. All the same, this world of wealth and privilege was reaching a conclusion. Looming around the corner in 1893 was a severe recession; scandals that would rock the families on the list of the Four Hundred (including Mrs. Astor); and a new wave of industrial innovation that would add another round of turmoil into society. As Jeffery E. Patterson noted of the revelation of the Four Hundred names and the days to come: "Although no one knew it, least of all its central figures, the age was burning itself out."[22]

The Political Punch Line

The political punch line to the age of excess was the emergence of an opposition, built up around those who felt threatened by the new economy and its financiers. Like the financial capitalists who rose around J. P. Morgan, this group also found the Darwinian struggles in U.S. industry disruptive, but on a far more personal basis as they were the ones that were fired, had their wages cut, had to pay higher fees, or were forced to go on strike. At the same time, the broad movement for change was poorly defined, with no single force. Western and Southern populists had different grievances than urban-based industrial Northern workers. The populists wanted to punish trusts, nationalize certain businesses, and demanded increases in the money supply through greater silver coinages. What did unify them though was their low opinion of government, which was at least partially justified considering the corrupt nature of much of the political class, with the possible exception of the presidents.

This served as a backdrop for Congress to pass the 1887 Interstate Commerce Act. This act was passed to address the growing and long-standing public frustration over railroad abuses, encompassing price fixing, kickbacks, and discriminatory freight prices. Although the Interstate Commerce Act was hardly perfect, it did address in some fashion the public's desire to make the rules of the game a little fairer for small business and farmers. Another important piece of legislation was the Sherman Anti-Trust Act of 1890. This provided the federal government with the authority to prosecute corporate monopolies. Simply stated, monopolies constituted unfair business practices.

By the time of the 1896 presidential elections, political emotions were running high. The Democrats had selected as their candidate the fiery orator from Nebraska, William Jennings Bryan. The Republican nomination was won by Ohio's William McKinley. Bryan was strongly backed by populists in the south and west and he set the campaign's emotional tone, proclaiming that the election was a conflict between "the idle holders of idle capital and the struggling masses."[23] This had a degree of resonance considering the brutal nature of the depression of 1893.

The so-called idle holders of idle capital soon rallied around McKinley, who proved to be a more astute political operator. Despite the highly emotional nature of the election, McKinley won by a half-million votes. Support for McKinley came from a growing urban middle class, who favored a more activist government capable of acquiring the legal authority and administrative capability to regulate a maturing industrial economy and protect the citizens from the more pathological behavior of large-scale capitalism, including the scandals on Wall Street.[24] Although McKinley was not to be the activist that this group wanted, he was a better choice than Bryan or the alternatives—Marxists, socialists, and anarchists. The irony is that in 1901, shortly after his reelection, McKinley was assassinated by an anarchist, Leon Czolgosz. Struck twice, McKinley was mortally wounded. The man to follow him was Theodore Roosevelt, who was to restore the presidency to the forefront of its power and advanced a very reformist agenda to curtail the power of big business. He would also level the power of Wall Street and make it deal with Washington on a more even basis.

Conclusion

As the Gilded Age came to an end, Wall Street became a more settled institution in the American economy. Although rogues would reappear in plenty in the future, some of the more wild aspects of the stock and bond markets were curtailed. The period of great bear raids was largely over. In a sense, Wall Street had become more structured, the rules of the game clearer, transactions a little more transparent, and the ability of speculators to form pools more challenging. Central to this was the rise of financial capitalists, who favored a more stable environment. This did not mean that Wall Street's new leaders were not inclined to power struggles and strong-arm methods, but that options other than the total destruction of the competition were a possibility. Instead of panicked battles over cornering the gold market or Erie stock, agreements could be made over glasses of scotch while sailing up and down the Hudson River, or over a friendly game of golf. To some degree financial capitalism channeled the vast energy at work in U.S. industry and rationalized the process. It became harder for outsiders to disrupt the market. All the same, the whiff of scandal would not go away and the next round would come from within the circles of the financial capitalist themselves.

Notes

1.   Indeed, the period lasting from the end of the War Between the States in 1865 to around the end of the century was called the Gilded Age, a term coined by Mark Twain to dramatize the excesses of the post-Civil War generation. The press certainly provided a mosaic of shady characters, plotting in smoke-filled rooms and motivated by greed. The *New York Times* exposed the corruption linked to "Boss" William Macy Tweed, the head of the nefarious Tammany Hall political machine that dominated New York City on a regime of siphoning of public funds, kickbacks, strong-armed toughs, and patronage. Although Tweed was arrested in

1871 and died in a New York City jail in 1876, the corrupt nature of local politics and Wall Street—or at least an unscrupulous yet influential part of it—dominated the public perception of high finance well past Boss Tweed's demise.

While the antics of Boss Tweed and certain Wall Street financiers provided for colorful fare, the scandals surrounding the Grant administration in Washington, D.C. became a benchmark for government corruption. The Credit Mobilier scandal, which was exposed in 1872, involved bribery of influential congressmen (possibly including future president James A. Garfield) and Vice President Schuyler Colfax. In 1869, speculators Jim Fisk and Jay Gould (both known to be acquaintances of Boss Tweed) attempted to corner the nation's gold market, enlisting the assistance of Grant's brother-in-law. Indeed, Gould had met one-on-one with President Grant in an effort to unsuccessfully sway him to help in the gambit. And then there was the Whiskey Ring (which involved bribery of government officials by distillers not wishing to pay taxes) and the Indian Ring (in which Grant's Secretary of War William Belknap accepted bribes from companies with licenses to trade on the reservations of many Native American tribes). The frequency of these scandals led to the use of the term "Grantism," a word that became synonymous with greed and corruption.

2.   Michael Korda, *Ulysses S. Grant: The Unlikely Hero* (New York: Harper Collins, 2004), pp. 131-132.

3.   William S. McFeely, *Grant* (New York: W.W. Norton & Company, 1982), pp. 490-491.

4.   Robert Sobel, *Panic on Wall Street: A Classic History of America's Financial Disorder* (New York: E.P. Dutton, 1988), p. 211.

5.   Quoted from Jean Edward Smith, *Grant* (New York: Simon & Schuster, 2001), p. 620.

6.   Sobel, *Panic on Wall Street*, p. 215.

7.   President Chester Arthur at least presided over the reform of the federal civil service in an effort to clean up the patronage system.

8.   Sobel, *Panic on Wall Street*, p. 232.

9.   Geoffrey Perret, *Ulysses S. Grant: Soldier and President* (New York: The Modern Library, 1999), p. 415.

10.   See President Garfield and Arthur's challenges with Congress in Zachery Karabell, *Chester Alan Arthur* (New York: Henry Holt and Company, 2004), pp. 55-59.

11.   As historian Robert H. Wiebe noted: "For regardless of the official deference he received, the President was still just a factional leader, a chieftain among peers, whose election gave him considerable power through his control over Federal offices but in no way raised him to leadership of the entire party." From Wiebe, *The Search for Order 1877-1920* (New York: Hill and Wang, 1967), p. 29.

12.   Ibid., p. 33.

13.   Ibid., p. 5.

14.   Amelia Sturges was known for her vivacious personality. Two years J. P. Morgan's senior, her outgoing personality helped ease his shyness. Clearly, he was enraptured with this attractive, lively brunette, who was known to everyone as Mimi. Sadly, their happiness was short-lived. In 1861, Mimi was diagnosed with tuberculosis. As her health rapidly declined, Morgan pleaded with her to marry him, believing a Mediterranean honeymoon cruise would help her. Mimi finally consented. They were married in her parents' home in Manhattan and promptly embarked for Europe. Mimi was to die four months later in Nice, France. A widower at twenty-four, Morgan was crushed. Mimi's memory would be with

him for the rest of his life. Every year he would visit her grave, either on their anniversary or on her birthday.

15.   Ron Chernow, *The House of Morgan: An American Banking Dynasty and the Rise of Modern Finance* (New York: Simon & Schuster, 1990), p. 54.
16.   Ibid.
17.   Matthew Josephson, *The Robber Barons* (New York: Harcourts, 1962, reprint of the 1934 edition), p. 235.
18.   Chernow, *The House of Morgan*, p. 54.
19.   Thomas Kessner, *Capital City: New York City and the Men Behind America's Rise to Economic Dominance, 1860-1900* (New York: Simon & Schuster, 2003), p. 293.
20.   Ibid.
21.   Consuelo Vanderbilt Balsan, *The Glitter and the Gold* (Maidstone, Kent: George Mann, 1953), p. 19.
22.   Jeffery Patterson, *The First Four Hundred: Mrs. Astor's New York in the Gilded Age* (New York: Rizzoli, 2000), p. 7.
23.   Quoted from Sobel, *Panic on Wall Street*, p. 236.
24.   Elizabeth Sanders, *Roots of Reform: Farmers, Workers, and the American State 1877-1917* (Chicago: The University of Chicago Press, 1999), p. 1.

5

Teapot Dome Erupts

"Oil was once a word that lubricated the jaws of the nation. Newspapers screamed it, preachers damned it, Mr. Average Citizen swallowed it and was shocked. That was back in 1923 when the Senate was airing the Teapot Dome and Elk Hills oil scandals of the Harding Administration. Soon the tumult died, the people forgot, and the wheels of justice began to churn ponderously."—Time, *October 11, 1926*

Warren Harding, the twenty-ninth president of the United States, was well-loved during his years at the helm of the country (1921-1923). Coming into office following the chaotic final year of the Wilson administration (complicated by Wilson's stroke), Harding reinvigorated the presidency and helped set the stage for the great economic boom of the 1920s. Harding, however, would not be around to enjoy the boom. In early 1923, Harding was hit by the flu—as well as what was probably an undiagnosed heart attack. With the extent of his illness not fully grasped, he soon set out on a "Voyage of Understanding" to Alaska and the West Coast. Faced with enthusiastic audiences for the first president to visit the northernmost U.S. state, he briefly rallied, but after Alaska, his health slumped again and within days, on August 3, he was dead. This was a great shock to an adoring public. Some nine million Americans lined the railroad tracks to witness his funeral train as it passed on its way back to the East Coast.

Although Harding's death stunned the nation and his departure was deeply mourned, his legacy was not to last. Soon a string of long simmering scandals boiled over into the public light. This left one biographer to comment: "Warren G. Harding is best known as America's worst president."[1] The reasons for this sour legacy were many, but the one that boils to the top was the Teapot Dome scandal, which historian J. Leonard Bates has called "the greatest scandal of United States history."[2]

While most great American financial scandals occurred around Wall Street, this was not the case of the Teapot Dome scandal. Far removed from the narrow confines of Manhattan's lower end, Teapot Dome was the name of an oil field in Salt Creek, Wyoming. According to popular lore, it was given that name because of a teapot-shaped rock formation that stood atop a subterranean geological dome that contained oil. The scandal revolved around two of Harding's cabinet secretaries and two of the leading figures in the budding U.S. oil industry. It was a mix of opaque government dealings with the private sector, sealed by friendships and complicated by greed. In the end, Harding's reputation would be sullied, one of the members of his government would be the first cabinet minister to go to jail, and the tale of scandal would become a staple of American history.

The American Stage—The Progressives Seek to Level the Playing Field

The Teapot Dome scandal came at a moment in U.S. history when many questions were still bubbling: Should capitalism be unbridled, should it be guided, or should it be regulated with a view that the government would function as a referee, seeking to maintain a level playing field for all players? The era of unbridled capitalism—of the earlier Gilded Age—had burned itself out in the antics of Gould, Fisk, Vanderbilt, and Drew. In its place came the guided financial capitalism of J. P. Morgan and his elite of bankers and insurance interests. Financial capitalism, however, raised serious questions about Wall Street's dominance over industry vis-à-vis all other economic actors, a cast of characters including farmers, labor, and small and medium-sized businessmen. Wall Street's guided capitalism and the power it represented were not to go unchallenged. In one of history's ironic twists, the anarchist's bullet that killed President William McKinley in 1901 was to set off a revolution in government activism that eventually led to Teapot Dome.

The man to succeed McKinley was his vice president, Theodore R. Roosevelt. With his beefy features, well-defined mustache, and toothy smile, Roosevelt was charismatic, filled with energy, and held a firm belief that government was responsible for promoting the common welfare of the American citizen. Roosevelt and other Progressives were sensitive to the concentration of the nation's financial resources in the hands of a small elite, largely built up around New York's private banking houses.

Roosevelt felt that it was necessary to regulate the great industrial monopolies for the public interest. During his years in office, Roosevelt used the Sherman Anti-Trust Act to break up monopolies and regulate large corporations. A number of other laws were to follow, including the

Hepburn Act (1906), the Pure Food and Drug Act (1906), Meat Inspection Act (1906), and Immunity of Witness Act (1906).[3]

Roosevelt's antitrust policy was spearheaded by his Justice Department, which was ordered to prosecute companies pursuing monopolistic practices. The first case was brought against the Northern Securities Company, a railroad holding corporation created by J. P. Morgan. The Roosevelt administration then went after Nelson Rockefeller's Standard Oil Company. At the end of his time in office, Roosevelt's Justice Department had brought indictments against twenty-five monopolies.

Roosevelt and his immediate successors, William Taft and Woodrow Wilson, created what has been called the regulatory or administrative state. The guiding philosophy of this was the notion that a complex industrial society required rules and regulations, combined with agencies capable of enforcing these rules to maintain and enhance democratic free enterprise competition. It was one thing to have rules and regulations; it was equally important to actually enforce those rules and regulations. Both Taft (a Republican) and Wilson (a Democrat) followed through with key reforms that deepened the power and reach of the administrative state. Indeed, Taft was active in antitrust actions. His administration also presided over the creation of the Federal Reserve System in 1913, which was followed by the Clayton Anti-Trust Act of 1914, which improved the old Sherman Anti-Trust Act by protecting labor unions and farm cooperatives from prosecution.

The financial elite in the country was also changing. Although President Roosevelt was forced to rely on J. P. Morgan to stop the Panic of 1907, the great banker died in 1913. His son, John Pierpont Morgan II (1867-1943) took over upon his father's death, but young John never had the same clout and charisma of his father. Jacob Schiff, sometimes regarded as one of the few figures to rival the older J. P. Morgan, and the dynamic head of Kuhn, Loeb and Company, died in 1920. Anthony Drexel, who had worked closely with J. P. Morgan, died in 1893. Among the august financial elite, Henry Clay Frick died in 1919 and Solomon Loeb passed away in 1903. The next generation of financial leaders was no less dynamic, but they inherited a much more institutionalized system.

The Rise of Harding

The last year of the Woodrow Wilson administration was not a great year for the United States. Many Americans associated Wilson with the higher cost of living, higher taxes, immigration problems, and unwelcome entanglement in foreign affairs. Although the United States survived the postwar global economic downturn better than most countries, activity slowed and President Wilson was incapacitated by a stroke. Complicating matters was the concealment of the stroke from the public and most of the government, in effect leaving the president's wife Edith, Wilson's personal doctor, his private secretary, and secretary of state running the nation's affairs. In many regards the country appeared to be adrift. It was in this atmosphere that the election of 1920 was fought.

Harding had long been an active and visible force in the Republican Party, a factor that helped move him toward the presidency in a crowded field. A popular senator from Ohio, the home of six of the ten previous presidents, Harding was well connected as publisher of a major newspaper, the *Marion Daily Star*. Even so, the death of Teddy Roosevelt in 1919 had meant that the party had no clear-cut successor, and Harding was not the obvious choice. Indeed, General Leonard Wood, the commander of Roosevelt's Rough Riders, appeared to have a slight advantage, though two other strong contenders emerged before Harding threw his hat into the ring.

The Republican National Convention was a tough four-way contest. In what appeared to be a deadlocked convention, Harding surprisingly emerged as the winner. While his home state of Ohio was an important consideration, Harding was also regarded as humble, easygoing, and with few enemies. In addition, he was not an unknown: He had nominated President Taft at the 1912 Republican National Convention, been elected to the Senate in 1914, and was keynote speaker of the 1916 Republican National Convention. Considering that the Republicans badly wanted to be back in power and that each of the other candidates was seen as more controversial, Harding was an ideal compromise.

Harding also benefited from the political acumen of Harry Micajah Daugherty, described as "a small-time but canny political operative in Ohio," who "was a colorful, hard-drinking figure about whom stories abounded."[4] Supremely self-confident, he was the key actor in Harding's campaign, willing and able to work the smoke-filled rooms of the Republican convention. Upon Harding's selection he emerged as one of the key insiders in the next administration.

Harding's campaign was conducted in a "front porch" style reminiscent of President McKinley, also from Ohio. Although it appeared that Harding spent his time meeting America from the front porch of his home, giving numerous speeches, he also vigorously campaigned in ten states to defeat fellow Ohioan Governor James Cox, taking thirty-seven out of forty-eight states and capturing 60 percent of the popular vote.

When Harding went to Washington, D.C. he clearly believed that he had a mandate for change.

Good Intentions and the Path to Hell

Harding came into office with a strong pro-business bias. He publicly stated that the "high cost of living is inseparably linked with high cost of government." Along these lines, he proposed "less government in business as well as more business in government."[5] This translated into reducing federal regulations and supervision over American industry.

From the point of view of Harding and many other Americans, the years of Progressive legislation under Roosevelt, Taft, and Wilson ultimately weakened the ability of business to be profitable. As the three prior presidencies witnessed a more activist executive leadership and antitrust legislation, Harding meant to free up business and loosen controls. The motivation for this was to return the U.S. economy to growth.

Where Harding got into trouble, though, was with his appointments for office. As many chief executives did, he turned to his friends, including a strong contingent from his home state of Ohio. Some of these individuals would form the nucleus of the so-called "Ohio Gang," who would do much to sully Harding's name. Part of the reason for his selection of such people was Harding's personality. Although he was regarded as looking very "presidential," he was ultimately a small-town politician made good. As one of his contemporaries (and historian) Frederick Lewis Allen noted: "The truth was that under his imposing interior he was just a common small-town man, an 'average sensual man,' the sort of man who likes nothing better in the world than to be with the old bunch when they gather at Joe's place for an all-Saturday-night session, with waistcoats unbuttoned and cigars between their teeth and an ample supply of bottles and cracked ice at hand."[6]

At the same time, Harding's government posts were top-heavy with well-known industrialists, in particular, people from the oil industry. This included Andrew W. Mellon (Gulf Oil) as secretary of the Treasury, Theodore Roosevelt Jr. (Sinclair Oil) as assistant secretary of the Navy, and Will Hays (Sinclair Oil) as postmaster general. This chumminess with big oil was also evident in the new Secretary of the Interior Albert Fall's setting up a meeting between his friend oilman Edward Doheny and President-Elect Harding. Doheny's motives were comprehensive: His operations in Mexico were threatened by that country's revolution and as the gasoline engine eclipsed all other fuel-burning technologies, there was a scramble for oil sources in the United States. Having the upcoming president's ear was not such a bad thing. It was no wonder that the Democrats called the incoming Harding administration the "Oil Cabinet."

The first rumblings of scandal came from the Department of Justice. Daugherty, who became Harding's attorney general, was accused of covering up illegal activities, such as selling alcohol and profiting from not enforcing other laws (in particular antitrust laws). Prohibition was, after all, the law of the land. Lawmakers sought to impeach Daugherty, but Harding remained loyal and the storm passed.

Other scandals soon arose. Charles R. Forbes, director of the Veteran's Bureau, and Jesse Smith, a friend of the president, both were caught out. Forbes was not the best selection for the Veteran's post as he had actually deserted the Army, had been arrested, and while in office sold government medical supplies to private companies at artificially low prices. Forbes also influenced contracts for the construction of new hospitals. Harding ultimately had to force Forbes to resign, but never publicly denounced him nor did he make public his criminal actions. Needless to say, eventually this came to be seen as evidence of an administration tendency to cover up such scandals. The perception was only reinforced when Forbes left the country for a "vacation" to Europe.

In all fairness to Harding, he had little proof of Forbes' criminality. At the same time, the president promptly appointed a new director at the Veteran's Bureau, with a mandate to clean house. It was also reported that at Harding's last meeting with Forbes, the six-foot plus president was seen with his hands on Forbes' neck and shaking him "as a dog would a rat," while shouting "You double-crossing bastard."[7] Based on this story (if true), Harding was keenly aware of Forbes' transgressions.

Jesse Smith was equally enterprising. A friend of the president's from Ohio, he worked with Attorney General Daugherty in a number of capacities, including as secretary and accountant. Smith's notoriety, however, came with what was called "the little green house on K Street." The green house was located in the backyard of the residence and allegedly was where the conspirators met. K Street was and (still is) known as the power corridor in Washington, D.C., filled with the offices of powerbrokers, advisers, and consultants.

Smith set up shop to arrange deals giving access to the Department of Justice. In a sense, he functioned as a fixer. He apparently earned up to $250,000 per deal in which he worked to receive favorable treatment in a court case or to avoid arrest for selling alcohol. It has been strongly suggested that Daugherty was involved in the green house activities, where he made money selling confiscated alcohol.[8] Indeed, many believe that Smith was Daugherty's bagman. Together with the owner of the K Street house, Howard Mannington, a newspaper editor and would-be politician from Urbana, Ohio, this trio made up the core of the Ohio gang. As one historian noted, the gang was more of a "collection of rank opportunists who worked together as a matter of expediency... They looked for a quick buck, and not sustained graft."[9] Smith was eventually discovered and in the summer of 1923 committed suicide.

While these scandals were problematic and were known in Washington, they were not entirely out in the open in the rest of the country. Harding's reputation probably could have survived these cases, friends arguing that he was guilty of nothing more than running his administration with a light hand and too trusting of his friends. Teapot Dome, however, was a much larger affair, as it pointed to the upper reaches of the administration. When it seeped out into the public realm it did substantial damage to Harding's memory.

The Drama Unfolds

Teapot Dome centered around oil. As the U.S. Navy made the shift from coal-burning ship engines to oil early in the twentieth century, oil reserves became strategically important. Consequently the Taft administration put aside two sites of oil-rich deposits on federal land at Elk Hills and Buena Vista, both in California. Wilson followed the same policy, but added a third reserve at Teapot Dome, Wyoming in 1916. There was also an element of conservation involved as these natural resources were to be protected and maintained for future generations.

When Harding came to Washington, one of his first acts was a review of government to enhance efficiency. Under this process, the new secretary of the Interior, Albert B. Fall, suggested that his department assume control of the oil reserves from the Navy. The secretary of the Navy, Edwin Denby, did not vocalize any opposition to this. Indeed, Denby was under intense pressure to bow to Fall's request. First and foremost, Teapot Dome and other naval oil reserves were being drained by privately-owned oil wells on neighboring lands. To Denby's thinking, the Interior Department with Fall at the helm would be in a much better position to lease the lands and thus make money for the Navy. In addition, any oil production and storage infrastructure built by private oil companies would become useful in case of a war. Harding agreed and the oil reserves fell under Fall's authority.

Albert Bacon Fall

Who was Albert Bacon Fall? Every scandal needs a villain and Fall was to be the main villain in the Teapot Dome scandal. Although Fall remains one of the most besmirched individuals in the telling of the Teapot Dome story, he was also a creature of his time and place—a robber baron in the American southwest at the turn of the century. Along those lines, he was driven, ambitious, and ruthless. Moreover, he had worked his way up from very little to become a key member of the American political establishment. As one of his biographies noted: "[H]e was a rag-to-riches story and no matter who you were, he left an impression."[10]

Born in Frankfort, Kentucky on November 26, 1861, Albert Fall came from relatively modest beginnings and a limited education. After an assortment of different jobs, he went west, attracted by the dry, warm weather, which was expected to help his respiratory problem. Starting as a cowboy and a chuck wagon cook, he eventually ended up in northern Mexico, working in mines and becoming a fluent Spanish speaker. Fall, however, was destined for bigger things: He studied law and by 1889 was admitted to New Mexico's Territorial Bar. From there he entered local politics as a Democrat.

Fall's political career reflected the rough and tumble of frontier life. Political loyalties were sharply defined and often backed by hired guns. Fall was active in defending small ranchers, while his main rival, Albert Fountain, a Republican, sided with the large ranchers and Mesilla (the largest town in the area) residents. One of the nagging questions about Fall's involvement in politics was the mysterious disappearance in 1896 of his rival, Albert Fountain, and his wife. It was suggested, but never proved, that Fall had his rival eliminated. Fall briefly served in the Spanish-American War between 1898 and 1899 and changed party affiliation in 1904, joining the Republicans. In 1912 New Mexico became the forty-seventh state and Fall won the election to the Senate, where he served from 1912 to 1921. By that time, he was widely known as the "Political Boss of Southern New Mexico." It was during Fall's years in the Senate that he became acquainted with Harding, who sat next to him in the upper house.

Harding had a high opinion of Fall, regarding him as forceful, effective, and tough. At the height of his power, Fall was described as wearing "a large black hat and a string tie; a cigar usually hung from the corner of his mouth; his eyes were narrow, blue and cold…[and] he spoke with a drawl which could become disagreeable whenever he met opposition."[11]

Fall also campaigned for Harding. When it came time to fill cabinet posts, Fall was high on Harding's list and was given the Department of the Interior. Like many Westerners of the time, Fall was a firm believer in making use of the country's natural resources. As David H. Stratton, his biographer, commented: "His belief in the unrestricted and immediate disposition of the public lands was as typically western as his black, broad-brimmed Stetson hat."[12] Consequently, Fall was very open to private sector management of natural resources. This included the Navy's oil reserves, the transfer of control of the national forests from the Department of Agriculture to the Interior, and opening Alaska for development.

Fall's connections to big oil were well-established. During his Washington years, Fall emerged as the Republican Party's major critic of Wilson's non-interventionist policy in Mexico. He believed that U.S. oil interests were not getting a fair deal from President Wilson's policy of not sending in troops to quell the political turmoil south of the border. Fall presided over hearings in the Senate in which oil tycoon and chum Doheny appeared as a witness and advocate for sending in the troops. Upon Fall's appointment to the Interior Department, Doheny sent him a letter: "We greet and congratulate you and through you the President upon the culmination of the event which marks the beginning of a new epoch in Americanism and we believe a period of progress and prosperity for our country."[13]

Fall's appointment was quickly decried by one of the leading conservationists Gifford Pinchot, who stated: "It would have been possible to pick a worse man for Secretary of Interior, but not altogether easy."[14] Nevertheless, Fall prevailed.

On May 31, 1921, responsibility for the Navy's oil reserves was officially transferred to the Interior Department. Fall was quickly in touch with his friends in the oil industry. In April 1922, very quietly and without competitive bidding, leases were sold to the oil companies.

Fall and Big Oil

Fall's first sale was to Edward L. Doheny (1856-1935), the owner of the Pan-American Petroleum and Transport Company. An old friend of Fall's, Doheny was an entrepreneur who is often credited with the development of Los Angeles' first oil boom and the development of Mexico's oil industry. Much like Fall, Doheny came from humble beginnings and had worked his way up, having spent time in Arizona and Mexico as a silver miner. In 1893, however, he embarked upon the oil industry in

California and never looked back, eventually having operations in Mexico and South America. By 1921, Doheny was wealthy and well-connected. Always on the outlook for new business opportunities, he was keenly interested in the naval oil reserves in California.

An exchange of money in November 1921, however, was to prove unfortunate. At that time, Doheny made what he and Fall would later define as a "loan" to the secretary of the Interior. Accordingly, Doheny had his son Ned draw $100,000 in cash from his son's account, wrap the bills in paper and put them in a little black bag. Ned then proceeded to Fall's room at the Wardman Park Hotel in Washington, D.C. and gave the money to the secretary of the Interior. Doheny was later to claim that he been given a note from Fall for the money. Eventually the oil tycoon produced a note, but the signature had been torn off.

Following the exchange of money, in early 1922, Doheny's company leased portions of California's Naval Reserve Number One (Elk Hills) and Number Two (Buena Vista). Under the terms of the agreement, Doheny was expected to construct storage tanks at Pearl Harbor as well as fill them and erect a refinery in California. In addition, his company was obliged to construct a pipeline from the naval reserves to the refinery. For all of this work, Pan-American Petroleum was given exclusive rights to exploit about 300,000 acres of proven oil lands. Doheny would later claim that he earned a profit of $100 million on the transaction.

It was also later reported that two other oil companies had indicated an interest in the naval reserves. However, they insisted that Congress approve the proposed contract before it went into effect, a condition that Fall rejected.[15]

Fall was also busy negotiating a deal for Teapot Dome, Wyoming with Henry F. Sinclair and Mammoth Oil. Sinclair was, in many regards, the face of big oil to many Americans. In a 1928 *Time* profile of Sinclair, it was noted: "His energy was tremendous. His big smile and loud, harshly good-natured laugh would persuade strong men to work and inspire other gamblers' confidence. But, if necessary, Harry Sinclair could drive strong men to work and outsmart the money fellows. He was, and still is, as shrewd as they come in the whole shrewd oil game. His big laugh and heavy hands are the foils of a cunning mind."[16]

Sinclair's story certainly was entertaining fare. The son of a small town druggist in Kansas, Sinclair demonstrated little inclination to follow in his father's footsteps. Instead, a shooting accident that cost him a toe brought him insurance money of $5,000. Young Sinclair invested the money in the logs that were being used to bolster oil derricks. Using the profits made there, he invested in an Oklahoma oil pool from which he emerged with $100,000.[17] From that transaction, Sinclair became one of the oil industry's wheeler-dealers, with holdings throughout the United States, Mexico, Central America, Angola (then part of Portuguese West Africa), and Russia. Rounding out the Sinclair empire were baseball teams, race horses, and yachts. When Harding was elected, Sinclair became a frequent visitor to Washington, including stays at the White House. He was wealthy, well-connected, and ambitious, sharing many of the same characteristics as Fall, whom he came to know as a senator.

In December 1921, Fall lavishly entertained Sinclair and his attorney, Colonel J. W. Zevely, their wives, and several others at his sprawling ranch at Three Rivers, New Mexico. One is given the impression of significant conversations over cigars and whisky. Business was obviously discussed as well as Fall's cattle needs. This was made evident as Fall soon received six heifers, a yearling bull, two six-month-old boars, and four sows from Sinclair. In addition, Sinclair sent a thoroughbred house for Fall's foreman.

The drama then moved to Washington, where Fall and Sinclair were busy wrapping up their deal. On February 3, 1922, Fall and Admiral John Robinson (chief of the Navy's Petroleum Reserves) and Sinclair met in the secretary's office to outline an agreement. Under the agreement Teapot Dome would be leased to Mammoth Oil, which would construct a pipeline from the Teapot Dome oil fields. The proceeds from the Navy's share of oil from the reserve were to be used by Mammoth to build storage tanks on the Atlantic coast and fill them with fuel oil. Questions were raised about the legality of the agreement, but Fall again indicated that it was not necessary to bring Congress into the picture. On April 7, 1922 Fall and Sinclair signed a lease for all of Teapot Dome.

In March—as word about Fall's dealings percolated into the Senate—the Interior secretary sent his son-in-law, M. T. Everhart, to visit Sinclair in the oil mogul's private railroad car. Sinclair gave Fall's son-in-law $198,000 in Liberty Bonds. This was followed shortly thereafter by another $35,000 worth of the same issue of bonds from Sinclair to Everhart. To give these transactions a fig-leaf of legality, Everhart also gave Sinclair a check for $1,100 to pay for the livestock earlier shipped to Fall's farm. He also advised Sinclair that Fall would like a "loan," so the oil baron provided $36,000 in cash.

For Fall the deals cut two ways. On one side, he stayed true to his firm belief in developing U.S. natural resources by the private sector. On the other side, he had collected from Doheny and Sinclair an estimated

$409,000 in cash and bonds, as well as new additions to his ranch's livestock.

Although not known at the time, Fall was in financial trouble. The Mexican Revolution deprived him of his income from copper mines in that country, and he was forced to sell off many of his business interests. Moreover, he was in arrears on his property taxes as well as indebted to the tune of over $100,000. As the historian Margaret Leslie Davis noted: "Doheny's loan and the additional gifts from Sinclair enabled him to pay back his back taxes as well as a $140,000 debt owed to the M.D. Thatcher Estates Company at Pueblo, Colorado. He even purchased the adjoining ranch owned by N.W. Harris. Fall now began to plan extensive improvements for both properties, including the construction of a hydroelectric plant, irrigation systems, and new roads."[18] Washington was good for Fall—at least until things unraveled.

The Scandal Breaks

The deals that Fall struck were not to go unnoticed. While the commercial rivals of Doheny and Sinclair were aware that something was going on, members of Congress were also tipped off. Upon hearing of Sinclair's newfound control of Teapot Dome, one small oil operator from Wyoming sent a letter to his senator asking what were to be the core questions in the entire scandal: Why was the Navy's land being leased, and why was the secretary of the Interior permitted to independently dispose of Naval reserve lands?[19]

Also, Fall's rise to political fame in New Mexico had brought him some enemies. News gradually filtered from New Mexico to Washington that Fall was buying more land and improving those properties he already owned. Had he suddenly come into some money?

Fall, however, was prepared. His first response was to argue that "secrecy" had been necessary during the lease-hold negotiations because of national security considerations. When members of the Senate started to press harder with inquiries, President Harding covered both Denby and Fall with a long letter of explanation that the latter had prepared. Accordingly, the president's letter stated: "The policy decided upon and the subsequent acts have at all times had my entire approval."[20] After Harding's death, these words certainly came back to haunt the president's memory.

Despite the presidential seal of approval, members of the Senate smelled blood. They were also pushed along by conservationists, who hated Fall. On April 15, 1922 the Senate passed Resolution 277, requesting the secretary of the Interior and his counterpart from the Navy to provide any information on negotiations and conditions pertaining to the oil reserves. This eventually led to a full-scale Senate investigation under Senator Thomas J. Walsch.[21]

A List of the Teapot Dome Actors

- **Warren Harding:** Twenty-ninth president of the United States. It was on his watch that the Teapot Dome scandal occurred. Although not directly involved, he appointed the key culprit, Albert Fall, as secretary of the Interior. In addition, Harding's administration was to be forever tainted by the Teapot Dome scandal.
- **Albert Bacon Fall:** A senator from New Mexico, he was a close friend of the oil industry and became Harding's secretary of the Interior, from which position he leased naval oil reserves to two friends. He was put on trial, found guilty of bribery, and became the first member of a presidential cabinet to go to jail.
- **Harry Sinclair:** Oil tycoon, head of Mammoth Oil Corporation, and friend of Fall. Accused of bribery, but was charged and found guilty in a contempt of court and sentenced to six months in prison.
- **Edward L. Doheny:** Head of Pan-American Petroleum and Transport Company, friend of Fall, and given credit for being one of the key players in Los Angeles' first oil boom. Indicted on conspiracy and bribery charges, he was acquitted. When he died, he left behind a considerable legacy in Southern California, including two libraries (one at the University of Southern California).
- **Harry Micajah Daugherty:** Small-time Ohio politician who helped win Harding the Republican nomination in 1920 and became the new president's attorney general. He was regarded as corrupt and a leading member of the so-called Ohio Gang. He exited Washington shortly after Harding died.
- **Calvin Coolidge:** Harding's vice president, who followed him as the thirtieth U.S. head of state. He inherited Teapot Dome and worked quickly to clean up the mess.
- **Atlee Pomerene:** A Democratic politician from Ohio, he served as senator and was appointed by Coolidge to serve as a special counsel to deal with the Teapot Dome scandal. He later ran unsuccessfully for the Democratic nomination to the U.S. presidency in 1928.
- **Owen Roberts:** Former law professor and Republican appointed along with Pomerene as special counsel to investigate Teapot Dome. Later was appointed and served on the U.S. Supreme Court of Justice.

Although initially Fall was able to push off the Senate investigation by sending a truckload of documents that took a year to digest, the clouds were gathering by early 1923. Under attack by the Senate and increasingly isolated from the president, as Harding began to distance himself, Fall finally resigned on March 4, 1923. He was, however, not off the hook—the Senate investigation was ongoing.

Investigation

Harding's administration had started with a spirit of promise. Under the weight of scandals, it was quickly becoming a mockery of the public's high expectations. Moreover, the stress did little to help Harding's health. Although he was not feeling well, he decided that the trip to Alaska and the West Coast was necessary to revive his administration. The positive responses of the crowds briefly reenergized him, but Harding's health was in a terminal spiral. His mental health was not helped by a coded telegram from Washington, D.C., which indicated that the scandals within his administration were far worse than he initially suspected. No doubt this weighed heavily on his mind and probably contributed to his deteriorating health. On August 2, 1923 he died; the official cause was a stroke.

The high level of respect that the American public had for their late president was not to last. As the elements of scandal began to leak out into the media, the hidden contours of the Harding presidency slowly emerged. The Senate investigation gained momentum, pushing the new president, Vermont's Calvin Coolidge, to nominate two special counsels, a Republican and a Democrat, to investigate and pursue the civil and criminal cases arising from the Senate's allegations. Coolidge eventually appointed Ohio Democrat Atlee Pomerene and Republican Owen Roberts, both of whom were affirmed by the Senate.

For Coolidge, Teapot Dome was both a shock and a potential political nightmare. Some thought that Coolidge, who had sat in on cabinet meetings, not only was aware of what was going on, but may have been involved himself.[22] Moreover, as he was an unexpected president of unknown nature, members of the Congress could be tempted to regain some power at his expense. But on the other hand, if Coolidge acted forcibly and quickly, he could take the moral high ground and use the scandal to his advantage. The bipartisan special counsel shrewdly bypassed the Daugherty Justice Department, itself very badly tainted by scandals. Indeed, Daugherty himself supported the appointment of special counsel, as this took him out of a potential conflict of interest. Coolidge, however, was deeply concerned over Daugherty's ongoing presence in his administration, considering all the rumors (some of which were true) about his involvement in various "questionable" activities. Daugherty soon resigned.

The trials from the Teapot Dome scandal were to drag on for years. The Department of Justice initiated five suits—two to void the Elk Hills and Teapot Dome leases, and three criminal suits, charging Fall, Doheny, and Sinclair with various counts of bribery and conspiracy to defraud.[23] Fall was finally indicted for conspiracy and accepting bribes. For this he was sentenced to prison for a year, making him the first member of a presidential cabinet to be sent to prison. He was also forced to pay a $100,000 fine.

In the drama surrounding Fall's trial, it was his son-in-law Everhart's testimony that sank the former senator and Interior secretary. Special Counsel Pomeree's questioning was damning when it came to Everhart's visit to Sinclair's private train car.

Pomeree's question: When you got to Mr. Sinclair's private car, what if anything, did Mr. Sinclair give you?
A. He gave me a package of bonds.
Q. A package of bonds?
A. Yes.
Q. What kind of bonds?
A. They were three and one half percent Liberty Bonds.
Q. Were they counted there in your presence, in his car?
A. No sir.
Q. Where did you take them?
A. I took them to the Wardman Park Hotel.
Q. Who lived there?
A. Secretary Fall.
Q. To whom did you deliver them?
A. To him.[24]

Doheny and Sinclair were initially acquitted, but the latter was subsequently sentenced to prison for contempt of the Senate and for employing detectives to shadow members of the jury in his case. Although Doheny was acquitted of bribery and conspiracy charges, the lengthy ordeal weakened his health. By the time of his final acquittal he was seventy-three years old. Shortly thereafter his only son, Ned, Jr., was murdered, a severe emotional blow to the aging man. He died in 1935, after being bedridden for two years.[25]

One of the stranger twists in the Teapot Dome scandal was the outcome of the trials. Whereas Doheny was acquitted, it was acknowledged that he had "lent" the money to Fall. On the other hand, Fall was guilty of taking a bribe. How could one man be guilty and the other innocent? *Time* magazine attempted to answer this issue by explaining that the $100,000 loan that Doheny gave Fall was a "corrupt bribe." The magazine went on to state: "Bribery, like adultery, is a peculiar crime in fact if not in law. Injury is done to a third party. And culpability between partners is not always equal before the law... A bribe-taking official is more punishable, because he has betrayed a public trust, than the bribe-giver, who is under no specific oath of honesty."[26] It should also be added that Doheny hired an excellent lawyer, and his age and appearance created a degree of sympathy among the jury.

As for Fall, he went to prison for a brief spell, spending most of the time in the correctional facility's hospital. Following his prison sentence, Fall moved back to El Paso, where he was forced to sell most of his assets. His wife Emma died in 1943 and he passed away in his sleep in 1944. Throughout the trials and after, Fall and his family maintained his innocence. Although Fall's actions were in the wrong, he was a product of an environment that generally condoned such wheeling and dealing. As such, he fit the role of the heavy for the press and the American public, no doubt making him a scapegoat for the affair, especially following the unexpected departure of President Harding.

As for the oil fields, Doheny and Sinclair were forced to return those properties to the U.S. government, following a Supreme Court decision in 1927. In 1998, Elk Hills was sold to Occidental Petroleum for $3.5 billion, the largest divestiture of federal property in the history of the federal government.

Conclusion

Teapot Dome ranks high as a major financial scandal that rocked Washington, making one wonder what would have happened to Harding's tenure in office if he had lived.

Part of the blame for the scandal clearly goes to Harding. The president was relatively complacent, not well informed, and a poor judge of friends. Although no one questioned Harding himself, he was the ultimate authority in an administration that was increasingly plagued by scandal. At the same time, Fall decidedly made a set of deeply flawed judgment calls, especially in light of the way money and other valued assets traded hands. The irony is that when Teapot Dome is discussed, it is Harding who is remembered and tainted, while Fall is largely forgotten, passing away quietly in a hospital, his memory still revered by many as a builder of the American West.

Notes

1. John W. Dean, *Warren G. Harding* (New York: Henry Holt and Company, 2004), p. 1.
2. J. Leonard Bates, *The Origins of Teapot Dome: Progressives, Parties and Petroleum, 1909-1921* (Urbana: Ill.: University of Illinois Press, 1963), p. 236.
3. The Hepburn Act expanded the membership of the Interstate Commission from five to seven. That body could also set its own fair freight rates, had its regulatory power extended over pipelines, bridges, and express companies, and was empowered to require a uniform system of accounting by regulated transportation companies. The Pure Food and Drug Act prohibited the manufacture, sale, and transportation of adulterated or fraudulently labeled foods and drugs in accordance with consumer demands. The Meat Inspection Act provided for federal sanitary regulations and inspections in meat packing facilities. And the Witness Act meant that corporate officials could no longer make a plea of immunity to avoid testifying in cases dealing with their company's illegal activities.
4. Margaret Leslie Davis, *Dark Side of Fortune: Triumph and Scandal in the Life of Oil Tycoon Edward L. Doheny* (Berkeley: University of California Press, 1998), p. 126.
5. Congressional Record, 67th Congress, 1st Session, p. 170.
6. Frederick Lewis Allen, *Only Yesterday: An Informal History of the 1920s* (New York: John Wiley & Son, 1997, reprint of the 1931 edition), p. 126.
7. Robert H. Ferrell, *The Strange Deaths of President Harding* (Columbia: University of Missouri Press, 1996), p. 121.
8. Jonathan L. Thorndike, *The Teapot Dome Scandal Trial* (Berkeley Heights, N.J.: Enslow Publishers, Inc., 2001), pp. 43-44.
9. Robert K. Murray, *The Harding Era: Warren G. Harding and His Administration* (Minneapolis: University of Minnesota Press, 1969), p. 434.
10. M. R. Werner and John Starr, *Teapot Dome* (New York: Viking, 1959), p. 6
11. Burl Noggle, *Teapot Dome: Oil and Politics in the 1920s* (New York: W.W. Norton, 1965), p. 13.
12. David H. Stratton, *Tempest Over Teapot Dome: The Story of Albert B. Fall*, p. xv.
13. Edward L. Doheny to Albert B. Fall, telegram, March 6, 1921, Albert B. Fall Papers, Manuscript Collection 8, Rio Grande Historical Collections, University Library, New Mexico State University, Las Cruces (RGHC).
14. Thorndike, *The Teapot Dome Scandal Trial*, p. 50.
15. Werner and Starr, *Teapot Dome*, pp. 84-86.
16. "Long, Long Trial," *Time Magazine,* April 9, 1928, http://www.time.com/archive/previewlo,10987,787077,00.html.
17. Ibid.
18. Davis, *Dark Side of Fortune*, p. 146.
19. Francis X. Busch, *Enemies of the State* (New York: Bobbs-Merrill, 1962), p. 96.
20. Ibid.
21. Walsch (1859-1933) was a Democratic senator from Montana from 1913 until his death. He was actively engaged as a legislator, being involved in writing the Eighteenth and Nineteenth Amendments. He was also strongly opposed to child

labor and sought to have it abolished. A strong debater and with considerable experience in Washington's ways, he was tapped to head the Senate Investigating Committee (1922-23).

22.   Robert Sobel, *Coolidge: An American Enigma* (Washington, D.C.: Regnery Publishing, Inc., 1998), p. 260.

23.   "Dome Comes Home," *Time Magazine*, October 24, 1927, http://www.time.com/archive/preview/0,10987,736904,00.html.

24.   *U.S. v. Fall*, Trial Testimony, Vol. 8, at 818-819 (October 15, 1929).

25   The Doheny legacy in California is considerable. Two libraries carry the family name: the Edward L. Doheny, Jr. Memorial Library at the University of Southern California, built as a memorial to Doheny's son Ned; and the Edward L. Doheny Library at St. John's Seminary in Camarillo, California, built in Doheny's memory by his second wife, Carrie Estelle Doheny (1875-1958), herself a noted collector of rare books, nineteenth-century paintings, and Western Americana. In addition, the Doheny name lives on in the Estelle Doheny Eye Foundation, a research laboratory and eye bank created by Mrs. Doheny at St. Vincent's Hospital in Los Angeles. The Dohenys also left behind two of the area's landmark buildings: their elegant residence at 8 Chester Place in the West Adams District (later willed to the Catholic Church), and the fifty-five-room Greystone Mansion in Beverly Hills. The latter was regarded as the "dream palace" built by Doheny in 1928 as a wedding present to his son. Greystone is currently owned by the city of Beverly Hills. Finally, the Dohenys financed construction of the magnificent St. Vincent's Church at Adams Boulevard and Figueroa Street south of downtown Los Angeles.

26.   Quoted in Davis, *Dark Side of Fortune*, pp. 263-264.

6

Empires Undone:
Samuel Insull, the Emperor of Utilities

"What I did, when I did it, was honest; now, through changed conditions, what I did may or may not be called honest. Politics demand, therefore, that I be brought to trial; but what is really being brought to trial is the system I represented."—Samuel Insull

Time was running out for Samuel Insull. Sitting in a jail in Istanbul, Turkey in April 1934, he pondered the string of events that had brought him to these crossroads. His hair was gray and his health was fragile. His heart, in particular, felt heavy—no doubt reflecting the acute levels of stress that had dominated his life and foretelling a series of heart attacks that would ultimately kill him. He had not seen his wife Gladys for several days and he longed for the tumultuous events surrounding his life to settle. He was in exile from the United States, a place where he had made his fame and fortune as the so-called "Emperor of the Utilities." Sitting in his cell, awaiting extradition to New York, the emperor was clearly deposed.

Insull understood that the wheels for his extradition were in motion, but he probably did not know of the personal involvement of President Franklin Delano Roosevelt himself. On April 10, 1934, the president and Secretary of State Cordell Hull had signed a warrant empowering Burton Yost Berry, a young U.S. diplomat, and W. Habel, master of the S.S. *Exilona*, to take Insull into custody in Turkey, transport him to the United States, and turn him over to the proper authorities. Roosevelt personally regarded Insull and others of his ilk (generally Wall Street bankers and industrialists) as the root causes of the Great Depression. This was, after all, turning out to be one of the worst economic dislocations in American history, a situation worsened by climatic change in the West, which had resulted in the Dust Bowl. In signing the papers to retrieve this villain who played a role in one of America's most troubling economic downturns ever, Roosevelt was doing his part in bringing justice to the common man against the obtuse machinations of big business.

Mr. Berry proceeded to Istanbul, where he notified Insull that he would be escorting him back to Chicago to stand trial on charges of a) transferring property in advance of bankruptcy in violation of the bankruptcy laws; b) fraud by an officer or director of a corporation; and c) using the mails to obtain money and property by means of false and fraudulent pretenses. Insull must have found the charges maddening as he maintained his innocence. All the same, Mr. Berry accompanied Insull on the S.S. *Exilona* to Chicago, an almost ever present, yet polite shadow. On entering New York Harbor, the press was ready and this round of American kabuki was enacted. Insull, old and in poor health, his hair more white than gray, met the press, read his prepared remarks—proclaiming himself innocent of all charges—and quickly headed off, with his son and Mr. Berry, on the train to Chicago.

Insull's meteoric rise had, until then, embodied the American dream. As a youth Insull had worked for the famous inventor Thomas Edison in New York and later moved to Chicago, where he soon brought electrical power to rural America. He became a recognized member of Chicago's high society, a frequent visitor to the prestigious halls of the Chicago Club. Insull hated New York bankers, which led him to create a number of interconnected and opaque companies designed to allow him to elude takeovers—a byproduct of an earlier unpleasant experience with J. P. Morgan.

By 1930, Insull's complicated shell game of power companies possessed assets of over $2.5 billion and served more than 45 million customers. Although Insull's power empire survived the stock market crash in 1929, Insull was eventually caught between large debts and a downturn in revenues due to reduced electricity use. He was eventually forced to go to New York bankers for help, and, just as he feared, they used the weakened state of his finances to oust him from his companies, discredit his name, and assume control over prime utility assets. Insull quietly slipped out of the country, but he eventually was extradited to the United States. He went to court and was acquitted, but his reputation was destroyed. Following the trial, Insull returned to Paris, where he died on July 16, 1938, one of the more misunderstood characters to be included in the history of American financial scandals.

Insull's Rise

How was it that a young Englishman, the son of a Congregationalist minister in Oxford, was to go down in American history as one of the major villains of the Great Depression? This very same villain, who was attacked by the Roosevelt administration as representative of the evils of the 1920s boom, also embodied the American dream of upward social mobility, based on hard work and thrift.

Insull was born in the United Kingdom in 1859. Apparently an intelligent child, he was sent to a good private school. At the age of fourteen, he left school and became a secretary and bookkeeper at an auction firm. However, four years later young Insull was pushed out to make room for the son of one of the firm's major clients. That unfair development, though, paved the way for Insull to get a new job—working for George A. Gouraud, a banker and one of Thomas Edison's agents in England, and for Edison's chief engineer in England, Edward Johnson. Johnson quickly recognized the younger man's keenness, his quickness at grasping the principles underlying technical problems, and his ability to systematize complex business affairs.[1] Gouraud was also duly impressed with his young protégé and helped Insull move to the United States in 1881, where he became an assistant to Thomas Edison himself.

Edison, of course, was one of the spearheads of the U.S. industrial revolution. In 1879 he invented the first commercially practical incandescent electric lamp and built the first electric motor. That was followed shortly by Edison's gradual move to put a utility empire together. Along these lines, he built the first electric power plant in New York City in 1881-1882. Consequently, when Insull arrived in New York, the Edison revolution was well in motion, forever changing the form and substance of industrial development.

Insull and Edison made an odd couple. At their first meeting, Insull arrived prim and proper; Edison was ill-shaven, his hair long and shaggy. Insull later noted of the great inventor: "With my strict English idea as to the class of clothes to be worn by a prominent man, there was nothing in Mr. Edison's dress to impress me. He wore a rather seedy black diagonal Prince Albert coat and waistcoat, with trousers of dark material, and a white silk handkerchief knotted around his neck and falling over the stiff bosom of a white shirt somewhat worse for wear."[2] Insull spoke with a cockney accent, which Edison had trouble understanding. In turn, Insull struggled to understand Edison's Midwestern accent. Yet, there was something in the chemistry between the two men that worked.

Insull was deeply impressed by the man who had invented the stock ticker, the multiplex telegraph, the mimeograph machine, the phonograph, and the transmitter that made the telephone practical. But Edison was also a poor business manager. For all of his innovations, Edison was constantly troubled by a lack of cash flow and usually seemed only two or three steps ahead of insolvency. Thus Edison was attracted by Insull's financial acumen. Within twenty-four hours Insull was able to come up with a plan to get Edison the capital he needed to continue his technological experiments. At twenty-one years of age, Insull became the great Thomas Edison's business manager.

As Edison's business manager, Insull was put into direct contact with New York's bankers, a group of people that Insull did not hold in deep trust. In particular, Insull was to take a pronounced dislike of J. P. Morgan, who was then very much the power on Wall Street. Although Morgan had invested in Edison securities, he was a very reluctant lender, and even in the early days he had an irritating tendency to call in the loans at difficult times. As a consequence, Insull openly resented the great banker. Loyal to Edison, Insull probably saw Morgan as a threat to the investor's control of his enterprises. By the same token, Morgan probably had little respect for the considerably younger Insull, who had yet to prove himself. At one point Morgan reprimanded Insull for his disrespectful attitude, something the young Englishman never forgot. He soon took revenge on Morgan in a proxy battle over the control of the Edison Light Company. Insull commented: "There is no one more anxious after wealth than Sam Insull, but there are times when revenge is sweeter than money."

With Morgan unresponsive to the pressing need to find financing for Edison's collection of decentralized companies, Insull was forced to go begging for loans among New York's banking community. As one observer noted: "This frantic nerve-racking experience disgusted Insull. He never lost a deep-seated animosity for banks and bankers, especially those in New York and more specifically the Morgan Bank."

What evolved was an impasse between Edison-Insull and Morgan. Edison-Insull did not want to surrender their emerging industrial empire, but badly needed funding. Morgan, with his railroad experience, believed he could make Edison's businesses into a consolidated money-maker. But this meant that Morgan would assume control and that Edison's role would be diminished—a nonstarter from the inventor's point of view. The deadlock between Edison-Insull and Morgan was broken by Henry Villard, a German-born speculator, well-known in New York's financial circles.[3] Villard had come to the United States in 1853 and spent many years as a journalist. He married the daughter of antislavery campaigner William Lloyd Garrison, made money on the railroads, and by 1881 was able to acquire a controlling influence in the New York *Evening Post* and the *Nation*. He lost his fortune in the financial panic of 1883-1884 and left New York for Germany, but returned two years later, with the financial support of powerful German financial parties—Deutsche Bank, the Allgemaine Elektrialzilals Gesellschaft, and (electric inventors) Siemens and Halske.

Wealthy, known in New York society, backed by German deep pockets, and aware of major industrial trends, Villard understood Edison's business potential as well as his troubles. He saw that with greater financial order, Edison's gaggle of companies could be profitable. In 1888, Villard proposed the amalgamation of the various Edison companies into one consolidated firm to be called the Edison General Electric Company, something that Morgan could go along with. The banker, after all, remained very much in the mix, being a major creditor of the company. After considerable negotiating, Edison-Insull, Morgan, and Villard were finally able to reach agreement on this, a new "electrical trust." Edison later wrote: "Mr. Insull and I were afraid we might get into trouble for lack of money...therefore we concluded it was better to be sure than to be sorry."[4]

Although Edison remained, real control of the "trust" passed to Villard and Morgan (who had stepped up with money). By 1892, the company had dropped the Edison part of its name, simply becoming General Electric. Edison wandered off to pursue other inventions. Insull was offered a minor executive position, which he turned down for the greener pastures of Chicago. Ironically, Villard, who had been one of the major guiding forces in consolidating the Edison companies, was also forced out—by Morgan. The all-powerful banker calmly informed Villard that his "courteous resignation would be courteously received."[5]

Insull Heads to Chicago

Insull arrived in Chicago at the right time, with the right package of skills. The large Midwestern city was a major hub for agricultural produce and manufacturing. Close to abundant natural resources, the challenge was often to find a regular source of power. Coal had long held sway, but electricity certainly offered a far cleaner alternative; it could also be used for homes. As Insull was leaving New York, the Chicago Edison Company was looking for a president. The two parties met and Insull was soon head of the Chicago firm.

Insull combined an ability to accomplish real goals and to promote. Along these lines, he designed the first steam engine turbine, which enabled the commercialization of energy. He also benefited from a structural change in U.S. energy markets as technological advances made electricity cheaper and more available, undercutting coal and gas. As historian Harold L. Platt noted in the era after 1898: "Electricity was no longer a mysterious technology but a mere commodity—energy—to be sold like other products in an emerging urban culture of middle class affluence and leisure."[6] Indeed, the spreading of such conveniences as the electric elevator and improvements in refrigeration reinforced this trend. And Insull was ready and able to benefit from these developments, fully understanding the dynamics of the business and the politics of urban government with its layers of party machines, handouts, and manipulation.

By 1907 all of Chicago's electricity was generated by Insull's Commonwealth Edison Company, largely because he was able to convince the city government that he could meet all of its electric power needs. He was also flexible when it came to rate cuts, working with the local government and its officials. At the same time, Insull understood marketing and promotion. In one case, he bought 10,000 GE irons and gave them away to anyone who would sign up for electrical service. As Platt noted: "He realized that once the housewife had the convenience of the modern iron, had the electric lights in the house, that they would never give it up again. So once they were hooked up, they were hooked."[7]

Insull also expanded into streetcar companies, which had been badly managed, poorly funded, and caught up in the cesspool of Chicago's political corruption. Insull quickly moved to consolidate competing lines and to upgrade the company's equipment.

Insull had become a past-master of intricate and opaque financial engineering that would have earned him a place within the inner circles of Enron. In establishing Middle Western Utilities, Insull demonstrated an amazing ability to sell shares to the public, while still maintaining control of the company (as his brother Martin was the chief executive). As one historian noted:

> First, Insull sold his properties to the newly organized Middle West Utilities (also called Midwest Utilities) for $333,000. He then issued to himself as president 40,000 shares of preferred stock and 60,000 shares of common for which he paid $3,600,000—a price he himself established. This proved to be such a bargain that he was then able to sell the preferred shares and 10,000 of the common stock to the public for $3,600,000, recouping his investment. After the smoke settled, Insull still owned 50,000 shares which, in effect, cost him nothing, and he had control of the company.[8]

Riding to the Top

Middle West Utilities would eventually control some 12 percent of the nation's power market. But Insull was hardly finished with the development of his power empire. Over the next several years and into the 1920s, Middle West (which extended north into Canada) became one of a handful of powerful utility companies. The other companies were the Southern Company (led by James Duke) and the Morgan Group (later operating as United Corp and including companies like Consolidated Edison and Public Service of New Jersey).

Insull was riding the wave of success. From his base at Middle West Utilities, he could see only room for expansion. Success fed on success. His empire grew from a local to a metropolitan to a national basis. Momentum was on his side. As Harold Platt noted: "And so I think he sees he can do no wrong—that electric utilities were clearly the wave of the present and future. He could see that use would just get larger and larger and larger, so why not control more and more and more of this economic growth and have it under his own control?"[9]

Another leg of Insull's business strategy was to tap an emerging group of investors, his employees and customers. This constituted a sizeable audience who observed the value of Insull's utility stocks each time they flipped the light switch on. The attraction of owning a small part of American industry was strong. Considering that the stock market was on a wild upward ride, owning Insull's stocks seemed like a certain bet.

But at the same time, Insull and his counterparts were gaining some enemies. The combination of the Southern Company, Middle West, and the Morgan Group had considerable influence, something that did little to endear the power chiefs to members of the political class, especially those of a more populist orientation. Senator George Norris of Nebraska (Republican) regarded the power companies as "the greatest monopolistic corporation that has been organized for private greed... It has bought and sold legislatures. It has interested itself in the election of public officials, from school directors to the President of the United States."[10] Aware of such political sentiment, Insull was a major contributor to the Republican Party and made certain that he had his photo taken with President Theodore Roosevelt. At the same time, Insull was very much able to hold his own in Chicago's rough and tumble politics. He was known to be a cunning and intelligent businessman, who avoided making bribes, instead seeking to cultivate relationships with politicians and make them allies.

By 1929 Insull was one of the most powerful men in Chicago. His public utility companies controlled several hundred electric, light, and power plants serving 5,000 communities spread over a thirty-two-state area from Maine to Texas and Oklahoma. As one historian noted: "On the eve of the crash, this interlocking structure of local operating and interstate holding companies allowed him single-handedly to maintain an iron grip on the management of energy and transit services worth $3 billion. He affected the lives of over a million stock and bond holders as well as 41 million customers."[11] Having come from modest beginnings in England, Insull had worked hard, been thrifty, and climbed the ranks as a successful entrepreneur. In many regards, he fulfilled the ideal of what the United States was built around: the ability of an immigrant to achieve upward social mobility through hard work and thrift.

Insull's personal life also reflected his growing success. In 1897 he married Gladys Wallis, an aspiring actress. In 1900, Samuel Insull, Jr. was born. Along the way, the Insulls bought and maintained a large apartment in Chicago and in 1907 bought the Hawthorn Farm. By 1907, the farm had 4,000 acres and Insull had built a mansion on the location; he also bought a yacht. While he picked up many of the trappings of the wealthy, Insull was also active in donating money to various causes, which helped his image with the public. Rounding out the realm of successful mogul, Insull also became a force in Republican politics. Along these lines he unsuccessfully supported a presidential candidate against McKinley, supporting Republican presidential candidates as well as developing positive relations with the new Democratic president.

Outsmarting the Eastern Bankers

Insull's empire building put him in a position where he was in constant need of capital. This, in turn, took him to the banks. As he had a very strong dislike of New York's banks, he developed business relationships with the local Chicago bankers, key among these being Continental Illinois and the investment firm Halsey, Stuart & Company. In turn, the Chicago bankers liked doing business with Insull, especially since it came at the expense of the Eastern institutions. As one Midwest banker noted: "These New York fellows were jealous of their prerogatives, and if you wanted to get along you had to be deferential to them and keep your opinions to yourself. Mr. Insull wouldn't, and that made bad blood between them. But there was this ongoing problem with New York."[12]

What was to elevate Insull with Chicago's banking community was his ability to ride through the financial panic of 1896. During the summer of that year, William Jennings Bryan, a populist firebrand, had won the Democratic Party's presidential nomination. Bryan favored silver over gold to back the national treasury, something desired by the farmers and loathed by financial circles. The "Bryan panic" fundamentally killed capital markets, with bankers showing little inclination to extend credit. Only with the election of William McKinley in November did credit flow again.

Despite the dubious nature of U.S. financial markets in 1896, Insull was able to get funding for Chicago Edison. In a move that bypassed New York altogether, Insull traveled to London, where he successfully sold his company's bonds. Making good use of his story as a plucky young Englishman who had gone off to the colonies and made a name for himself, Insull added certain innovations to the bonds, making them more attractive to investors. Clearly, when Insull returned his standing in Chicago's financial community was higher. The emperor of utilities, however, had permanently earned the enmity of New York's powerful bankers, who were an unforgiving lot and willing to wait for their revenge.

The seeds of Insull's downfall came from another tycoon, who had made his mark in the rough and tumble of U.S. capital markets. Cleveland speculator Cyrus Eaton was born in Nova Scotia, moved to Cleveland, and had amassed a fortune, much of it through speculation. When Eaton decided to buy working control of a number of Insull's utilities, Insull was immediately suspicious. His response was to create an elaborate system of companies that were entangled with each other and loaded with debt, hence making them less attractive to interlopers like Eaton. Along these lines, in December 1928 Insull and Chicago-based investment bankers Halsey, Stuart & Company formed a new corporation, the Insull Utility Investments (IUI). This investment vehicle owned large blocks of shares in all the companies under the Middle West banner (which was managed by Insull's brother Martin).

Insull Utility Investments issued stock as IUI at $12 a share. On the first day of trading, IUI soared to $30 a share. By the spring, IUI had risen to $150 a share as an investing public decided to partake in Insull's seemingly brilliance in the utility industry. Yet, not everything was what it seemed. To finance IUI, Insull and his investment bankers Halsey, Stuart organized another company, the Corporation Securities of Chicago. Under this new structure, IUI owned 28.8 percent of the Corporation Securities of Chicago, which in turn owned 19.7 percent of IUI. The new entity and IUI gave Insull the ability to control Middle West Utilities and its 111 subsidies. Insull's complicated shell game included companies with assets of over $2.5 billion, which served more than 4.5 million customers.[13] As *Time* magazine was to note from the vantage point of 1934: "Thus Insull entered the great game of 1929, building towering corporate pyramids, buying the selling stock. He had been right so long the public thought he could never be wrong and so followed him blindly down the road to ruin."[14]

The mood of the time was also a critical factor in making Insull's stocks attractive. As the overall stock market boomed, the stock market beckoned and caught the imagination of the investing public. The press was also caught up in the excitement, trumpeting the central theme that the prosperity of the 1920s was produced by the genius of businessmen like Insull.

The Fall from Grace

But others were beginning to notice that something was amiss with the Insull empire. Owen D. Young, one of the famous lawyers of the time, and with a well-placed antenna to U.S. big business, clearly understood that the Insull empire was not as it should be. Before the market crash later in 1929, he noted of Insull's companies that it was impossible "for any man, however able, to grasp the real situation (of that vast structure)…it was so set that you could not possibly get an accounting system which would not mislead even the officers themselves."[15]

When the New York Stock Exchange crashed in September and October 1929, Insull's empire shook, but did not immediately crumble. Eaton backed off from his takeover attempt, his own financial empire starting to unravel. After all, customers still needed electrical power. Moreover, Insull's convoluted crossholdings of an empire made it somewhat difficult to accurately calculate—at least from the outside—how heavily in debt the entire affair was. Yet, the Eaton run on his companies had been costly, forcing Insull to buy up his own stock at very high levels. This drained him of available cash. At the same time, Insull's collection of companies was built around a system that depended on ongoing growth and, more significantly, on continuous sales of stock to give him the funds to pay his dividends.[16] As the Great Depression began to bite, investment in Insull companies declined, forcing him to borrow where he could to make interest payments.

There was one additional factor that was to play its part in the upcoming crisis: Insull's confidence that the economic downturn (which was to extend into the Great Depression) would not last too much longer. No doubt this view was reinforced by his attendance at President

Hoover's famous "business-as-usual" conference in November 1929 in which Insull and other leading business leaders pledged to spend more on capital investment. Consequently, Insull miscalculated badly in 1930—he expanded far more than turned out to be prudent, returned to debt financing and, after much persuading, bought Eaton's holdings in the Insull companies.[17] And Insull followed his usual line of having Halsey, Stuart & Company orchestrate the bond issues—something that did little to please New York bankers who were intentionally excluded from the deals. Adding insult to injury, Insull delivered a fiery speech in May 1930 against the concentration of financial power in New York at the annual dinner of the Chicago Stock Exchange. This was naturally taken up by the Chicago press as a declaration for the Midwest to seek its liberation from New York.

The past was beginning to catch up with Insull. Up to 1930, Insull had been able to conduct business without the help of New York bankers. That changed as Insull decided to expand his companies, though his Achilles heel was ironically through Continental Illinois. Continental Illinois was formed by a merger between Continental National Bank and Illinois Merchants Trust Bank. Illinois Merchants was long dominated by John J. Mitchell, a close Insull ally, who had earlier rejected an offer from Continental National to merge. However, Mitchell died and the management team that succeeded him opted for the merger. By 1930, the two banks were merged and the support for Insull, which was once close and personal, became a little more formal and open to outside pressures.

Although the new Continental Illinois was to remain Insull's bank, there was treachery afoot. One of the directors, insurance mogul Donald R. McLennan, was actively seeking to obtain business from Cyrus Eaton, holder of a sizeable amount of Insull stocks. Eaton had earlier offered to sell Insull the stocks, but the emperor of utilities refused. McLennan managed to persuade Insull to buy Eaton's shares, partly by offering for Continental Illinois to provide the necessary loans to transact the purchase. Unfortunately, the price that Eaton and Insull settled upon, $56 million, was beyond what Continental Illinois and other Chicago banks could finance. In what must have been a very painful decision, Insull was forced to borrow $20 million from Wall Street. He must have reasoned that as the economy would soon pick up, he would be able to generate enough cash to cover his costs until the stock market rose again.

But instead, the New York banks, led by J. P. Morgan (then under J. P. Morgan, Jr.), moved to drive Insull's stocks down with an eventual eye to a takeover. Strong negative momentum vis-à-vis Insull stocks developed in September 1931, a situation partially caused by an overall sharp market downturn related to London's decision to abandon the gold standard. In addition, the rumor popped up that Insull—then in London—was dead or dying. IUI, Commonwealth Edison, and Middle West saw their values plunge. This development, in turn, forced the companies to put up increasing amounts of securities as collateral against their bank loans. The bank creditors quietly gained control over the companies. Critically, the faltering Chicago banks were in no position to help Insull, as the banking crisis during the summer of 1931 revealed their dire state of affairs.

The New York bankers tightened the screws on Insull by changing the accounting system under which his companies operated and appointing a new auditor. These actions, in effect, made Middle West insolvent, allowing the bankers to portray Insull as an inept villain. This view was reinforced by disclosures from the auditors in early 1932 of a number of corporate indiscretions, in particular, inter-corporate loans.

There was another element of disclosure that raised the specter of financial fraud. Insull's broker, Russell, Brewster and Company, was under investigation by the New York Stock Exchange and was in danger of having its doors closed. Although Insull did not own any shares in the company, the perception was that he had a very close relationship. (Indeed, his brother Martin's account was insolvent, but the brokerage was working with him to liquidate it in a less painful fashion than declaring an Insull family member bankrupt.)

As the auditors went through Commonwealth Edison's books, a loan from ConEd to the brokerage house was discovered and disallowed. Insull biographer McDonald noted: "By the spring of 1932 the loan from Edison's subsidiary was worthless, and the circumstances surrounding the transactions were just confused enough to smack of fraud."[18] Insull was now personally tainted, which allowed the New York bankers, led by J. P. Morgan, to put the Insull companies into bank-controlled receiverships. Insull was forced to surrender control of over sixty corporations, including his first springboard to the apex of the utility industry, Commonwealth Edison. The implosion of Insull-related securities soon spread through the Chicago banking community, with runs forcing twenty-five banks to close in a matter of days.[19] Continental Illinois eventually was forced to seek government support to remain in business.

Equally devastating, the collapse of Insull's empire had a very damaging impact on small shareholders, who had put their life savings into what they perceived as a safe investment. Consequently, when Middle West Utilities entered into receivership in 1932, a large number of smallholders witnessed the elimination of their life savings. Insull soon became a widely hated man, closely associated with the misery of the times. Platt noted: "The smashed hopes of tens of thousands of local investors in his holding companies made his self-imposed exile abroad easy to understand."[20]

A Changed Environment

Considering the changing political environment—from the freewheeling capitalism of the 1920s to the grimness of the Great Depression—Insull soon emerged as a perfect scapegoat. He was in good company: As the depression deepened and the pain was widely felt, the public soon turned on the villains—real and imagined—who appeared to be responsible for their predicament. This led President Hoover to encourage a Senate investigation. While the Senate investigation was gaining momentum, the public's attention was suddenly riveted by the mysterious death of the Swedish "match king," Ivar Kreuger.

Kreuger was a millionaire who had climbed his way to fame and fortune by establishing monopolies for the making of matches. From his base in Sweden in 1917, Kreuger expanded his business throughout Europe. While the United States enjoyed an economic boom in the 1920s, Europe generally struggled with postwar reconstruction, debt, and a lack of economic growth. Kreuger companies would offer European governments loans and as a security the government would grant his company the local match monopoly.

But Krueger did not stop there. Soon he expanded into the United States and outside of matches, gaining control of most of the forestry industry in northern Sweden and acquiring a majority interest in the telephone company Ericsson, the mining company Boliden, and major interests in the ball bearing manufacturer SKF and a local bank. By 1931 Kreuger owned 200 companies and his fortune was massive—at least so it appeared to be.

The only problem was that Kreuger had looted much of his empire before the crash. And Kreuger's empire was not immune to the Great Depression. By 1932, rumors were spreading that something was amiss. The real shocker came on March 12, 1932, when Kreuger was discovered dead in a hotel room in Paris, probably a suicide. Although he was mourned at the time of his death, it soon became apparent that Kreuger's empire was constructed on deceit. Kreuger had issued bonds, backed by collateral—French government bonds; at a later date and without any notification, he substituted those bonds for those of Yugoslavia. By the time the Depression broke out, the Yugoslav bonds were almost worthless. For those American investors who had bought Kreuger bonds, this was a shock. The ensuing Kreuger crash was devastating to many Swedes and Americans who had invested in his securities. The entire situation only reinforced the public's negative sentiment about finance and financial leaders. And that was not all: Other foreign government bonds—Peru, Brazil, and Cuba—also defaulted.

Ferdinand Pecora: A Foreshadowing of Eliot Spitzer

Events in Washington reinforced Insull's concerns. In early 1932, the Senate Banking and Currency Committee appointed a short, dark-complexioned Italian lawyer out of New York City, Ferdinand Pecora, as counsel to hearings about financial wrongdoings related to the crash of 1929. Pecora was a Democrat and had worked as an assistant district attorney, prosecuting shoddy stock salesmen and businessmen. He had a reputation for being honest and hard working, and he clearly understood the connection between the law and politics. As Wall Street historian John Brooks commented: "Pecora, three quarters righteous tribune of the people, was one-quarter demagogic inquisitor." (Think Eliot Spitzer.) Certainly the public's mood was supportive and President Roosevelt was on the same page. And one of the first things that Pecora investigated was the Insull empire. He also was to expose the contempt in which much of Wall Street held the American public, and the self-serving and question-able antics of such bankers as Charles Mitchell, the head of City National Bank, who lied about his income taxes, made loans to bank insiders, and passed on worthless Cuban sugar bonds to unsuspecting investors.

Observing the rising public mistrust of the stock market and the manipulations of the corporate world and aware of the Pecora hearings, Insull decided that the heat was only going to intensify. This was brought home to him in a small mountain of threat letters and reinforced when someone shot at him (the bullet hit his chauffeur in the shoulder). Local politicians, both Democrats and Republicans, jumped on the bandwagon of public dislike and launched a number of investigations into his affairs. Facing a rising tide of hatred, Insull quietly slipped out of the country, first into Canada, and then departing from Quebec to Europe on the Empress in June 1932.

Insull even gained the attention of President Roosevelt, who was elected in November 1932. In a speech delivered at the Commonwealth Club in September 1932, Roosevelt, then a candidate of the Democratic Party, singled Insull out: "Whenever in the pursuit of this objective the lone wolf, the unethical competitor, the reckless promoter, the Ishmael or Insull whose hand is against every man's, declines to join in achieving an end recognized as being for the public welfare, and threatens to drag the industry back to a state of anarchy, the government may properly be asked to apply restraint."[21] He was to follow through with the same theme once he was elected. In his inaugural address in Washington, D.C. on March 4, 1933, Roosevelt indicated that more was to come in cleaning up Wall Street: "The money changers have fled from their high seats in the temple of our civilization. We may now restore the temple to the ancient truths. The measure of the restoration lies to the extent to which we apply social values more noble than mere monetary profit."[22]

The long hand of the law was soon in motion. The State of Illinois indicted Samuel Insull's brother Martin (who had fled to Canada and remained there) three times for embezzlement, and Samuel Insull twice for having permitted it. The federal government was not far behind. Government auditors went to work on the books and records of the In-sull companies. In February 1933, the U.S. government indicted Samuel Insull et al.—Sam Jr., brother Martin and sixteen of their associates—on charges of using the U.S. postal system to defraud, that is, selling the securities of Corporation Securities Co. through the mails as a "good safe and sound investment," whereas they knew the securities were not as represented.[23]

The federal government added another charge under the bankruptcy law. Considering that both Samuel and Martin left the country, they needed something that was an extraditable offense—embezzlement and misuse of the U.S. mail system did not do the trick. Consequently, the In-sulls were accused of knowing that Corporation Securities was insolvent six months before it failed and therefore of having acted "feloniously and fraudulently," in declaring preferred dividends and putting up additional collateral on bank loans.

Congressional investigations also led to charges that Insull's Chicago banker Halsey, Stuart and Company had been employed by the utilities king to maintain the price of his shares while he was negotiating bank loans. According to historian Charles Geest: "Halsey did not bother to mention that it too had sizable holdings in the Insull companies. Apparently, the financings and the subsequent fall of the businesses had been at the investors' expense, which ran somewhat counter to Insull's public image of personal generosity that derived from his lending money to overextended employees at the time of the crash."[24] Insull became fearful of being roasted by the Senate.

Exile and Home

Despite his losses, Insull was not easy to corner. It was a vast under-statement to say that he had little intention of returning to the United States, where he had been humiliated, lost his fortune, and was under the threat of arrest. Insull first settled in Paris. Although much of his wealth was gone, he still had pension money granted to him by his old companies. Paris, however, was not to be peaceful. He was soon hounded by the press and learned that back in Chicago he was the center of a political campaign with the political class clamoring for his blood. Moreover, the U.S. government indicated to its French counterparts that it wanted the fugitive industrialist. Before the net could be closed, Insull, with his son, crept out of Paris late one night.

Insull's next stop was Milan, but that city was not safe either. Parting company with his son, the senior Insull journeyed to Athens. Eventually even Greece became questionable, leaving Insull to take a ship first to Romania, which refused him entry, and then to Turkey, where he was spirited off a Greek ship by the local authorities. In Istanbul, he was put in jail, waiting extradition. *Time* commented: "Instead of bravely facing the music, he had elected to become a hounded man, to ask hospitality of aliens, to finagle with outlandish courts and people, to flee on a scummy little freighter, to lie in shabby hotels, and finally to be cornered in a common jail in Istanbul and carried home captive."[25]

Insull returned to the United States in 1934. Along the way home, in Morocco, he had a mild heart attack, but he recovered on the voyage across the Atlantic. In New York, his son Sam met him—along with a large group of reporters. The seventy-year-old turned to the press and stated: "I have erred, but my greatest error was in underestimating the effect of the financial panic on American securities and particularly on the companies I was working so hard to build. I worked with all my energy to save those companies. I made mistakes, but they were honest mistakes. They were errors in judgment but not dishonest manipulations."[26]

Under guard the Insulls, father and son, were placed upon a train to Chicago. The next day in Chicago, after being fingerprinted and suffering another mild heart attack, the former utility king was arraigned. Unable to make the $200,000 bail (which was four times that which was demanded of Al Capone), Samuel Insull found himself in the hospital ward of Cook County jail, where he spent the next several months as he waited for his trial.

In many regards, the results of Insull's trial were an anticlimax. Instead of finding that Insull was a cunning manipulator along the lines of Jay Gould, the investigation revealed that Insull had pursued a policy that was favorable to the public. In particular, as prices had increased and costs were brought down, Insull had pursued a policy of lowering rates. Moreover, Insull's operating companies were well-run and remained in business. As Insull himself noted: "The financial troubles of the business have been mainly with the holding companies and investment companies, and, not as a rule, with the operating companies."[27]

Insull's weakness, though, was his breach of the public trust and mismanagement of his own financial empire of holding companies. Although his holding companies had indeed held off takeovers, they were clearly pyramid schemes, requiring ongoing inflows of new money to maintain the outward flow of dividends. At the same time, Insull's success at widely selling his stocks—including to ordinary people who normally could not afford to invest in stocks—was his crime to the public. The former great hero of the 1920s had left them in the 1930s with lots of worthless paper, much of it purchased with hard-earned and hard-to-replace savings. Yet, under the laws of the time, it was very difficult to successfully prosecute Insull.

The jury acquitted Insull in a relatively quick fashion. While it was understood that he had made mistakes in the creation of pyramids and that this did have a negative impact on the public good, it was also acknowledged that Insull believed in what he was doing. The intention was not to cheat the investor, but to maintain control over his empire. As historian Platt commented: "And the fact that he threw so much of his own personal fortune into a black hole, basically, to try to shore up Commonwealth Edison, is fairly substantial proof that he was not trying to defraud people—that he really believed in his own vision."[28]

Released from jail, Insull quickly retreated from the public light. Vilified by President Roosevelt and still hated by the public, Insull was in poor health. His once vast fortune was gone, though there was enough left for him to move back to Paris. On July 16, 1938 he died of a heart attack, waiting for a subway. According to most reports, his body was not identified for several hours, because someone stole his wallet. The official police statement indicated that he had nothing in his pockets, with the exception of a silk handkerchief with his initials and a few French coins.

The Insull saga did have one important additional element. In the aftermath of the wild free-for-all markets of the 1920s and loose controls over the public utility sector, the American kabuki cycle of excess was followed by a round of regulation and press vilification, true to form. One consequence of the Insull era was the passage of the Public Utility Holding Company Act of 1935. That act stipulated that all holding companies owning public utilities must register with the Securities Exchange Commission, and gave the SEC the authority to break up large monopolies or near-monopolies. It could also be interpreted as giving the SEC the power to dictate the size of a utility company—something that clearly raised a subtle but critical question over the role of the state in economic affairs. As Geest noted: "Congress was in the mood to regulate those industries deemed vital to the public welfare, and the utilities industry had had too many strikes against it since the turn of the century."[29]

Conclusion

The Samuel Insull saga represents the rise and fall of one of America's greatest industrial entrepreneurs. Indeed, during his trial the prosecution compared Insull's rise and fall to that of Napoleon, as the industrialist, like the French leader, had become intoxicated and corrupted by power. Despite the very questionable structure of his various financial companies, Insull hardly deserved the vilification that followed the market crash of 1929. In many regards, he made an important contribution to the industrial development of the United States. More specifically, Insull reinforced the idea that every home should have access to cheap electricity. In addition, his decision to create opaque, pyramid-like structures was probably founded more on his well-placed distrust of New York's financial elite and of Samuel Eaton than personal greed and aggrandizement. This is not to argue that wealth was not a motivating factor—Insull clearly enjoyed the good life. It also might be argued that he firmly believed that the good times of the 1920s would continue and there would be no day of reckoning. Sadly, all booms eventually go bust and Insull had a lot of company.

Notes

1.   Forrest McDonald, *Insull: The Rise and Fall of a Billionaire Utility Tycoon* (Washington, D.C.: Beard Books, 1964, reprint 2004), p. 17.
2.   Samuel Insull, *The Memoirs of Samuel Insull: An Autobiography* (Polo, Illinois: Transportation Trails, 1992), p. 29.
3.   For more information on Villard see Alexandra de Borchgrave, *Villard: The Life and Times of an American Titan* (New York: 2001).

4. McDonald, *Insull*, p. 40.
5. Ibid., pp. 50-51.
6. Harold L. Platt, *The Electric City: Energy and Growth of the Chicago Area, 1880-1930* (Chicago: University of Chicago Press, 1991), p. 87.
7. Ibid., p. 157. As Platt explained: "In perhaps his best-known publicity stunt, he had a truck laden with ten thousand irons tour the residential districts of the city. Huge signs draped on its sides announced that the mountain of appliances piled on the vehicle would be given to new customers for a free trial. A small army of salesmen followed up with a systematic canvass of the neighborhoods. In exchange for the free use of the iron for six months, the householder agreed to install central station service."
8. George H. Garrison, Jr., "Do It Big Sammy, Part II," *Friends of Financial History*, p. 26. Article supplied by the Museum of American Financial History.
9. PBS interview of Harold Platt in 2002 provided on PBS website http://www.pbs.org/greatprojects/interviews/platt.1html.
10. Quoted from Brian Trumbore, "Samuel Insull," Buy and Hold (2002), http://www.buy-and-hold.com/bn/en/education/history/2002/sam_insull.html.
11. Platt, *The Electric City*, p. 272. Along the same lines George H. Garrison, Jr., "Do It Big Sammy," *Friends of Financial History*, p. 1 was to comment: "Few men in the United States wielded a mightier influence than this man who was sitting on the U.S.'s power switch."
12. Quoted from Trumbore, referenced to Geest, *Wall Street,*
13. Robert Sobel, *Panic on Wall Street: A Classic History of America's Financial Disorder* (New York: E.P. Dutton, 1988), p. 232.
14. "Old Man Comes Home," *Time*, May 14, 1934, p. 3.
15. Garrison, "Do It Big Sammy, Part III," *Friends of Financial History*, p. 24.
16. Garrison, "Do It Big Sammy, Part IV," *Friends of Financial History*, p. 4.
17. McDonald, *Insull*, p. 284.
18. Ibid., p. 298.
19. Chicago's banks were already a little shaky before the collapse pf the Insull empire. An agricultural downturn in the 1920s resulted in the collapse of a number of smaller banks in the farm states. Because these banks were part of a correspondent banking system, they began to withdraw their balances, which, in turn, weakened the balance sheets of Chicago banks. When the Great Depression struck, it found a shaky banking system. From 1929 to 1930 more than thirty Chicago banks failed. "Banking, Commercial," Encyclopedia of Chicago, http://www.enclopedia.chicagohistory.org/pages/108.html.
20. Platt, *The Electric City*, p. 273.
21. Franklin Delano Roosevelt: "Commonwealth Club Address," September 23, 1932, San Francisco, California, quoted from http://www.americanrhetoric.com/speechjes/fdrcommonwealth.htm.
22. Quoted from Franklin Delano Roosevelt, "First Inaugural Address, Washington, D.C., March 4, 1933," in John Grafton, editor, *Great Speeches: Franklin Delano Roosevelt* (Mineola, New York: Dover Publications, Inc., 1999), p. 30.
23. "Old Man Comes Home," *Time*, May 14, 1934, p. 4.
24. Geest, *Wall Street*, p. 223.
25. Ibid.
26. Ibid.
27. Insull, *The Memoirs of Samuel Insull*, p. 271.
28. PBS interview of Harold Platt.
29. Geest, *Wall Street*, p. 242.

7

The Decade of Greed: Michael Milken,
Junk Bonds, and Insiders (1980s)

On March 3, 1991, world-renowned financier Michael Milken removed his precious toupee and checked into the federal minimum-security prison in Pleasanton, California. For the next twenty-two months he would exchange his designer suits for prison jumpsuits, and his X-shaped trading desk for a thirty-seven-hour work week in maintenance and construction. Fellow Wall Streeter Dennis Levine served his term at a federal prison in central Pennsylvania, where he complained that he was ostracized as a "squealer," but was perhaps compensated by a star turn on *60 Minutes* soon after his release. Ivan Boesky served two years of a three-year term in Lompoc prison, and emerged with a flowing white beard and shoulder length hair; while in prison, he reportedly paid other inmates to do his laundry.[1]

These famed symbols of the 1980s, the Decade of Greed, ended their Wall Street careers in ignominy and isolation (though, in true American fashion, resurrection was not too far away). Still, the defining symbol of the decade was not Michael Milken in prison stripes, but rather the annual Predators' Ball, so ably chronicled by Connie Bruck in her 1988 bestseller (a book that Milken reportedly did his best to suppress). Bruck writes,

> In the third week of March 1984, the faithful, fifteen hundred strong, came to Beverly Hills to pay homage to Michael Milken, the legendary junk-bond guru of Drexel Burnham Lambert whom many of his followers simply called "the King." For the next four days, they would savor the world he had created for them.
> By five-thirty each morning, an armada of about one hundred limousines glided into position around Beverly Hills. Dozens of them ferried guests from the lush green-and-pink medley of the Beverly Hills Hotel—then owned by arbitrageur Ivan Boesky, his wife and his in-laws, and completely booked by Drexel for these four nights—through the city's wide, stately, palm-tree-lined streets. Their destination was the Beverly Hilton, where the annual Drexel High Yield Bond Conference—by now known as the Predators' Ball—was being held, just a few blocks from Drexel's West Coast office...[2]

The energy, excess, and glitz of the Decade of Greed were not confined to the annual Predators' Balls. Owners of savings and loans (S&Ls) around the country leaped onto the good-times bandwagon as well, funding their pleasures by using depositors' money as their own personal piggybanks. Long-time U.S. financial observer Martin Mayer writes about Don Dixon, owner of Vernon Savings & Loan in Texas:

> ... In 1983 [Dixon] and his wife used depositors' money to tour Europe with friends in a rented Rolls-Royce and Learjet, dining every night in a different Michelin three-star restaurant. His S&L hired prostitutes to entertain customers and directors. (Vernon's president pleaded guilty to this one, though his lawyer argued at the sentencing that one of the most important recipients of said gift, a regulator, couldn't get it up, anyway, and therefore wasn't really bribed.) He bought a half-dozen Learjets and the sister ship to Franklin Roosevelt's presidential yacht, Sequoia. This he kept at anchor in the Potomac, to be used for congressmen for entertaining friends and raising money...
>
> Dixon redecorated a gorgeous house in Del Mar, next to La Jolla in the "big money" suburbs of San Diego, all at the expense of his S&L because, after all, he entertained borrowers there. Many of his borrowers were his friends. He spent more than $5 million for art to hang in his office and in the house in Del Mar. There was also a ski chalet in Beaver Creek...[3]

But while the great financiers were fiddling, Rome was burning—and by the end of the decade it had all come crashing down. The bemused but increasingly indignant American taxpayer was clamoring for action—any action—after the indignities of:

- the October 1987 stock market crash;
- a never-ending chain of insider trading scandals that extinguished some of Wall Street's leading lights;
- a massive meltdown in the S&L industry that threatened to cost the American public hundreds of *billions* of dollars;
- a series of giant corporate buyouts culminating in the $24.9 billion takeover of RJR Nabisco—which generated almost $1 billion in fees for the greedy Wall Street dealmakers; and
- investment bank Drexel Burnham Lambert's guilty plea to criminal fraud and subsequent bankruptcy.

What next? worried Main Street America. The messes were especially alarming since Reagan had swept into office in 1980 sounding a clarion call for deregulation and free markets, which would cure every ill and put a Porsche (or at least a Ford Taurus) in every driveway. Reagan's eight years in office were supposed to be a new era of great hope and optimism in the financial world—a time of easy money, laissez-faire government, and faith in the fundamental rightness of markets.

A Cheerleader for Capitalism

The likable and sunny Reagan was a wonderfully effective cheerleader for capitalism. Unlike his predecessor, Jimmy Carter (who had actually set financial deregulation in motion but was best remembered for his worries about America's malaise and his tendency to lust in his heart), Reagan was a true believer. He arrived at the White House pledging to cure the economy of its depressing plunge into stagflation—both inflation and unemployment were soaring—by "getting government off our backs." And befitting his gift for Teflonization, even though some of the most important deregulation of the 1980s was actually launched by the Carter administration, Reagan was widely credited with stimulating the U.S. economy by tackling—and defeating—big government. (The painfully high interest rates that actually won the battle against inflation were blamed on Fed Chairman Paul Volcker.)

For Reagan, small government was both a fiscal need and a moral imperative. Thus he championed free markets and railed against government programs, according to Charles Schultze of the Brookings Institution, because of this happy intersection of budgetary constraints and true belief. But the Great Communicator went even further. Carter may have ushered in deregulation, but Ronald Reagan became its chief crusader, whose words mattered much more than his actions. As another Brookings scholar explains, "he changed the conversation."

So just as Reagan fundamentally altered labor-management relations when he fired striking air traffic controllers, he fundamentally altered the national mood toward capitalism when he pledged to streamline government and unfetter the markets. By the mid-1980s, most Americans agreed, for example, that relaxation of government regulations was necessary to revitalize the ailing S&Ls.[4] As Martin Mayer put it, Reagan "extolled the magic of the market"[5]—and such were his preaching skills that Americans rose up in his wake and shouted hallelujah.

And indeed, the 1980s were years of "tremendous innovation in financial markets and wealth creation" beyond our wildest dreams, both on Wall Street and beyond. A wave of corporate takeovers, mergers, and leveraged buyouts consumed the imagination and attention of the financial world, resulting in dramatic corporate restructurings that would sharply improve the profitability and efficiency of corporate America, setting the stage for a lengthy economic boom. And many of these transactions were made possible by high-yield (or junk) bonds, a financial innovation pioneered by none other than Michael Milken and Drexel, which provided a valuable financing alternative for growth companies in growth industries.[6]

A Bloody Mess

But unfortunately for Reagan and the Main Streeters, there is no magic in financial markets. In the end, even Reagan was not able to change the basic rules of finance—high rewards still come only after high risks—and there are still no free lunches. The Reagan revolution, though, did manage to set the tone for the greed-is-good times, exalting the rise of a new financial era that has been dubbed the "casino economy."

Michael Lewis captures this stage better than anyone else in his book *Liar's Poker*, which chronicles his adventures as a young trainee and trader on Wall Street during the heady years of the mid-eighties. Lewis describes Wall Street in those days as a "modern gold rush" where a "new pushy financial entrepreneurship" reigned supreme. He writes, "Never before have so many unskilled twenty four year olds made so much money in so little time as we did this decade in New York and London. There has never before been such a fantastic exception to the rule of the marketplace that one takes out no more than one puts in."[7]

In other words, the no-free-lunch rules had been repealed. Or had they? With capital available in seemingly unlimited supply, the traditional gatekeepers—bankers, investors, and financiers—"abandoned historical yardsticks of value" and ladled out money with scant regard for boring old notions like business plans, value creation, and ability to service debt.[8] They assumed that the economy would grow its way out of any problems that arose; with the pie expanding so quickly, the occasional bad deal could be easily fixed.

Like the Internet boom of the 1990s, the results were depressingly predictable. (As John Kenneth Galbraith has noted, "The financial world is characterized by explosions of wealth and then, for those involved, a very sad day of reckoning."[9]) The day of reckoning was upon many by the end of the decade, triggered by a crisis in the S&L industry, the bankruptcy of a leading Wall Street investment bank, the jailing of some of the financial world's best and brightest, and a widespread loss of confidence in the fairness of financial markets.

As historians pointed out, this was nothing new—just one more chapter in a never-ending but depressingly familiar cycle of scandal and reform. Wall Street chronicler Charles Geisst commented, "I can't think of a previous boom period, whether it was the 20's, the 60's or the 80's, where it hasn't ended up a bloody mess, with declining asset values and cases of fraud." Geisst and others argue that the emergence of fraud and scandal at the end of a market bubble is inevitable; everyone understands the business cycle, he says, but far less is known of "capitalism's cycle of scandals."[10] John Kenneth Galbraith warned, "History is repeating itself,"[11] and how right he was!

By the turn of the decade, business schools were introducing classes in ethics (skeptics may well wonder how effective this was), and Congress was rushing (once again) to legislate its way out of the mess. But what really happened during these tumultuous years? Was Michael Milken an instrument of Satan or a financial genius? Was his employer, Drexel Burnham Lambert, an inspired innovator or a rogue institution? And were regulators asleep at the switch, or simply facilitating the operation of free markets?

An Anonymous Letter from Caracas

It all began to unravel, improbably enough, with an anonymous letter sent to Merrill Lynch's New York headquarters from Caracas, Venezuela. "Dear Sir," the deceptively innocent-looking missive read, "Please be informed that two of your executives from the Caracas office are trading with insider information…"

At first, the bombshell landed with a soggy thud. But Merrill Lynch's compliance department doggedly followed the money, triggering an SEC investigation that eventually turned up a chain of piggybacking that meandered throughout the Southern Hemisphere.[12] Bahamian brokers executing trades for Dennis Levine, a New York investment banker, recognized a winner and "piggybacked" on his trades—bought the same stocks for their own accounts. The brokers' brokers, no slouches themselves, promptly followed suit, creating a trail of trades from New York to Caracas. Once alerted, the suspicious officials essentially worked backwards, following this chain of trades back to New York and Levine, who worked for high-flying investment bank Drexel Burnham Lambert. Levine was duly arrested in May 1986.

Investigators immediately suspected that Levine's remarkable trading record was founded on inside information about upcoming deals, rather than dumb luck or brilliant research. He was, in the end, a relatively minor figure in the story, but his confession set off the investigation that ultimately brought down some of Wall Street's biggest players. Most important, he fingered Ivan Boesky, the Street's top arbitrageur (someone who invests in the stock of companies that are likely to be takeover targets), netting a reduced jail sentence for himself in the bargain.[13]

Boesky was a big fish indeed—a man at the very heart of Wall Street, involved in many of the Street's biggest and splashiest deals. He bought two million shares of Getty Oil, for example, and resold them to Texaco for nearly twice what he had paid when Texaco acquired Getty, netting an estimated $100 million on that transaction alone. James Stewart describes his 1985 speech at Berkeley's business school commencement:

> Boesky...looked out of sorts as he waited impatiently in the wings of Berkeley's Greek Theater, the outdoor amphitheater that serves as an open-air setting for the University of California's commencement ceremonies.
> After welcoming remarks by the dean, Boesky stepped to the podium, greeted by enthusiastic applause... Then, when it seemed as though he would lose his audience permanently, he galvanized the crowd with just a few sentences.
> "Greed is all right, by the way," he said, raising his eyes from his text and continuing with what seemed like genuinely extemporaneous remarks. "I want you to know that I think greed is healthy. You can be greedy and still feel good about yourself."[14]

Even after his exit from prison (and investigations that unearthed overwhelming evidence to the contrary), Boesky continued to insist that he never traded on or divulged inside information. He remained proud of his accomplishments while at Drexel, explaining that he matched "capital to entrepreneurs who could use it effectively."[15]

But there was a seamier side to Boesky's exploits as well, most painfully exposed when investigators closed in on a third character, Martin Siegel. No dead-end loser, Siegel was in fact another of Wall Street's stars, an investment banker who specialized in defending companies from hostile takeovers. Over the course of his career, he helped negotiate more than five hundred corporate mergers. But Siegel too had fallen prey to the hubris and greed that was enveloping Wall Street; he was charged with selling secret information about upcoming deals to none other than Ivan Boesky. (Perhaps most intriguing, Siegel earned $2 million fair and square in 1985, the same year that he picked up another $700,000 in illegal payments from Boesky—often delivered in suitcases of cash on Manhattan street corners. Bewildered friends wondered aloud why Siegel, a Harvard Business School graduate with a promising future in investment banking, was drawn into such a life.)

The arrests of Siegel and Boesky marked a sharp escalation of the scandal. On November 14, 1986 (dubbed Boesky Day by shaken market insiders), officials announced that Ivan Boesky had agreed to plead guilty to insider trading, pay $100 million in fines, and cooperate with the government in its ongoing investigation. Wall Street was staggered. This was no longer a case of petty misbehavior among some fringe players, entertaining but not particularly momentous; now, investigators were pulling in "senior officers of major firms." Marty Siegel, for example, was the head of mergers and acquisitions at Kidder Peabody. Insider trading had moved from the outliers of Wall Street right into its core. As one observer noted, this was "no longer a matter of individual misbehavior. It now implicates the central functions of the investment banks."[16]

And then, the ultimate prize: Boesky led investigators to Michael Milken. In the end, a scandal that began with insider trading among bit players metastasized into a widespread crazy-quilt of wrongdoing including market manipulation, companies being tricked into mergers, secret deals that allowed insiders only to profit, and much more—at the hands of Wall Street's highest fliers. As James Stewart lamented in the classic *Den of Thieves*, "…a cancer was eating away at the moral fabric of Wall Street and the American economy."[17] Levine, Boesky, and Milken all went to prison, and Drexel Burnham Lambert went bankrupt.

A sad ending to their once-glorious careers. But to this day, it is not entirely clear whether these figures, especially Milken, were more sinning or sinned against. Even Boesky, despite a guilty plea and jail sentence, appears to genuinely believe in his innocence. Milken, too, genuinely does not appear to believe that he broke the law.

Are these men simply deluded? Or is the story more complicated than it first appears? To evaluate these questions, we need to start at the center of the Wall Street universe in the 1980s: Michael Milken, and Drexel Burnham Lambert (DBL).

Drexel's Long, Strange Trip

At its peak in the mid-1980s, Drexel was the fifth largest investment bank in America and the fastest-growing powerhouse on Wall Street. (It replaced Salomon as Wall Street's most profitable investment bank in 1986, earning a staggering $546 million on revenues of around $4 billion.) Milken, its star and chief moneymaker, was widely regarded as the most influential financier since J. P. Morgan. The junk bond market, which was dominated by Drexel, had exploded from less than $1 billion in 1981 to a whopping $175 billion in 1988, largely under the stewardship of Milken and Drexel. And Drexel owned this market: By the mid-1980s DBL was responsible for underwriting 73 percent of new junk bond issues, and accounted for 70-75 percent of secondary market trading as well. Milken and his cronies were lionized by the press, and worshiped by their grateful clients.

They worked hard and partied hard. In 1978 Milken moved his operation out to Beverly Hills, essentially shifting Drexel's cash-generating center out of its New York headquarters and into the warm California sunshine where he and his wife had grown up. His westward migration had another pleasant byproduct as well—it removed him from any pretense of supervision or oversight by his so-called bosses. His working hours were legendary: He was at his X-shaped trading desk by 4:30am (and expected his associates there as well) in time for the New York market opening, and remained there long after the closing bell had rung.

The partying was just as intense. Drexel—that is, Milken—hosted an annual "junk bond convention" that had become a wild bacchanalia by 1985. The 1500 guests that year included some of the most important players in U.S. financial markets, such as T. Boone Pickens, Carl Icahn, Sir James Goldsmith, and Ronald Perelman. Author Connie Bruck writes about what came to be called the annual Predators' Ball, which became ever more extravagant as the money poured in:

> What all these men did share, of course, were enormous egos and appetites. On the second night of the Predators' Ball, while the lower-ranking troops (money managers and executives of medium sized companies) were sent in buses to a show at a movie lot, some one hundred of the real players—takeover entrepreneurs, major investors, arbitrageurs, deal lawyers—attended a cocktail party at a bungalow at the Beverly Hills Hotel. From there they were chauffeured to dinner in a private room at the swank Chasen's in Beverly Hills.
>
> In addition to Drexel's female employees, there were a number of extremely attractive young women at this dinner—so good-looking, in fact, that one takeover lawyer…remarked to a companion, "I've got to hand it to these guys—I've never seen so many beautiful wives."
>
> In fact few if any wives attended this dinner. An assessment closer to the mark was made by arbitrageur Martin Weinstein who, noting that Irwin Jacobs had been deep in conversation for hours with one of these women at the far end of the room, commented to a friend, "Tell Irwin he doesn't have to work so hard. She's already paid for..."
>
> … Following the dinner at Chasen's, many of the guests and the women had repaired to Bungalow 8 at the Beverly Hills Hotel where the cocktail party had been held earlier that evening… As one participant who partied there late into that night puts it, "All these big takeover guys were in that place together, and we've all got tremendous egos, we're all trying to prove ourselves all the time, to show we can get the girl we didn't get in high school, we're basically a bunch of exhibitionists—things just got out of hand."[18]

Various top-of-the-line entertainers wowed the crowds as well. Frank Sinatra appeared one year, costing Drexel a cool $150,000. Diana Ross showed up too; she "sang a medley of Motown hits and managed to change outfits twice." Perhaps most impressive for the era, "J. R. Ewing" made a surprise appearance. He was the main character of a then popular television show, depicting the exploits of a ruthless and wealthy Texas oil patch family-run empire. J. R., played by Larry Hagman, was well-known for making such comments as "All that matters is winning." "As the strains of the 'Dallas' theme filled the room, Larry Hagman strode onto the screen, flashing a 'Drexel Express titanium card.' The card 'has a ten billion dollar line of credit,' J. R. drawled. 'Don't go hunting without it.'"[19]

Colossal pay packages matched the colossal egos. Milken earned an unheard-of $550 million in 1987, and more than $1 billion in a four-year period—making him the highest paid person in America. One reporter calculated that Milken earned $1,046 for every minute that he drew breath, awake or asleep. (Once the dominos started to fall, even Wall Street's most hardened professionals were stunned by the revelation of his income.)

But Drexel's chief executive officer, Frederick Joseph, defended Milken's pay, and indeed, in some sense it reflected the cold hard truth that Milken, and Milken alone, was responsible for Drexel's meteoric rise from a third-tier investment bank at the dawn of the 1980s to its position at the very heights of Wall Street by the middle of the decade. Milken's power was second to none in the bank (arguably including Joseph, his nominal boss). *Forbes* reporters called Milken "the man who runs America's economy" in 1984[20]; certainly his junk bond department was the engine of growth at Drexel.

Much has been written about Milken the man. His relatively austere lifestyle—he owned two cars and lived in a house in Encino that he bought for $700,000 in 1978—stands in sharp contrast to his prodigious appetites in business. (He famously engaged in a shouting match with Joseph over a $15,000 commission in 1987, the same year that he earned a cool $550 million.) *Forbes* compared Milken in a 1990 article to Samuel Insull (see chapter 6), another "fallen hero facing a federal court…a symbol of capitalist greed and excess." The men shared similar personality types—hot-tempered, impatient, brilliant, controlling. Indeed, *Forbes* founder B. C. Forbes described Insull as a "brilliant man who accomplished much but came to think of himself as exempt from limitations of ordinary human beings." When Insull died in 1938, the *New York Times* commented, "…his unbridled lust for power led to his financial undoing and personal disgrace."[21] The parallels to Milken are obvious.

Trolling Through the Trash

And yet, to a large extent Milken's hubris was well-deserved. Even his detractors acknowledge that he was a brilliant and innovative banker, whose financing techniques enabled many companies and entrepreneurs to realize their dreams. His "penetrating insights and fifteen-hour workdays" raised billions of dollars for corporate powerhouses like Turner Broadcasting, MCI, Time Warner, and Rupert Murdoch. He achieved this through a devastatingly simple formula: junk bonds.

Milken's genius was to recognize that junk bonds—high yield debt issued by high risk companies—often carried less default risk than their hefty interest rates would suggest. In other words, the yield offered by these bonds was more than adequate to compensate holders for their risk. Inspired by solid academic evidence that these supposedly risky bonds were in fact good investments, he turned this vision into a reality by single-handedly creating and growing a vibrant market for such instruments.

Guided and nourished by Milken, the junk bond market exploded. He wove an intertwined web of buyers and sellers with himself solidly in the center, partly by encouraging his junk bond issuers to invest their idle cash into the junk issued by other corporations. The business was immensely profitable for Drexel, because junk bond issues carry huge fees (three to four percent of face value, compared to less than one percent for higher-grade bonds). And it was good for the economy, too, funneling cash into the hands of hungry, high-octane entrepreneurs who would otherwise be starved of funds needed to help build their companies.

But Milken's deeds had a darker side as well, as investigators eventually discovered. In October 1988, after three long years of digging, the SEC finally filed charges against Drexel, Milken, his brother Lowell Milken, and four others. The charges alleged that they:

- traded on inside information;
- manipulated stock prices;
- filed a false disclosure form with the SEC to disguise who really owned a block of stock;
- filed fraudulent offering materials;
- kept false books and records; and
- defrauded their own clients.

Milken's legal problems were only beginning. Eventually he pleaded guilty to six felonies (the government dropped ninety-two other charges, including the insider trading rap, as part of his plea bargain agreement) and paid a fine of $600 million—keeping an estimated $1 billion in personal and family wealth. He served a relatively light sentence in prison (twenty-two months), partly on the argument that his pioneering work in creating the junk bond market had been a contribution to society. In 1992 he paid an additional $500 million to settle lawsuits related to savings and loan collapses (more on that later).

Drexel fared even worse. The firm pleaded guilty to multiple criminal charges and paid $650 million in fines—but it was not enough. Drexel Burnham Lambert, one of Wall Street's most high-flying names, went bankrupt in the early 1990s and its name disappeared forever.

To the investing public, Milken became a symbol of everything that was wrong in the 1980s—greed, market manipulation, hostile takeovers, savings bank collapses, and more greed. It was the ultimate victory of speculation over productive investment, a return to the rough and tumble days of Fisk and Gould. Thomas Jefferson would have surely disapproved. Although in the end he pleaded guilty to relatively technical legal transgressions rather than gross criminal activity, he seemed to epitomize the push for more and more money, bigger and bigger deals, that characterized the era. Mirroring the public image of the 1930s (and, later, the early 2000s), Milken and the industry he embodied were widely regarded as corrupt, unfair, and heavily larded with cronyism.

Milken: Financial Genius or Barbarian?

Close examination of what Milken actually did in the financial markets reveals a much more nuanced picture. Let's look at the popular charges against him with regard to his role in the:

1. Junk bond market,
2. Hostile takeover boom, and
3. Savings and loan collapse.

Milken the Financial Genius

Any unbiased discussion of Milken's impact on the financial world has to begin with an acknowledgment of his very serious contribution to the high-yield debt markets. Indeed, the morality play of Milken and Drexel, at a very important level, "offers crucial insights into the underlying challenges of managing innovation and how the most successful innovations can lead to the most spectacular disasters." (See Samuel Insull.) Whatever else one may say about Milken, he was indisputably a brilliant innovator. The junk bond market, which he single-handedly pioneered and dominated, peaked at more than $200 billion in the 1980s—reshaping the world of finance as we know it. By the end of the 1990s, junk bonds had become a widely accepted staple of international capital markets, providing funding for issuers all around the world.

Milken's innovations, like many others before and after him, also set the stage for massive conflicts of interest. Fees were excessive; insider trading was an irresistible temptation. Throughout history, in fact, financial market innovations have been driven by the need to create profits for investment bankers at least as much as the need to solve problems for the client.[22]

Milken's Junk

Milken's greatest innovation, of course, was his reinterpretation of the high-yield bond market. He did not invent high-yield bonds, but he redefined their utility and, in the process, created a whole new universe of financing and investment for financial market participants. As one observer explains, he "became the most important financier of the 1980s by pioneering the high-yield, low-rated bonds that helped fuel a takeover boom, forced companies to restructure and, in some cases, gave them the funds to grow."[23]

As noted above, his strategy was based on sound research, which found that high-yield securities historically had a good track record, with few defaults. Based on this research, Milken came to believe that the high yield on such securities was more than adequate to compensate investors for the risk. Simply put, junk was a good investment. As he explained to a *Forbes* reporter, "People forget that today's junk is often tomorrow's blue chip. And these reversals take place fast these days. Look at Wal-Mart and Sears…" (Indeed, the gradual shift in investors' vocabulary from "junk bond" to "high-yield bond" reflects the extent to which these instruments have morphed into respectability.)

Milken had good timing, too. Fed Chairman Paul Volcker had announced in 1979 that from now on money supply would be fixed; instead, interest rates would fluctuate in line with the business cycle[24] (previously, interest rates had been more or less steady, and money supply had fluctuated). And fluctuate they did—interest rates began to swing wildly, so bond prices (which are directly related to interest rates) swung as well. This meant that bonds were transformed from boring, conservative investment vehicles into objects of speculation. Michael Lewis explains, "Overnight the bond market was transformed from a backwater into a casino." A casino whose rules Michael Milken understood better than anyone else—indeed, he had invented many of them.

Indisputably, Milken did much good. Thanks to the use of Milken's junk bonds, many medium-sized but quickly growing companies—which would otherwise have foundered due to a lack of bank financing—suddenly had access to huge pots of capital. Between 1977 and 1989, Drexel's high-yield unit raised nearly $100 billion in public issues. (Milken received up to 35 percent of each transaction as his commission, based on a formula that he had negotiated in the late seventies.) So Milken's argument that he used financial engineering to create value, build companies, and provide jobs bears up under scrutiny.[25]

Hostile—Very Hostile—Takeovers

While the long-term impact of financing corporate growth with high-interest junk bonds is open to controversy, nothing gripped the public imagination more than the use of junk in corporate takeovers. The 1980s were a decade of ever larger, ever more dramatic takeover battles involving multibillion dollar sums of money, gargantuan egos, and larger-than-life boardroom battles taking place in the public arena.

And some of these huge takeover bids were financed by none other than Michael Milken's junk bonds, the "high-octane financial fuel that powers many of [the decade's] most daring Wall Street deals."[26] Thanks to Milken, takeover bids that once were possible only for giant corporations, backed by traditional bank financing, were now possible for aggressive individuals like T. Boone Pickens, Carl Icahn, and Irwin Jacobs. Milken had democratized the hostile takeover—much to the dismay of many.

For better or for worse, Milken was credited with "almost single-handedly [sparking] the frenzy of takeovers and buyouts that has given the Roaring Eighties their name."[27] In fact, though, the data fail to support this. Junk bonds provided only five percent of takeover financing overall.

Trash or Treasure?

What, then, were the funds used for? One Drexel report pointed out that very few companies were strong enough to qualify for investment-grade bonds in the mid-1980s; only 800 out of 23,000 American companies with sales of over $25 million could win the coveted status. This left a vast universe of underfinanced companies, and Drexel argued that it performed a public service in stepping up to fill this gap. Studies by Drexel and others during the decade indicated that junk bond finance was mainly used as a catalyst to help small and medium sized companies grow—companies that would otherwise be woefully underfunded.[28] MCI, for example, credited Milken with raising $2.4 billion for the ambitious company at a time when everyone else turned it down.

On the other hand, the simple fact is that junk bonds—by definition—carry high interest rates, putting a heavy burden on these growing companies. Corporate debt in the United States soared from $965 billion in 1982 to a painful $1.8 trillion by 1988, climbing from 32 percent to 37 percent of gross national product. Economists argued that this high debt level was unsafe for the entire economy, not just for the individual companies struggling to service their debt. High debt servicing costs reduce the cash available for companies to invest in productive investments, reducing efficiency and growth potential. Moreover, management lost any margin for error—they had to hit every target, every year, in order to raise enough cash to pay the interest.[29]

Time magazine summarized the concerns swirling around Milken and his Wall Street cronies as follows:

- …the relentless focus on dealmaking rather than on long-term investment,
- the apparent disregard for company employees and the communities in which firms are located,
- the rapid pileup of debt that has alarmed everyone from small investors to Federal Reserve Chairman Alan Greenspan, who recently called for measures to curb borrowing,
- the cost to the American taxpayers, who wind up underwriting the buyouts to the tune of billions of dollars because interest payments… are [tax-deductible].

Time put it into historical perspective by remarking: "Seldom since the age of the 19th century robber barons has corporate behavior been so open to question."[30]

By the end of the decade, it was clear that at least some of these concerns were well-founded. Lust for massive fees on the part of dealmakers and investment bankers had produced a series of deals that generated little or no productive investment—just paper shuffles and unimaginably huge payoffs for the financiers lucky enough to get a piece of the action.[31] Profits and productive investments had been sacrificed to meet cripplingly high interest expenses. Many companies had gone bankrupt or were forced to undergo painful restructuring. Bondholders and shareholders lost billions, and thousands of workers were jobless.

Part of the trouble, as academics pointed out, was that Milken's historical analysis of junk bonds was based on so-called fallen angels, the once highly-rated debt of once-sound companies that had fallen on hard times. As the investment ratings of these companies declined, their debt costs rose—to levels that more than compensated investors for the riskiness of these instruments. But Milken was venturing into new and untested territory with his junk bonds, underwriting *new* bond issues with initial below investment-grade ratings. The performance of these issues was likely to be different from that of issues that started out with a higher rating and then declined, academics suggested. And they were right.

But on the other hand, it could also be argued that the undeniably painful process of restructuring had strengthened corporate America, laying the groundwork for the boom of the 1990s and the many jobs that it would create. Wasn't it possible that high debt had forced companies to make extraordinarily careful use of their scarce resources, wringing out profligacy and actually promoting efficiency?

Moreover, Milken was also right about the inadequacy and inaccuracy of the bond ratings system. Recognizing that bond ratings were

- based on the past, rather than the future, and
- gave investors a phony sense of safety, appealing to the overly risk-averse,

he exploited the opportunities provided by this flawed system. Milken observed, for example, that bond ratings appeared to be related to company size; only Fortune 500 companies received AAA or AA ratings. This failed to even pass the common-sense test! Further, he calculated that using the current bond ratings system, barely 15 percent of U.S. companies would receive investment-grade ratings.

Combined with the fact that most investors were unwilling or unable to buy sub-investment grade securities, this meant that the public debt markets were completely dominated by investment-grade—that is, Fortune 500—issuers before the late 1970s. The small junk bond market, as noted above, was made up of fallen angels whose creditworthiness had plummeted.

Then Millken came along. By the late seventies Drexel had developed a technique for analyzing the credit quality of these lower-grade bond issues, and had pioneered the underwriting of new high-yield bond issues for these companies. All of a sudden, young or highly leveraged firms—which had previously been limited to pricey commercial bank lending, private placements, or equity—had a new, seemingly unlimited source of cash. Between 1977 and 1984 the junk bond market tripled in size, amounting to more than a third of all public corporate debt issued in 1984.

By any measure, this was a positive and lasting contribution to financial markets. By educating the investment community about the exceptional returns available on junk bonds, and by providing a secondary market to trade the bonds as needed, Drexel persuaded a broad range of institutions into this market. And overall, the results confirmed the rightness of Milken's approach. Solid academic studies in the mid-eighties provided overwhelming evidence that yields on junk bonds were more than enough to compensate investors for default losses—just as Milken had said they would be.

All was not perfect in Milken-world, though. For one thing, by mid-decade corporate raiders such as T. Boone Pickens and Carl Icahn were increasingly apt to use junk bonds to finance their highly publicized hostile takeovers. You didn't need a Ph.D. to figure out that these deals were mostly about creating gargantuan payoffs for the armies of investment bankers and top executives who fed off them, rather than actually creating value in the form of new production and new jobs. (Quite the opposite, in fact.)

The debate over which side is right goes to the heart of the debate over Milken's legacy. But the most damaging, important—and ultimately controversial—charge against him probably revolves around his role in the savings and loan industry debacle of the 1980s.

Notes

1. James Stewart, *Den of Thieves* (New York: Simon & Schuster, 1991), pp. 530-531.
2. Connie Bruck, *The Predators' Ball* (New York: Simon & Schuster, 1988), p. 7.
3. Martin Mayer, *The Greatest-Ever Bank Robbery: The Collapse of the Savings and Loan Industry* (New York: MacMillan, 1990), p. 9.
4. William A. Niskanen, "Reaganomics," The Concise Encyclopedia of Economics, available at www.econlib.org.
5. Mayer, *The Greatest-Ever Bank Robbery.*
6. Daniel Fischel, *Payback: The Conspiracy to Destroy Michael Milken and His Financial Revolution* (New York: Harper Collins, 1995), p. 7.
7. Michael Lewis, *Lair's Poker* (New York: W.W. Norton & Company, 1989), p. 2.
8. Seth Klarman, "Blundering Down Wall Street," *Washington Post*, November 25, 1990, p. C3.
9. Kurt Eichenwald, "Wages Even Wall Street Can't Stomach," *New York Times*, April 3, 1989, p. D1.
10. Kurt Eichenwald, "After a Boom, There Will Be Scandal," *New York Times*, December 16, 2002, p. C3.

11. Eichenwald, "Wages Even Wall Street Can't Stomach."
12. David Colbert, *Eyewitness to Wall Street: Four Hundred Years of Dreamers, Schemers, Bust and Booms* (New York: Broadway Books, 2001), p. 225-227.
13. Ibid.
14. Stewart, *Den of Thieves*, p. 260.
15. J. W. Michaels, "My Story—Michael Milken," *Forbes*, March 16, 1992, p. 78.
16. Michael Kinsley, "Wall Street's Other Scandal," *Washington Post*, March 5, 1987, p. A27.
17. Stewart, *Den of Thieves*, p. 529.
18. Bruck, *Predators' Ball*, pp. 14-15.
19. Stewart, *Den of Thieves*, pp. 136-8.
20. Colbert, *Eyewitness to Wall Street*, p. 220.
21. J. W. Michaels, "History Lessons," *Forbes*, December 24, 1990, p. 38.
22. Michael Schrage, "Drexel's Demise Should Be A Warning About Financial Innovation," *Washington Post*, February 16, 1990, p. C3.
23. Paul Richter, "Ranking Milken Among the Rouges," *New York Times*, April 29, 1990, p. D1.
24. Lewis, *Liar's Poker*.
25. Michaels, "My Story."
26. Barbara Rudolph and John Greenwald, "Where's the Limit?" *Time*, December 5, 1988, p. 66.
27. Ibid.
28. David A. Vise and Steve Coll, "Drexel Study Says Junk Bonds Make Companies Grow," *Washington Post*, May 20, 1987, p. 64.
29. Rudolph and Greenwald, "Where's the Limit?"
30. Ibid.
31. Ibid.

8

The Decade of Greed, Continued: Where the Money Is

Q. Why do you rob banks? A. "Cause that's where the money is."—Willy Sutton, Bank Robber

The S&L mess began far away from Milken's Beverly Hills trading desk, in the dimly lit cloakrooms and congressional hearing rooms of Washington, D.C. The stage was set by a series of well-intentioned moves to deregulate the struggling thrift industry beginning in the early 1980s. Battered by sky-high interest rates and intense competition, the thrifts had fallen on hard times. In the drive to restructure the thrift business and make it more market-driven, greed was allowed to go unchecked, leaving the savings and loan sector to be one of the biggest financial scandals to rock the U.S. financial system in decades. Compared to some of the S&L and thrift business leaders, Willy Sutton, the famous bank robber, was a small time operator.

Tough Times in Thrift Land

Thrifts were created to take in retail deposits and provide long-term, fixed-rate mortgages for residential homeowners. (The first known mortgage transaction took place in 1831, when lamplighter Comly Rich borrowed $381 to buy a house that still stands in the Philadelphia suburb of Frankford.) Solidly based on the Main Streets and byways of small-town America, until the mid-1960s the thrift business was secure, profitable, and dull.

But the S&L credo of 3-6-3 (borrow at 3 percent, lend at 6 percent, be on the golf course by 3pm) began to erode in the late 1960s as interest rates rose and, worse, started to fluctuate more widely. The S&Ls, which lent at long-term fixed rates but had to pay ever-increasing short-term rates to depositors, saw their comfortable niche begin to disappear. Their problems multiplied when Fed Chairman Paul Volcker decided to rely on high and volatile interest rates to combat inflation beginning in 1979. The ailing thrifts were stuck paying as much as 15 percent to depositors, while earning just 7-8 percent on their low, fixed-rate mortgages.[1]

From the moment that the Fed lifted interest rates in October 1979, the S&Ls hemorrhaged cash. By the time that Reagan took office, it was estimated that barely 100 of the nation's 4000 thrifts were truly solvent, and government officials judged that only dramatic action could rescue the industry. The path they chose—in tune with the Reagan mantra of getting government off our backs—was deregulation.

1. First, in 1980 Congress voted to phase out interest rate ceilings on commercial banks and S&Ls over the next six years. The legislation also allowed thrifts to expand their investments into consumer loans, commercial paper, and corporate bonds. The importance of this shift for S&Ls—humble hometown banks that had been created for the purpose of providing home loans—cannot be overstated.

2. Second, over the next few years a series of congressional and bank oversight board decisions under the laissez-faire Reagan administration continued to ease regulations on the S&L industry, while at the same time increasing its safety net. One of the most important moves involved deposit insurance. In 1934 President Franklin Delano Roosevelt had created the Federal Savings & Loan Insurance Corporation (FSLIC) to insure savings accounts at thrifts up to a limit ($5000 originally). This government-sponsored, government-run insurance system was to be funded by the industry itself through a federally mandated fee.

    The deposit insurance scheme, which mirrored that put into place for commercial banks, had obvious benefits, but a risky side effect as well—the so-called moral hazard of reducing incentives for good management. If bank officials and depositors know that they will be bailed out in the event of imminent failure, what is their incentive to behave conservatively?

    During the 1980s, the moral hazard was compounded when the government raised the deposit insurance limit to $100,000 per account from its earlier $40,000 level. This decision followed a massive lobbying effort, including hefty campaign contributions, on its behalf by the thrift industry, especially the major California thrifts.

3. Finally, in 1982 Congress passed another bill to deregulate the industry. The Garn-St. Germain Act, which was also heavily influenced by the hard work of industry lobbyists, allowed S&Ls to move even further afield from their original purpose of home lending. Basically, S&Ls would now be allowed to invest up to 90 percent of their assets in commercial bank-type, or nonresidential mortgage, activities.

The result of all this deregulation was an S&L industry awash in high-cost money (thanks to the higher interest rate ceilings), chasing too few low-risk investments. Inevitably, higher-risk investments—such as junk bonds—became more alluring, especially since deposits were now insured up to $100,000 per account.

Enter Michael Milken

The match of Milken's high-yield investments and S&Ls desperately seeking yield was made in heaven, and Milken was quick to consummate the union. Drexel aggressively courted thrifts and recruited them as both issuers and purchasers of junk bonds. It was not unusual for Drexel to finance an S&L via junk bonds, and then persuade the newly cash-rich S&L to invest in junk issued by other Drexel clients.

But junk-bond investments were only one piece of the S&L puzzle, as the 1980s progressed and "the thrift problem changed from bad interest rates to bad judgment by managers."[2] Deregulation had opened a Pandora's Box for the S&Ls, and it was only a matter of time before the system staggered under the weight of unscrupulous operators and badly overmatched regulators. Daniel Fischel appraised the situation in these terms:

> The combined effect of these legislative and regulatory initiatives was to eliminate whatever market discipline existed in the thrift industry. Weak or insolvent thrifts, allowed to remain in existence by lowered capital requirements and accounting gimmickry, now could choose among a wide menu of investment alternatives... And depositors were more than willing to invest in thrifts, no matter how weak, because of deposit insurance... Thrifts now had incentives to raise large amounts of money and take big risks. This incentive was strongest for those thrifts...at or near insolvency with little or no capital of their own at risk. These thrifts had nothing to lose by adopting a "shoot the moon" strategy and pursuing the most speculative investment ventures.[3]

Thus S&L operators believed that they faced an unlimited upside with virtually no downside risk.

Even as interest rates fell in 1983 and many S&Ls returned to profitability, the industry was embarking on a joyride of no return. High-cost deposits overwhelmed the industry, but few knew what to do with the now-abundant cash sitting in their vaults. Too much capital, too little expertise in the newly available realms of construction and real estate development lending, too little supervision, and too few internal policies to ward off corruption and fraud led to an increasingly perilous position. Eventually, it became clear that the so-called construction loans were in fact a form of real estate speculation that left the hapless thrifts exposed to tremendous risk. Lax ownership requirements had made S&Ls a target for every major real estate developer and speculator in the country; with virtually no downside risk, deregulation had created a situation rife with moral hazard.

The first signs of disaster appeared in Mesquite, Texas at Empire Savings in 1984. The bank had expanded by an extraordinary 1000 percent over the past few years but failed because of bad real estate loans (no one wanted to buy the projects it had financed). Empire turned out to be a veritable template for many subsequent bank failures, featuring:

- no reserves against bad loans;
- a willingness to lend 100 percent of a project's value;
- astonishing asset growth; and
- lax regulation (bank examiners remained remarkably unaware of the bank's accounting tricks and extreme leveraging until the bitter end).

Soon, the trickle of thrift collapses turned into a torrent. The industry lost $6.23 billion in 1989, and the Resolution Trust Company was created to handle failed thrifts; it was to become the biggest owner of real estate and junk bonds in the country, responsible for running one-third of the thrift industry. By the decade's end, the cost to the taxpayer of industry bailouts was variously estimated from $170 billion to as high as $1 trillion. Eventually, banking expert Martin Mayer would call the thrift industry collapse "the worst public scandal in American history." Compared to earlier scandals, he maintains, "the S&L outrage makes Teapot Dome and Credit Mobilier [look like] minor episodes."[4]

Faced with a disaster of such proportions, observers cast about for someone to blame—and scrutiny soon fell upon Michael Milken. Some of the biggest failed thrifts, including Lincoln and Columbia savings and loans, had invested heavily in junk bonds at their own peril. CenTrust, for example, which was seized by the government in early 1990, had $1.2 billion invested in junk bonds.

So in 1989 Congress passed one more piece of legislation, the Financial Institution Reform and Recovery Act (FIRREA), which ordered the S&Ls to unload their junk bond investments over the next five years. The result, inevitably, was panic selling, which drove down the price of junk bonds even more dramatically and forced thrifts to liquidate their holdings at a huge loss.

Finding the Villains

Who was to blame for this debacle? At first, public opinion centered on Milken and his junk bonds. Editorial pages argued—and many prominent economists agreed—that S&Ls should never have been involved in the junk bond market, lacking the expertise, risk tolerance, and capital base for such inherently risky investments. The obvious mismatch of small-town home lenders and Milken's sophisticated financial instruments cried foul too loudly to be ignored.

But, as with everything else about Milken, the truth is undeniably more nuanced. The abovementioned CenTrust, for instance, suffered from many other serious management failures—including a chairman who spent $122,000 of the firm's money on a party and $29 million on paintings. At many failed thrifts, it seemed that the lunatics—or, at least, the crooks—had taken over the asylum. One government study of the twenty-six most costly S&L insolvencies in 1987 found that all twenty-six had violated the law, resulting in eighty-five criminal referrals. The government eventually concluded that 60 percent of the institutions that had failed by 1990 were plagued by "serious criminal behavior."[5]

The Best Way to Rob a Bank

Examples of outrageous behavior—even looting their own banks—on the part of S&L executives abound. As a California regulatory official noted, "The best way to rob a bank is to own one."

In *Big Money Crime*, authors Kitty Calavita, Henry N. Pontell, and Robert H. Tillman report on a few of the most egregious cases. Thomas Spiegel, director and CEO of Columbia S&L in Beverly Hills, made at least four trips to Europe; purchased guns, ammo, and accessories totaling $91,000; bought several condos and resort villas; and purchased a jet aircraft for $5.6 million—"all paid for by federally insured Columbia deposits." (Miscellaneous personal expenses listed in the charges against Spiegel also included "$1953 for silverware and table linens...$8600 for towels...$19,775 for 16 cashmere throws and three comforters...$1800 for the installation of a stereo into a Mercedes-Benz 560 SEL.")

Then there was Janet McKinzie and Duayne Christensen of North American S&L. Both had a Rolls Boyce; McKinzie charged hundreds of thousands of dollars of clothes from Neiman Marcus

---

to the bank; and they spent "$125,000 for a gold eagle statue, $18,000 for a letter opener, and $500 for a solid gold paper clip. On McKinzie's birthday they hosted a five-course dinner party for several hundred guests, with Sammy Davis, Jr. providing the entertainment." All paid for by the bank's unwitting depositors, of course.

And let's not forget Ed McBirney at Sunbelt S&L. McBirney, who reportedly ran the "Animal House version of a savings and loan," spent over $1 million of Sunbelt's money on Halloween and Christmas parties, including a $32,000 payment to his wife for planning the parties. She planned well. "At his 1984 Halloween party McBirney went as a king, and the dinner featured broiled lion, antelope, and pheasant to fit the medieval theme. The next year the theme was an African safari, complete with a 'jungle' and real elephants." McBirney apparently specialized in entertainment of all sorts; he "produced prostitutes for his customers the same way an ordinary businessman might spring for lunch." Courtesy of McBirney's depositors and the federal deposit guarantee program.

From *Big Money Crimes* (Berkeley: University of California Press, 1997), pp. 58-60.

But if evidence of rampant crooked behavior at the failed thrifts is clear, it is much less clear that Milken and junk bonds caused the S&L collapse, or even played a major role in it. In fact, very few S&Ls actually were big junk bond investors. In 1989, only 183 of the nation's 3000 S&Ls held any junk bond investments at all, and most of those put just a small amount of money into the market. Thirty institutions accounted for 90 percent of all junk bonds held by thrifts, and just ten held 80 percent of the industry's total in junk bond investments. So it was a few players who took most of the pie.[6]

And their piece of the pie was not particularly impressive overall, either. The 3000 thrifts held only $7.2 billion in junk bonds by 1986, a tiny share of the total $1.1 trillion in assets in their portfolios. These facts led the *Wall Street Journal* to editorialize that "Michael Milken is serving here as someone else's $500 million scapegoat," pointing out that junk bonds accounted for just 1.2 percent of the thrift industry's total assets, and that only 5 percent of all thrifts owned junk.[7]

Second, the government's eventual decision to force all thrifts to liquidate their junk bond holdings (which accounted for 7 percent of the
total junk market) by then ignited a fire sale and locked in heavy losses
that otherwise would probably not have occurred. The panic selling—at
a time when the market was already struggling to cope with recession,
as well as the reverberations of Drexel's death rattle and Milken's legal
woes—was devastating.

And probably unnecessary, as things turned out. By mid-1992, prices
in the junk bond market had recovered to the levels that prevailed before
the thrifts were forced to sell. The *Wall Street Journal* noted tartly: "There
are no congressional hearings to ask what would have happened to the
bailout's price tag if the S&Ls had been allowed to hold their junk portfolio through the recession."[8] Another analyst commented that "If thrifts,
the Resolution Trust Company, and insurers lost their shirts in the junk
bond market, it was not due to Michael Milken's alleged manipulation of
the market, but to government regulations that forced them to sell their
junk bond debt at the bottom of the market."[9]

On the other hand, it is clear that the thrifts were woefully unprepared
to play in the big leagues of the bond market. If every market needs a
sucker, Milken certainly found his suckers in the S&Ls. Michael Lewis
points out: "The 3-6-3 Club members had not been stress-tested for the
bond market; they didn't know how to play Liar's Poker."[10]

As a result, Milken became a popular scapegoat for the pricey S&L
disaster. A lawyer representing bondholders who were suing the failed
Lincoln S&L remarked that "the whole Milken-takeover-junk bond thing
was intertwined with the collapse of the thrift industry,"[11] and Milken
suffered accordingly from this widespread (mis)perception. Eventually,
he forked over $500 million to settle the vast array of claims against him
arising from the S&L collapses.

But the controversy remains. Postmortems suggest that corruption
played a critical role in most of the bank collapses, and most analysts
conclude that the government's role was far more influential—and
damaging—than Milken's. Deregulation, which allowed the industry to
invest in highly speculative assets without adequate risk management
skills or supervision, was at the center of the debacle. Politicians of all
stripes had, in essence, created a "system distorted by deposit insurance
and phony accounting,"[12] which was a tempting target for unscrupulous
operators of all kinds. Add to that a heavy dollop of political influence—the biggest thrifts were extraordinarily well-connected—and
you have a foolproof recipe for disaster. Junk bonds were just the icing
on the cake. If that.

Big Brother Is (Not) Watching

In fact, government played a remarkably unhelpful role in this scandal-ridden decade of greed. As noted above, its role in the S&L collapse was especially pernicious. First, the emphasis on deregulation reflected an "uncritical acceptance—so much in fashion at the time—that regulation meant inefficiency and that free-market policies would work to everyone's benefit"[13] (a feature of the free-wheeling 1990s as well). This argument failed to consider, of course, the fact that the S&L market was hardly free of government intervention, since the government was essentially insuring its depositors!

Indeed, the so-called "deregulation" of the S&Ls was so haphazard that the government completely controlled the industry right up till the bitter end. As Martin Mayer points out, "...players entered the game through a government charter and continued to play, however severe their losses, in violation of all capitalist principles—courtesy of a government that continued to insure their borrowings." He adds, devastatingly: "Deposit insurance has proved to be the crack cocaine of American finance."[14]

Second, the wave of deregulation meant that very few overseers were equipped to supervise and regulate the newly emboldened thrifts—as often occurs in periods of financial innovation, the bankers' creativity evolved much faster than anyone's ability to supervise it. Many S&L directors did not fully understand the sophisticated new transactions well enough to question the banks' aggressive managers, especially since the economy was booming and (paper) profits looked impressive.

Auditors were similarly befuddled (again, a precursor of the nineties). In the wake of the industry collapse, Ernst & Young eventually agreed to pay $440 million to settle claims relating to its thrift audits (without admitting or denying any wrongdoing). Ernst & Young's predecessor, Arthur Young, had given Vernon Savings & Loan of Texas a clean state-ment just five days before the government seized control of the ailing thrift. Laventhol & Horwath, the nation's seventh largest accounting firm, collapsed in 1990 under the weight of thrift audit-related lawsuits, in an eerie foreshadowing of Enron auditor Arthur Anderson's demise a decade later. And the industry's prime regulator, the FSLIC, was so heavily influenced by industry insiders and lobbyists that one official commented it seemed to work for the thrifts, rather than supervising them.[15]

As the industry's troubles mounted, the S&L insiders wielded their considerable clout in Washington to influence policy. Members of

Congress, it appeared, were enthusiastically protecting their favorite S&Ls and intervening on their behalf with regulators. These practices were epitomized by the infamous Keating Five, a group of five senators who were skillfully manipulated by Lincoln Savings & Loan's Charles Keating into browbeating bank regulators on Lincoln's behalf.[16] (Fortunately, the senators "didn't accomplish anything except to hurt their own reputations."[17])

Lobbyists, Politicians, and Regulators

Indeed, bank regulators faced a wave of derision and anger as the industry faced collapse. But, in truth, the role of the regulators was far more subtle than the obtuseness and sleepiness they were accused of. Powerful politicians repeatedly told the regulators to get off the backs of "over-regulated" businesses, urging them to pressure the industry toward self-regulation instead. So there was a division in both Washington and in state capitals scattered around the country, between the actual troops working in a regulatory capacity, who firmly believed in their mission of prudent supervision—and their political masters, who were driven in quite another direction by both ideology and pragmatism. Also, the S&L supervisors, as has been noted above, were badly out of their depth in dealing with financial innovations like junk bonds. Told to back off by their political chiefs, and accustomed to dealing with sleepy, uncomplicated S&Ls, these regulators were hopelessly outmatched.

S&Ls were not the only operators to cultivate powerful friends inside the Beltway, underlining the inevitable corruption of a political system where the costs of running for office are so high. James Stewart chronicles Drexel's political connections with his usual perspicacity:

> Drexel had no Washington office or registered lobbyists before 1985. Then, however, Congress had begun rumbling about hostile takeovers. During the Unocal raid, Representative Timothy Wirth, the powerful Colorado Democrat who chaired the Subcommittee on Telecommunications, Consumer Protection, and Finance, introduced a bill outlawing greenmail. Drexel, opposed to the measure, hired a former White House aide and opened an office in Washington. It retained Robert Strauss, a former Democratic National Committee chairman, and John Evans, a former SEC commissioner, as lobbyists. Contributions from Drexel's political action committee rose from $20,550 in the 1984 elections to $177,800 in the 1986 elections.
>
> At the 1986 Drexel bond conference, the once-critical Wirth was featured speaker. Drexel executives gave $23,900 to his successful Senate campaign, and Wirth became a defender of junk bonds. His earlier attempt to prohibit greenmail went nowhere, and he didn't reintroduce it. Drexel invited other influential politicians to speak, including Senators Bill Bradley, Alan Cranston (the recipient of $41,750 in Drexel money that year), Edward Kennedy, Frank Lautenberg, and Howard Metzenbaum. Most of them seemed as dazzled by the aura of mega money as the lowliest

pension-fund manager. For good measure, Drexel executives contributed $56,750 to Senator Alfonse D'Amato of New York, then chairman of the securities subcommittee.[18]

Fortunately for Drexel et al., the prevailing winds under the Reagan administration of the 1980s favored free markets, deregulation, and unbridled capitalism. If greed was necessary to make the capitalist carousel go round, then Ivan Boesky was right—greed was good.

The Reagan years were a time, much like the mid to late 1990s, when markets were celebrated and government's primary role was to get out of the way. Reaganites emphasized free markets, deregulation, and relaxed supervision. And the markets rejoiced; the "Reagan dollar," for example, reached amazing heights in foreign exchange markets as capital poured into the United States from all over the world.

As discussed above, deregulation in the savings and loan industry had an electrifying effect: freeing up the thrifts to invest in all sorts of non-thrifty assets, including junk bonds, and eventually laying the groundwork for the industry's collapse. (Or as Martin Mayer puts it, the collapse of "institutions that had been conservative pillars of their communities until the U.S. government insanely invited them to take a flier.") One amazing S&L, American Diversified in California, took advantage of deregulation to rack up unheard-of losses. "A company with $11 million in assets lost $800 million," explained one analyst. This is "…tantamount to a news report that a drunken motorist has wiped out the entire city of Pittsburgh." Not to be outdone, when the state of Texas seized Vernon S&L in 1987, "96% of its loans—a Guinness Book of World Records number—were delinquent."[19]

On Wall Street as well as Main Street, financiers' creativity moved much faster than the regulators' ability to control it. Even when problems appeared at some of the Street's most important investment banks, such as Kidder Peabody and Drexel, regulators were reluctant to act. The Securities and Exchange Commission (SEC), after all, has the power to put a firm out of business by simply revoking its broker-dealer's license. But throughout this scandal-ridden era the SEC only used this power for small, fringe players. The big fish, deemed too big to fail, were allowed to go on playing.

And once the authorities stepped in, matters often got even worse (recall the thrift industry's disastrous junk bond selloff). As the decade drew to a close and the drumbeat of scandal grew ever louder, the balance of power shifted, at least temporarily, back to the government. A favorite target of legislators, for example, was the wave of hostile takeovers that dominated press headlines and captured (unfriendly) public attention. So congressmen set their sights on new legislation aimed at curbing takeovers, or at least takeovers financed with junk bonds. Public outrage notwithstanding, it is difficult to conceive of legislation better suited to curbing the entrepreneurial engine that has fueled American business for so many years.

Crime and Punishment

Fortunately for all, this legislation foundered as cooler heads prevailed, and officials turned to the more serious work of ferreting out and punishing the true wrongdoers of the era. At the top of their list, of course, was Michael Milken—the man who had been called the most important financier in America, and who now also looked to be the greatest financial scoundrel in America.

So in 1988, the SEC filed a complaint against Milken alleging securities fraud and a host of other violations including defrauding his own clients, market manipulation, insider trading, concealing the ownership of securities, and filing false statements about the purpose of securities purchases. As noted above, he ended up serving twenty-two months in jail and paying around $1.3 billion in restitution; other players also served time and paid various, smaller amounts.

Did the punishment fit the crime? Milken's $1.3 billion payment sounds huge—but his personal and family fortune upon his exit from jail in 1992 was variously estimated at anywhere from $500 million to $1.2 billion. Certainly he remained a very, very wealthy man by any standard. And Milken was not alone: James Stewart notes, "Michael Milken may be an extreme example, but every major participant in these crimes emerged from the experience a wealthy man... Such results have understandably led many to question whether justice was served, and whether future scandals will be deterred."[20] (Certainly anyone who lived through the late 1990s can answer that question with an unequivocal no, but more on that later!)

Also, the damage done to investors, taxpayers, innocent workers who lost their jobs, and, most important, to the integrity of the U.S. capital markets, undoubtedly far exceeds even the billion-plus in restitution that was eventually paid. So did the punishment fit the crime? Certainly not with regard to offsetting the losses suffered by so many. Did it provide an adequate deterrent to future financiers? As Stewart further points out: "The Wall Street criminals were consummate evaluators of risk—and the equation as they saw it suggested little likelihood of getting caught."[21]

And even if they did caught, maybe a cool billion or so might be worth twenty-two months in minimum security.

A Fickle Public

To all of this there was a willing handmaiden in the press, which lionized and then vilified the Wall Street players. During the boom of the 1980s, Milken and his colleagues became folk heroes in the financial papers, widely credited with revitalizing the U.S. economy and sending the dollar soaring. *Forbes* called him "the man who runs America's economy," while Ivan Boesky's "greed-is-good" commencement address at Berkeley's business school drew adoring cheers.

As scandals emerged and the economy soured, though, public opinion turned against Milken with a vengeance as Milken et al. quickly became the villains of the piece. Milken was widely blamed for the recession that set in by 1990, as well as the savings and loan debacle; truly, he was "the embodiment of a decade of greed."[22]

S&L operators were similarly vilified as reporters fell over themselves to expose their excesses. But this attention followed years of media inattention to the gathering storm clouds over the thrift industry. The boring, technical issues were deemed sure losers in the world of if-it-bleeds-it-should-lead (truly, even the most eager business student's eyes would glaze over after plowing through an article peppered with references to capitalized interest, retained operating loss carryforwards, duration-matched spreads, and pushdown purchase accounting). The alphabet soup of U.S. government agencies involved in the S&L industry was even more stupefying; an incomplete list would include the FSLIC, RTC, FDIC, NCFIRRE, GAO, OTS, FHLB, DIDC, OMB, and OCC. Not to mention Ginnie Mae, Freddie Mac, and Fannie Mae. Really, who wouldn't rather read—and report on—Nancy Reagan's astrologer? *Rolling Stone* reporter P. J. O'Rourke wrote:

> Government officials [in the S&L mess] can do anything they want, because any time regular people try to figure out what gives, the regular people get bored and confused, as though they'd fallen a month behind in their algebra class.[23]

By decade's end, of course, it was a different story as reporters eagerly reported on the extravagance and excess of the former high-fliers. In a frenzy of self-disgust, Wall Streeters and Main Streeters turned on their fallen heroes. As jobs were lost and business activity slowed, revelations about obscenely large executive payoffs were particularly infuriating. Milken, who had earned some $550 million in 1987, was a fat target, as was Ivan Boesky with his $100 million pay package in the same year. Excessive compensation captured the public attention, as people pondered the fact that the securities industry had joined entertainment and sports as the only other arena in U.S. business where multimillion dollar paychecks were routinely given out to employees far below the senior management level. Greed, it seemed, was no longer good.

Neither was "deregulation." As noted above, by the dawn of the 1990s various government bureaucrats were scrambling to plug the regulatory holes that had let all of this happen in the first place. But the problem was that very few people, including President Reagan, really understood deregulation and the free market fantasy in the first place. The fact is, free markets work perfectly only under certain impossible conditions—like perfect information, rational people, and zero government intervention. Even the most cursory glance at conditions in the 1980s makes it clear that none of these conditions was even close to being met. So the rush to re-regulate, just like the earlier rush to de-regulate, was based on silly premises and a fundamental misunderstanding of what makes markets work.

Even more powerful than revelations of executive greed, though, was public outrage about the enormous fees earned and companies overturned in the takeover mania of the 1980s. And there was no better catalyst for this widespread disaffection with business practices than the well-publicized, bitterly-contested battle for RJR Nabisco. In late 1988, the battle culminated with a $24.9 billion buyout spearheaded by Kohlberg Kravis Roberts—partly financed by Drexel—which generated as much as $1 *billion* in fees for the army of Wall Street investment bankers and lawyers lucky enough to get a piece of the deal. Wall Street economists and Washington politicians alike worried that the system was out of control—how could these fees, so out of proportion with the (dubious) value created by the deal—contribute to the well-being of the U.S. economy?

The RJR deal (ably chronicled in *Barbarians at the Gate*), crystallized popular disgust with the alarming takeover trend and fueled "public fears that greed, debt, and buyouts are all spiraling out of control."[24] Dismay at the buyout focused on its:

- focus on financial deal-making rather than long-term, productive investment;
- rapid pileup of debt; and
- cost to taxpayers, who effectively subsidized the deal because billions of dollars in interest payments incurred to finance the deal were tax-deductible.

RJR Nabisco: The Art of the Deal

When Ross Johnson's Standard Brands merged with Nabisco to form Nabisco Brands in 1981, Johnson did not waste any time replacing Nabisco's staid corporate culture with the flashy lifestyle he and his band of Merry Men had enjoyed at Standard Brands. Following the 1985 merger with RJR, Johnson came to head a corporate powerhouse boasting a stable of high-profile brands ranging from Oreo cookies to Winston cigarettes; Reynolds Tobacco alone generated $1 billion in cash every year. (As Johnson famously commented, "Some genius invented the Oreo. We're just living off the inheritance.") Johnson took full advantage of the company's bulging coffers to supply himself and his executives with lavish perks (think Jack Welch)—a $12 million airplane hangar, twenty-eight celebrity spokespeople for Team RJR, eight airplanes, and more. Johnson himself observed, "a few million dollars are lost in the sands of time."

The notion of a leveraged buyout (LBO) for RJR Nabisco arose as early as the summer of 1986. Johnson went so far as to meet with Henry Kravis, the already legendary young buyout star of Kohlberg Kravis Roberts (KKR), but had little incentive to shake up his privileged life as CEO of RJR Nabisco. Just a year later, though, with the market crash of 1987, RJR became a tempting takeover target thanks to its steady inflow of cash plus its newly cheap stock price.

Realizing that a play on his company was inevitable, Johnson set to work. At first, he engaged Shearson Lehman Hutton to draw up defense plans that could ward off unwanted suitors, including "golden parachute" provisions amounting to more than $50 million for the top executives. But as external interest in the company intensified, a newly invigorated Johnson asked Shearson to put together plans for a management-led LBO.

Negotiations between RJR management and the bankers were sticky. Johnson demanded that he and his management team pocket 20 percent of the profits from the deal (estimated at up to $3 billion), that he be given veto power and equal representation on the board, and that Shearson loan him the necessary equity stake that managers would need to finance their portion of the deal.

Johnson's conditions were unprecedented. But Shearson caved, determined to lead the biggest LBO deal in history, and the battle was joined. Soon Shearson's $75 per share bid was easily topped by KKR's $90 tender offer, other suitors had emerged, and the media was transfixed by this drama playing itself out in full view of a fascinated public. KKR was handicapped, though, by the impossibility of due diligence under these circumstances; without management on board, it was extraordinarily difficult to analyze the company's financials. In this case, insiders feared, KKR was just throwing darts—it was nearly impossible to determine how much debt the company could sustain.

In the meantime, the management-led team gained momentum—until the disputed management agreement was made public. When newspapers revealed the $2.5 billion that Johnson and six other executives would share over the next six or seven years, anti-Johnson sentiment began to grow. Kravis was delighted as Johnson and his team quickly became poster children for corporate greed and excess. Under pressure, Johnson began to concede crucial elements. As the bidding war mounted, more fat had to be trimmed. Johnson agreed to cut the management stake from 8.5 percent to 6.5 percent plus incentives. Meanwhile, Kravis, who had struggled to model the company's cash flows without management assistance, caught a lucky break. Jack Greeniaus, who had viewed himself as Johnson's successor until the LBO offer emerged, made himself available to KKR analysts to interpret financial statements. Kravis learned that they had been off by at least $1.5 billion in estimating the company's value before Greeniaus showed up.

When the dust settled and final bids were submitted, the management group had bid $101 per share and KKR bid $106. KKR appeared to have won, but Johnson's advisers at Shearson were not ready to throw in the towel. They went public with a last-ditch bid of $108, using more paper and less cash so as to increase the bid without increasing the cash requirement. Kravis, who had arrived at 9:45am to sign the final paperwork, was forced to cool his heels while the board deliberated. To buy some time, the board agreed to pay KKR $45 million for an extension of the deadline to 2:00pm.

It was time to play the last cards. The board approached the management group and Kravis with the same question: How high were they willing to go? The management's response was $112; Kravis said $108. Now the board had the two final bids. But without a Shearson guarantee on the value of the stock included in the management offer, the board valued the Johnson-led bid at only $109-$112. They went back to KKR. Would they go any higher? Kravis threw in one more dollar, topping out at $109, and sweetening the deal with provisions that seemed more favorable to RJR shareholders and employees. At 10:36pm, Kravis called his wife and told her that KKR's $109 bid had won.

But in the end, the real winners were the Wall Street investment bankers and lawyers who pocketed up to $1 billion in fees, including:

- $227 million to Drexel,
- $109 million to Merrill Lynch,
- $325 million to other investment banks, and
- $75 million to KKR.

KKR sold off RJR Nabisco in an initial public offering (IPO) a few years later, generating more fees for the Wall Street few, but the firm failed to prosper during the 1990s, producing lower-than-expected earnings and consistently disappointing analysts. In June 1999, RJR shed its tobacco operations through a spinoff of stock to the shareholders, tacitly admitting how badly the food side had been dragged down by the tobacco liability. The name reverted to Nabisco, bringing the firm back full-circle to its humble start in the food business.

Source: *Barbarians at the Gate*

Symbols for an Era of Excess

By the time that Milken was negotiating with prosecutors, he had joined RJR Nabisco's chief executive Ross Johnson and the most infamous S&L operators as a widely vilified symbol for an era of greed and excess. Milken's lawyers undoubtedly feared that revelations about his obscene salary would hurt him at trial, and that he risked being punished for the era of greed rather than his actual crimes. Indeed, by the close of the era an outraged public was not differentiating between someone who was guilty of violating securities laws, and someone who was guilty of excessive greed (Martha Stewart, take note). As one economist observed, "In many ways it was Wall Street's excess of the 1980s that was on trial, not Mr. Milken."[25] And another commented, "It is part of a continuum of questionable behavior in the financial arena that starts with names like Ivan F. Boesky, Boyd L. Jefferies, Martin A. Siegel and Dennis B. Levine—cases where illegality has been established—and ends with names like RJR Nabisco, F. Ross Johnson and Henry R. Kravis, where the 'indictment' is for greed and excess."[26]

Wall Street According to Oliver Stone

Moviemaker and conspiracy buff Oliver Stone's classic movie *Wall Street*, which debuted in 1987, almost immediately became an iconic symbol for the Decade of Greed on Wall Street. Stone's "hero"—so to speak—is the lizard-like Gordon Gekko, a man whose slicked-back hair and pricey suspenders dovetail perfectly with his take-no-prisoners, greed-is-good philosophy. Roger Ebert's review says it all:

How much is enough? The kid keeps asking the millionaire raider and trader. How much money do you want? How much would you be satisfied with? The trader seems to be thinking hard, but the answer is, he just doesn't know. He's not even sure how to think about the question. He spends all day trying to make as much money as he possibly can, and he cheerfully bends and breaks the law to make even more millions, but somehow the concept of "enough" eludes him. Like all gamblers, he is perhaps not even really interested in money, but in the action. Money is just the way to keep score.

The millionaire is a predator, a corporate raider, a Wall Street shark. His name is Gordon Gekko, the name no doubt inspired by the lizard that feeds on insects and sheds its tail when trapped. Played by Michael Douglas in Stone's *Wall Street*, he paces relentlessly behind the desk in his skyscraper office, lighting cigarettes, stabbing them out, checking stock prices on a bank of computers, barking buy and sell orders into a speaker phone. In his personal life he has everything he could possibly want—wife, family, estate, pool, limousine, priceless art objects—and they are all just additional entries on the scoreboard. He likes to win.

Stone's *Wall Street* is a radical critique of the capitalist trading mentality, and it obviously comes at a time when the financial community is especially vulnerable. The movie argues that most small investors are dupes, and that the big market killings are made by men such as Gekko, who swoop in and snap whole companies out from under the noses of their stockholders. What the Gekkos do is immoral and illegal, but they use a little litany to excuse themselves: "Nobody gets hurt." "Everybody's doing it." "There's something in this deal for everybody." "Who knows except us?"

Although Gekko's law-breaking would of course be opposed by most people on Wall Street, his larger value system would be applauded. The trick is to make his kind of money without breaking the law. Financiers who can do that, such as Donald Trump, are mentioned as possible presidential candidates, and in his autobiography Trump states, quite simply, that money no longer interests him very much. He is more motivated by the challenge of a deal and by the desire to win. His frankness is refreshing, but the key to reading that statement is to see that it considers only money, on the one hand, and winning, on the other. No mention is made about creating goods and services, to manufacturing things, to investing in a physical plant, to contributing to the infrastructure.

What's intriguing about *Wall Street*—what may cause the most discussion in the weeks to come—is that the movie's real target isn't Wall Street criminals who break the law. Stone's target is the value system that places profits and wealth and the Deal above any other consideration. His film is an attack on an atmosphere of financial competitiveness so ferocious that ethics are simply irrelevant, and the laws are sort of like the referee in pro wrestling—part of the show.

So Milken, Drexel, Kravis, et al. came to symbolize the excess of the 1980s—an excess of optimism generated by their high-risk junk bonds, an excess of money exemplified by Milken's $550 million payout. But the question of their legacy goes far beyond that to the core issue of value creation: Did the high-flying financiers of the eighties engage in true financial building, or short-term financial juggling?

On this question, of course, the jury will forever be out. As one commentator notes, "This was no straightforward morality play of good and evil. Milken had been dangerous, but he had also been one of the most imaginative, visionary financiers of his time."[27] But in attempting to untangle his legacy, a few points can be made:

- First, a very small portion of Milken's huge income was ill-gotten. Most of it came the old-fashioned way—he earned it—by pioneering a new way of raising funds in the junk bond market, by brokering huge financial deals, and by working fifteen-hour days.
- The value of Milken's financial innovations to global capital markets is very real, if incalculable.
- On the other hand, the damage that Milken, Boesky, Levine et al. did to the financial markets is similarly incalculable. With much justice, observers worried that "...Wall Street's Watergate scandal has reached such proportions that the ethical foundation of the financial markets is in question."[28] Investors suffered, taxpayers suffered; indeed, by using his financial clout to aid "a favored few," Milken's financial schemes "corrupted the marketplace as a whole." Like the Enron debacle a decade later and Samuel Insull some decades earlier, the insider trading scandals of the 1980s were widely viewed as a cancer eating away at the heart of Wall Street, threatening the very foundation of capitalism. As Harvard law professor Alan Dershowitz pointed out, trying to compete against big players with access to inside information is "like playing darts with a blindfold."[29] If faith in financial markets as a level playing field is shaken, then the entire economy will suffer.

Whatever Became of Michael Milken?

After a five-year legal battle, Michael Milken was sentenced to ten years in prison on November 21, 1990. He entered the federal minimum-security prison in Pleasanton, California on March 3, 1991, and was released twenty-two months later to a halfway house. One month after that, he was released to home confinement, which he served until March 2, 1993; he was on probation through 1998.

As part of his plea agreement, Milken was barred from ever again participating in the securities industry. However, he skated close to the law by "facilitating" and "consulting on" various deals throughout the 1990s, including a $2 billion partnership deal between Rupert Murdoch's NewsCorp and MCI. This brought him to the attention of the SEC once more, triggering yet another investigation that ended with him paying $47 million to close the probe.

Following a bout with cancer, Milken now describes himself as a "philanthropist and financier." His Milken Family Foundation, variously viewed as an embarrassingly obvious public relations ploy or a genuine contribution to society, supports, among other things:

- programs for youth at risk,
- medical research, and
- the largest teacher-recognition program in the country.

He also serves as chairman of the Milken Institute, a think tank involved in research on global capital markets and economics.

Partly in recognition of his charitable endeavors, Milken's friends have lobbied vigorously for a presidential pardon since the late 1990s. When Bill Clinton left office in January 2001, he pardoned 140 convicts including, most egregiously, fugitive financier Marc Rich. Milken's supporters, with some justice, were outraged. Rich, they pointed out, fled the country instead of serving his time in jail, and never contributed to social welfare as Milken undeniably had. Even New York Mayor Rudolph Giuliani, who had prosecuted Milken for securities fraud a decade earlier, told the *Wall Street Journal* that he favored pardoning Milken. But Milken remains both unpardoned and unrepentant; to this day, he still does not concede any wrongdoing.

Since Milken pleaded guilty to just six counts, the government never really had a chance to make its case against him—and Milken never had the chance to defend his. From a historical perspective, this is probably unfortunate. In the end, Milken will be judged on three points:

1.   *Whether his junk-funded companies prospered or collapsed.* The record is mixed, with some expensive failures and some shining successes. High-cost junk bonds impose a massive interest burden on companies that issue them, but they also impose some much-needed financial discipline on growing companies and democratize the marketplace.

2.   *Whether junk bond investments are decreed to have played a central role in the S&L collapse.* Here the verdict is less mixed: Only about 7 percent of all junk bonds were sold to S&Ls, and the biggest thrift disasters reflected disastrously poor, often corrupt, management rather than Milken's junk. Moreover, even those junk bond investments would not have been losers for the most part had the government not forced a fire sale at the bottom of the market.

3.   *Whether Milken's junk bond market outlives him and prospers.* By the early 2000s, junk bonds had spread to Europe and beyond, funding high-risk, high-growth companies (and countries) across the continents. In 2003, global market size was over $600 billion. On this measure, at least, the record is clear: Milken's contribution to finance will live long beyond his years.

But, in the end, are these achievements overshadowed by his ultimate abuse of the system, and his betrayal of so many—including his own clients? Milken cast a large shadow: His $600 million settlement of the securities charges set a record, as did his 1987 earnings of $550 million. Unlike many earlier scandals by "fringe operators" such as Charles Ponzi, which "said nothing at all about the integrity of the financial system,"[30] Milken and Boesky and their ilk illuminated a corruption at the very heart of the financial world. In that sense, Milken is in an (un)distinguished league apart from the rest, along with Credit Mobilier before him and Enron not long after, threatening the very integrity of the great U.S. financial system.

A disillusioned James Stewart concluded in 1991, "Fifty years passed between the scandals of the 1920s and their counterparts in the 1980s. If Wall Street escapes another major threat to its integrity for even half as long, the crackdown that culminated in Milken's conviction will have proven of historic value."[31]

In fact, barely ten years would pass before the next eruption.

Notes

1.   Alberto Moel and Robert C. Merton, "Savings and Loans and the Mortgage Markets," Harvard Business School Case #9-297-088, 1997.
2.   Kathleen Day, *S&L Hell* (New York: W.W. Norton & Company, 1993), p. 178.
3.   Daniel Fischel, *Payback: The Conspiracy to Destroy Michael Milken and His Financial Revolution* (New York: Harper Collins, 1995), p. 195.

4. Martin Mayer, *The Greatest-Ever Bank Robbery: The Collapse of the Savings and Loan Industry* (New York: MacMillan, 1990), p. 1.
5. Kitty Calavita, Henry N. Pontell, and Robert H. Tillman, *Big Money Crime: Fraud and Politics in the Savings and Loan Crisis* (Berkely: University of California Press, 1997).
6. Jerry Knight, "The S&L-Junk Bond Link," *Washington Post*, February 18, 1990. p. H1.
7. *Wall Street Journal*, Editorial, "The $500 Million Scapegoat," March 10, 1992, p. A18.
8. Ibid.
9. Glenn Yago, "The Regulatory Reign of Terror," *Wall Street Journal*, March 4, 1992.
10. Michael Lewis, *Liar's Poker* (New York: W.W. Norton & Company, 1989), p. 104.
11. Knight, "The S&L-Junk Bond Link."
12. Day, *S&L Hell*, p. 101
13. Jeff Gerth, "The Savings Debacle," *New York Times*, July 3, 1990, p. D5.
14. Mayer, *The Greatest-Ever Bank Robbery*, p. 56.
15. Day, *S&L Hell*, p. 221
16. The Keating Five consisted of five senators, representing all ends of the political spectrum: Alan Cranston (D, CA), Dennis DeConcini (D, AZ), John Glenn (D, OH), John McCain (R, AZ), and Donald Riegle (D, MI). These senators leaned hard on bank regulators to discontinue their investigation of Charles Keating's Lincoln Savings & Loan, which eventually collapsed in 1989, losing around $2 billion of investors' money in the process. Eventually, it turned out that Lincoln had donated $1.3 million to the campaign funds of those senators. Thus the Keating Five became known as the gang that supported a bunch of S&L bandits, and the phrase became synonymous with buying political influence in Washington.
17. Martin Lowy, *High Rollers: Inside the S&L Debacle* (New York: Praeger, 1991), p. 148.
18. James Stewart, *Den of Thieves* (New York: Simon & Schuster, 1991), p. 256.
19. Mayer, *The Greatest-Ever Bank Robbery*, p. 17.
20. Stewart, *Den of Thieves*, p. 527.
21. Ibid.
22. Stewart, *Den of Thieves*, p. 516.
23. Calavita et al., *Big Money Crime*, p. 46.
24. Bryan Burroughs and John Helyar, *Barbarians at the Gate* (New York: Harper Business Essentials, 2003), p. 2.
25. J. W. Michaels, "History Lesson," *Forbes*, December 24, 1990, p. 38.
26. Sarah Bartlett, "Curbing Excess on Wall Street," *The New York Times*, December 25, 1988, p. C1.
27. Connie Bruck, *The Predators' Ball* (New York: Simon & Schuster, 1988), p. 193.
28. Vickey Cahan et al, "What Is Insider Trading?" *Wall Street Journal*, November 18, 1987, p. 1.
29. Robert J. McCartney, "Michael Milken's Trail of Injured Parties," *Washington Post*, April 29, 1990, p. H1.
30. Paul Richter, "Ranking Milken Among the Rogues," *New York Times*, April 29, 1990, p. D1.
31. Stewart, *Den of Thieves*, p. 529.

9

The 1990s B.E. (Before Enron):
A Few Bad Apples, or Rotten to the Core?

Joseph Jett's arrival on Wall Street in the early 1990s was surely a triumph of opportunity over expectations. His father's family can be traced back to a slave named Fred Lattimore, born in Alabama sometime before the Civil War. Jett's great-grandmother Sarah (like her mother before her) was repeatedly raped by a white master, giving birth to a light-skinned daughter who was rejected by Sarah's husband. Jett's father grew up in a primitive shanty without running water or electricity; the only time he saw a white person, Jett writes, was "seeing one on a horse in the distance."

So Jett's meteoric rise on Wall Street was, from the very beginning, improbable. But his father joined the army and moved up quickly, becoming one of a handful of black master sergeants given command of white soldiers in Korea. Thanks to the GI Bill, he finished his high school education. He married and moved north, to Cleveland, where Joseph was born. But even his birth was racked by racism, as Jett describes in his book, *Black and White on Wall Street*:

> [I] was born at a local Catholic hospital because it had a reputation of treating black patients better than the other hospitals in Cleveland. But the North was far from perfect. When my mother was in labor with me, a white woman came into the ward with a twisted ankle. She insisted on a bed with privacy, so to make room for her, my mother's bed was pulled into a hallway. Workmen were sweeping when my father arrived to find my mother, in labor, breathing dust and debris in the public hall. Enraged, he began arguing and shouting and was nearly thrown out of the hospital. Incensed, Pops called a black attorney he knew, and together they forced the hospital to give my mother a room.[1]

Jett grew up despising welfare, affirmative action, or "any other system of dependence that weakened the will or lessened the ability of black men and women." Yet his arrival on Wall Street, by way of MIT and Harvard

161

Business School, was frequently shadowed by assumptions—bitterly resented by Jett—that he was the beneficiary of affirmative action. At a Disney World conference in 1993 for Kidder Peabody's top earners, he was devastated to find himself identified in the conference packet as a representative of the firm's affirmative action program, rather than a star trader.

So when Jett woke up one April morning in 1994 to find morning news reporters announcing that he had been fired from Kidder for perpetrating a massive fraud that shook the mighty firm to its core, in some ways he may not have been surprised. Jett—and others—would always wonder what role racism played in his precipitous fall. In the early days after the scandal broke, he found that he could avoid the throngs of reporters massed around his apartment building by just putting on a baseball cap and walking through them; no one expected Kidder's star trader to be African American.

Jett's journey from star trader to rogue trader—eventually contributing to the disappearance of the long-respected Kidder Peabody name from the annals of Wall Street—is long and strange indeed. But he is only one of a near-epidemic of rogue traders who shook financial markets in the 1990s, contradicting the overall sense that until 9/11 and Enron, the post-Milken decade was relatively clean.

A Decade of Blind Faith

Indeed, between the demise of Drexel Burnham Lambert at the beginning of the 1990s and the implosion of Enron at the end, it is certainly true that Wall Street investors enjoyed a long, raucous party for much of the decade. Yes, it was punctuated by a crash here and a scandal there, but for the most part it was a great ride.

In fact, the 1990s were an era of persistently rising markets—ten solid years of economic expansion, with investors pouring record amounts of money into stocks and earning double digit returns year after year after year. It was the longest bull market since World War II, so long and so strong that even economists wondered if we had permanently vanquished the business cycle.

Not surprisingly, faith in the fundamental rightness of financial markets reached new heights. Investors and policymakers alike gloried in the power of the markets to bring prosperity, democracy, and technology to people from Seattle to Sumatra. Everyone was an investor; by the end of 1997 U.S. mutual funds had total assets of $4.2 trillion, more than the combined gross national products of Canada, Sweden, and France. As Hughes wrote in 2002:

> Power brokers around the world have marched to a single drummer for the past decade and more. In the United States and Britain, left-of-center politicians Bill Clinton and Tony Blair moved their parties and countries decisively into the middle. In Mexico, when voters finally threw out the 70-year-old single-party rule of the Institutional Revolutionary Party (PRI), they rejected the presidential candidate of the left and chose their new president from the right-wing party of landowners and businessmen. Vietnam and China embraced, albeit clumsily, market economics; even Fidel Castro has permitted something of a market to develop in Cuba.[2]

Wall Street, the center of U.S. financial markets, took on near-mythic proportions. President Bill Clinton firmly believed in the power of the bond markets to make or break his fiscal policy; fifty million Americans owned shares; and dot-com companies without any assets or any products raised millions of dollars in seed capital. Normal precepts of prudence and caution were flung to the wind, in the ultimate triumph of the get-rich-quickly mentality. It was a world gone mad.

Blind faith in the glory of free markets, though, tended to sidestep the new and somewhat alarming realities of those markets. In fact, dramatic shifts in the fundamentals of Wall Street were taking place, shifts that would eventually send it spinning way out of control.

For one thing, the markets were infinitely more complex than they had been in the early 1980s. Back in Milken's era, capital markets were pretty simple animals, largely focused on the basics (stocks and bonds); even Milken's innovations, such as junk bonds and leveraged buyouts, were hardly rocket science. But during the 1990s the central focus of the markets shifted to derivatives—financial instruments whose value derives from some underlying assets—which are, by their very nature, highly complex and difficult to value. Even more important, arcane accounting rules meant that most derivatives could be held off the corporate balance sheets, so that they could essentially lurk underground—avoiding the scrutiny of both shareholders and regulators.

The development of ever-more complex derivatives products was enabled by the development of space-age technology. Even in the early to mid-1980s, financial professionals still relied on primitive tools: Lacking email, the Internet, and personal computers, most used handheld calculators to compute prices for simple derivatives such as options and futures. But a decade later, calculations were performed at the speed of light, and the pace of the markets hastened accordingly.

And a new breed of financial professionals came to dominate the trading rooms as well. While the 1980s witnessed the rise of the MBA trader, trading rooms in the 1990s were increasingly dominated by rocket scientists—quantitative wizards with advanced degrees in fields ranging from physics to engineering. Between their brains and the brawn of the computers, these rocket scientists (often called "Quants") churned out astonishingly complex financial products that befuddled most investors.[3]

At the same time, financial deregulation proceeded apace, most obviously in the dismantling of the decades-old separation between investment and commercial banking. Financial powerhouses like Citigroup and J. P. Morgan Chase emerged as leaders in the world of universal banking, able to deliver commercial loans, securities underwriting, investment advice, even insurance policies, under one roof. But hand-in-hand with the deregulation was a growing sense that financial malfeasance was rarely punished. To some, Michael Milken's relatively short prison stay seemed a low price to pay for the millions he got to keep—especially since he was back in the business, advising top corporate clients on mergers and acquisitions, by the mid-1990s.

Not only did financial wrongdoers seem to get off with a slap on the wrist, but those still in the market were encouraged to test the boundaries of what was permissible, over and over again, until the boundaries became virtually meaningless. (In this they were aided, of course, by an army of lawyers.) And even as the financial industry continued to push out the borders, there was very little pushing back from Washington.

And finally, faith in free markets and in the all-knowing abilities of top corporate managers (think Jack Welch) gave management the ability to operate almost without any strings. In many cases, control and ownership of corporations moved far apart, leaving even the most experienced investors without any real ability to influence senior managers. As an astonished public would eventually learn, there was a huge gap between what ordinary shareholders comprehended, and what actually went on in the boardroom (think Tyco, Enron, WorldCom, and Qwest).

"Financial Hydrogen Bombs"

The most important financial development of the early 1990s, without doubt, was the rise of the derivative.

As noted above, derivatives are financial instruments whose value is *derived from* some underlying asset. For instance, a contract in which two parties agree to exchange gold for dollars in thirty days—a futures contract—is also a derivative, because its value derives from the price of gold, an underlying asset. Plain-vanilla derivatives whose value can be easily understood, such as futures and options, were not uncommon in the 1980s. Indeed, derivatives were (and still are) often used to *hedge*, or reduce, risk by banks and other financial institutions.

But during the 1990s, at the frontiers of the industry, some derivatives morphed into huge, unsightly beasts that sometimes defied understanding and explanation, but still managed to take over the markets. As Wall Street guru Felix Rohatyn warned, "Twenty-six-year olds with computers are creating financial hydrogen bombs."[4]

Orange County in the Red

Orange County, California, home to more than 2.5 million people, has long been touted for its wealth, beautiful beaches, and conservative Republican politics. Millions of visitors descend upon Orange County every year to enjoy the surfing and sunbathing on Huntington Beach, which was immortalized by Jan and Dean and Brian Wilson of the Beach Boys as "Surf City, USA," as well as the Richard Nixon Birthplace and Presidential Library, Disneyland, and Knott's Berry Farm.

But in the mid-1990s Orange County, most improbably, also became synonymous with derivatives disaster. The tale begins with Robert Citron, a University of Southern California dropout with no formal training in finance, accounting, or economics, who nonetheless became county treasurer in 1972 and held that position for over two decades. Citron was an unlikely treasurer, let alone an unlikely financial hero. He had only been to New York four times in his entire life; according to one observer, "he kept investment records on index cards and a wall calendar, and used his wristwatch calculator more than any other financial software. Instead of developing computer pricing models, he consulted psychics and astrologers for advice about interest rates."[5]

Yet hero he became. By the early 1990s Citron was managing an investment portfolio of $7.4 billion, which made him one of the largest investors in the country. Moreover, he had racked up an outstanding track record. From the early 1980s until the mid-1990s Citron managed to outperform every other county investment manager in California, sometimes by several percentage points (which explains why the voters kept reelecting him!). Emboldened by his success, he borrowed even more ($13 billion) to invest, so that by early 1994 he had a whopping $20 billion tied up in the markets.

Citron's job was to invest the revenues paid to Orange County. And right up until the bitter end he seemed to be a star performer in this job; during his twenty-two-year tenure the average return on the Orange County Investment Pool (OCIP) was 9.4 percent, compared to the state pool's return of just 8.4 percent, which translated into a hefty $775 million more in profits than the state earned. One of the biggest and most successful municipal investors in the country, Citron was named one of the five best financial officers in America in 1988. Financial expert Philippe Jorion comments: "Citron was viewed as a wizard who could painlessly deliver greater returns to investors."[6] Such a wizard, in fact, that Citron had to turn down investors from outside Orange County who begged to invest in his pool, while some local school districts and cities issued short-term notes to reinvest.

These earnings were a critical source of revenue for Orange County. Local governments in California were increasingly strapped for funds as political sentiment turned sharply against higher taxes. By the early 1990s they were hit by a double whammy as interest rates also began to slip. Municipalities used to 5-7 percent returns were having to make do on 3-4 percent, with no prospect for a tax hike to ease the pain. In this environment, Citron's wizardry was immeasurably valuable.

But, unfortunately, in the end there was less wizardry than wishful thinking. Citron's $20 billion investment was nothing more and nothing less than a bet that interest rates would stay low—a bet that turned out to be painfully ill-advised. Jorion explains, "His portfolio…was supercharged with repurchase agreements and structured notes, [which] essentially implemented a bet on falling, or at least stable, interest rates."[7] All well and good, until the Federal Reserve started to raise rates in February of 1994.

The Fed raised rates six times in 1994, which created a bloodbath in the unprepared bond markets (as interest rates go up, bond prices fall). But throughout the year, an increasingly desperate Citron clung to his position, believing that the U.S. economic recovery was fragile and that the Fed would be forced to reverse its policy. As the year wore on, Citron's losses began to mount. By November, the Orange County Investment Pool was in crisis.

Author Jorion chronicles the events of early December:

On December 1, 1994, the Board of Supervisors officially announced a $1.5 billion loss in the fund. Less than a week later, after frantic attempts to sell the damaged portfolio came to nothing, Orange County declared itself bankrupt.

On December 4, a Sunday, [Assistant Treasurer] Raabe and several other county officials visited Citron at home. "He just looked extremely sad, befuddled," Raabe has said. "You can imagine a man who has run a portfolio for 20 something years, having people come in and say the loss has turned into a real loss and this is going to be the end of your career." After a few minutes, Citron agreed to sign a letter of resignation. Two women officials, Eileen Walsh and Lynne Fishel, stayed behind with Citron, awaiting the arrival of a psychiatric social worker, while the rest of the delegation returned glumly to City Hall.[8]

The losses, which in the end amounted to a staggering $1.7 billion, stemmed directly from Citron's wrong-way bet on interest rates through his investment pool, which was supposed to be a conservative but profitable way to manage the cash holdings of Orange County and some 240 local government entities. Instead, the pool turned out to be a California version of the roulette wheel. It was the largest municipal failure in U.S. history and a shocking blow to the prosperous taxpayers of Orange County.

Who to blame? A crash this dramatic had to have a villain, and the lawsuits were quickly flying. An obvious villain was Robert Citron himself, the college dropout who had managed Orange County into bankruptcy. Citron, who took enormous risks with taxpayers' money, was patently the wrong man for his position by the early 1990s, when markets exploded in complexity and sophistication. His wristwatch calculator was unequal to the task of evaluating complex derivatives that he clearly did not understand—but persisted in buying anyway. Afterwards, the broken Citron lamented that he was "not as sophisticated as I thought I was."

And Citron was duly punished for his sins. In the end, he pled guilty to six felony counts, including making misleading statements for the purpose of selling securities, misappropriating funds for the county, and falsifying accounting records. He paid a $100,000 fine, and spent nearly a year under house arrest.

But Citron was not a satisfactory villain. He appeared more befuddled and bewildered than evil, especially since, unlike Milken and the popular villains of the 1980s, he had reaped no personal gain from his actions. He had received no multimillion (or even thousand) dollar bonuses, he did not enrich himself or anyone in his family; he stole nothing; he enjoyed no thousand-dollar shower curtains or million-dollar birthday bashes. He was a failure, but not a crook.

The Sucker in the Market

Other villains were required, and the first to pop up on the radar screen were the salesmen from the top brokerage houses who had lured an unsuspecting Citron into the murky world of derivatives. Not surprisingly, his huge investment pool combined with his lack of financial sophistication made Citron a great favorite among Wall Street salesmen, especially those of Merrill Lynch. Between 1990 and 1993 Merrill earned an amazing

$100 million in profits from its transactions with Orange County, thanks to Citron. In effect, he had become the sucker in the market.

Lawsuits were inevitable. In January 1995 Orange County filed a $2.4 billion suit against Merrill Lynch, charging that the firm was culpable for steering Citron towards highly risky, unsuitable securities in violation of state and federal laws. Merrill never admitted wrongdoing, but it settled with Orange County for a hefty $400 million, explaining that it just needed to finish the costly, distracting litigation.

Tempting as it is to excoriate Merrill Lynch, in fact it is not at all clear that they are the villains of the piece either. The lawsuits revolve around two questions:

1.   Did Merrill Lynch give Citron adequate warning as to how exposed his investments were to the risk of an interest rate shift?
2.   Did Merrill Lynch sell Citron securities that were so unsuitable for its purpose as to be illegal?

Since the firms settled rather than go to trial, a definitive response to these questions will never be found. But one fact should give pause to those rushing to judgment: Merrill (and other bankers) had indeed warned Citron repeatedly between 1992 and 1994 to reconsider his risky interest rate bets. Citron, and Citron alone, was responsible for his decisions.

Supervisors & Watchdogs

One of the most curious elements of the Citron saga is how easy it was to predict—not even using the benefit of hindsight. In fact, an accountant named John Moorlach did just that: He launched an aggressive public campaign against Citron in spring 1994, warning voters about Citron's interest rate bets and predicting a billion dollar loss. But voters focused on Citron's remarkable track record and rewarded Moorlach for his remarkable prescience by reelecting Citron.

What of the other watchdogs—Orange County's supervisors, auditors, government regulators, and credit rating agencies? Despite four independent audits in 1994 alone, the auditors raised no red flags. Citron was directly "supervised"—the quotes are well-advised—by a county board with no financial background and even less financial sophistication. One county supervisor candidly admitted in spring 1994 that Citron "...is a person who has gotten us millions of dollars. I don't know how in the hell he does it, but it makes us all look good."[9] The supervisors ignored Moorlach's warnings and continued to support Citron, largely because of his winning track record. Like many before and after them, the hapless supervisors "failed to understand OCIP's strategy; neglected to look closely at the instruments being employed; and declined to question OCIP's extraordinary results."[10]

The credit rating agencies were equally clueless. Both Standard & Poor's and Moody's gave Orange County their highest ratings right up through December 1994 when the county filed for bankruptcy. It remains unclear whether this reflects incompetence, or a murkier conflict of interest issue (very high fees were involved in the rating process). But the fact remains that despite the obvious danger of trusting an unsupervised county official with no financial background to invest $20 billion in complex and sophisticated financial instruments; despite ample warnings from Moorlach during the 1994 electoral campaign; and despite admissions from supervisors themselves that they did not understand Citron's financial dealings—despite all this, the rating agencies backed Citron until the bitter end.

And the government? Citron and others had lobbied hard for the deregulation of laws that govern municipal investors (much like the S&L operators had done in the early 1980s). So the California legislature liberalized statutes for county treasurers so that Citron and his colleagues could invest in more exotic instruments—just like the S&Ls.

And in another parallel with the S&L crisis, Orange County wound up magnifying its losses by liquidating its portfolio in a painful and unnecessary fire sale. By selling off the pool's assets in December 1994, the county managed to lock in a loss of $1.6 billion. But since interest rates fell soon after, much of the loss could have been avoided had the county waited to dispose of its assets in an orderly and market-timed maneuver.

Financial Hydrogen Bombs

Obviously the system failed. But was failure inevitable in an environment dominated by complex, virtually incomprehensible financial instruments called derivatives—those financial hydrogen bombs decried by Felix Rohatyn?

In fact, Orange County itself fared pretty well in the end. The county exited bankruptcy in just eighteen months, thanks to a buoyant local economy that lifted tax revenues and filled the county's coffers. The reputation of financial derivatives, though, was not so easily mended. Media mavens zeroed in on the devastating role of derivatives in the OCIP debacle, concluding that derivatives themselves are inherently dangerous.

Certainly the instruments do lend themselves extraordinarily well to previously unheard-of rates of leverage (recall that Citron had leveraged $7.5 billion of invested capital into $20 billion of investments), and many are almost absurdly complex. Citron had invested heavily, for example, in structured notes—instruments with incredibly complicated embedded formulas that Citron had no hope of understanding (remember his wristwatch calculator). Frank Partnoy describes one such product, the "Quanto," marketed by investment banks in the early 1990s:

> In a Quanto, the investor received payments based on foreign interest rates, with the unique twist that all payments were in the investor's home currency. In other words, a U.S. investor could bet on European interest rates, but receive payments in U.S. dollars. In one typical deal, the Federal Home Loan Bank of Topeka, Kansas, issued $100 million of notes paying a coupon of twice U.S. LIBOR [London Interbank Offered Rate], minus British LIBOR plus 1.5 percent, all payable in U.S. dollars.

Looks simple enough, right? But in reality, Partnoy explains, it was "unimaginably complex," because of the correlations among the Quanto's variables.

> In simple terms, the amount to be converted at maturity into U.S. dollars (the currency variable) depended on the value of, say British LIBOR (the interest rate variable). [But] interest rates and currency rates affected each other, not only in the real world, but also in the Quanto. They could not be separated.

Armed with hardworking Ph.D.s and increasingly muscular computers, the investment banks' Quants figured out, for the most part, how to evaluate these risks. But for Citron, of course, it was impossible. "The techniques were sufficiently complex," Partnoy concludes, "that most clients had no hope of accurately evaluating Quantos."[11] And Citron wasn't "most clients"—he was the sucker in the market. It was a disaster waiting to happen.

Bankers to Trust or Not to Trust

The view that derivatives in and of themselves were unacceptably dangerous was bolstered by other debacles that came to light in the same 1994-95 timeframe. At the center of most—regrettably, from senior managers' point of view—was Bankers Trust.

Bankers Trust was a bank on the move. Under the stewardship of CEO Charlie Sanford, who took the helm in early 1988, BT was transforming itself from a sluggish commercial bank into an aggressive, innovative investment bank. It was banking on its quantitative financial skills and famously competitive culture to become a powerhouse in the trading arena, specifically in the trading of derivatives. To this end, BT had created a space-age risk management system and an army of whiz kids who could develop breathtakingly sophisticated derivative products—whose value and pricing only BT really understood.

The job of BT's salesmen, thus, became a quest to find the sucker in the market—a customer who would be content, nay, eager, to gobble up huge quantities of BT's incomprehensible financial instruments. Gibson Greetings fit the bill nicely. It was a middle-America (Cincinnati, Ohio) company that sold greeting cards, established in 1850 but running a very distant third in its market behind giants Hallmark and American Greetings (which eventually acquired Gibson in 2000).

Gibson was woefully unprepared to play in the derivatives markets with sharks like BT. Nonetheless, treasurer Jim Johnsen aggressively plunged in. Between 1991 and 1994 Gibson entered into an astonishing twenty-nine derivatives transactions with BT, in which Gibson placed huge interest rate bets and BT earned huge profits. BT had found its sucker.

Gibson's transactions with BT were space-age indeed. Partnoy describes one such deal:

> In a so-called Treasury-Linked swap, Gibson agreed, among other things, to receive the lesser of $30.6 million or an amount determined by the following formula: $30 million—(103 x 2-year Treasury Yield/4.88%)—(30-year Treasury Price/100). Another trade, called a knock-out option, became worthless when rates hit a specified level (it "knocked out" at that point). Financial economists would spend the next several years attempting to create pricing models for knock-out options. Still another Gibson trade, called a Wedding Band, was too complex to describe without a mathematician and a psychotherapist.[12]

From Cards to Soap

BT earned $13 million in profits on its swaps with Gibson. But other customers were even more valuable—among them, consumer giant Proctor & Gamble. P&G, unlike Gibson, was hardly a babe in the woods. The vast, prosperous soapmaker had a large and well-educated staff of finance professionals, as well as a sophisticated board of directors and an army of analysts and bankers watching its every move. But P&G too fell prey to BT's blandishments.

Since even the wealthy and sophisticated P&G was unable to evaluate BT's swaps properly, it too quickly became a favorite of BT's salesmen. One enthusiastic salesman, describing a swaps deal with P&G to a friend, exclaimed, "This is a wet dream!" Unfortunately for BT, its sales staff's conversations were being taped, and the inevitable lawsuits turned up a treasure trove of incriminating conversations. Consider this chat between BT salesman Kevin Hudson and his fiancée, Alison Bernhard, about a deal Hudson had just done with P&G:

> Bernhard: Oh, my ever-loving God. Do they understand that…what they did?
>
> Hudson: No. They understand what they did, but they don't understand the leverage, no.
>
> Bernhard: They would never know. They would never be able to know how much money was taken out of that.
>
> Hudson: Never, no way, no way. That's the beauty of Bankers Trust.

Hudson and his compatriots at BT were amply rewarded for their labors. Between 1990 and 1993 BT was the most profitable major bank in the United States, largely thanks to its derivatives engine. Derivatives volume at the bank by the end of 1991 stood at an amazing notional off-balance sheet total of $895 million (actual risk exposure was much less, though); by 1994, derivatives accounted for somewhere between 65 percent and 75 percent of total profits. CEO Charlie Sanford himself earned total compensation in 1990 of more than $5 million, making him, according to *Fortune* magazine, the thirteenth most overcompensated CEO in America (just behind twelfth-ranked Ken Lay at Enron).

But when the Fed started hiking interest rates in February 1994, the party was over. Gibson Greetings, P&G, and others joined Robert Citron in the bloodbath that ensued as their one-way bets on interest rates went very sour, very fast. Magnified by the magic of leverage and largely hidden thanks to accounting sleights of hand, those space-age derivatives resulted in huge losses for BT's unlucky clients.

The lawsuits came fast and furious. In the end, BT settled with P&G for $78 million, and with another three clients (including Gibson Greetings) for $93 million. An SEC investigation resulted in minor slaps on the wrist for BT and its people; most continued to work on Wall Street, and the fines imposed were minimal.

The damage to the reputations of both BT and derivatives, however, was considerable. Media coverage was almost uniformly negative, as reporters and politicians alike weighed in on the dangers of "financial hydrogen bombs" in the hands of BT's techno-crazed salesmen. Famed investor/trader George Soros warned the House Banking Committee in April 1994 about the dangers of derivatives: "There are so many of them," he opined, "and some of them are so esoteric, that the risks involved may not be properly understood by the most sophisticated investors."

According to this line of thinking, losses like those of Orange County and Gibson Greetings were inevitable given the spread of innovative financial instruments and strategies from Wall Street to "much less sophisticated venues."[13]

Headlines were filled with dozens of mini-Orange County disasters. Indeed, "in 1994 the House Banking Committee heard testimony by officials from Odessa College in Texas, Charles County in Maryland, and the Eastern Shoshone Tribe in Wyoming about why they had invested public funds in mortgage derivatives." So both bankers and derivatives became pariahs: One enterprising cartoonist pictured a man in a three-piece suit, holding a briefcase and a cup for begging, next to a sign that said "Dabbled in Derivatives." Another had a caption reading, "Hey, there's always tomorrow. Well, unless you're in derivatives." And one public relations firm sent out a Christmas card in 1994 showing Santa and his reindeer crashing into a building, with the caption, "Don't worry. He's got a derivatives contract from Bankers Trust. Happy Holidays!"[14]

Inevitably, stories of derivatives disasters were followed by calls for legislative and regulatory remedies. Several state legislatures proposed laws that would deem local governments "unsophisticated investors," or would prohibit all investments in derivatives by public investors.

Fortunately, cooler heads would prevail—since most of the proposed remedies would be much worse than the original maladies—and none of this legislation ever saw the light of day. Lobbyists from the International Swaps & Derivatives Association (ISDA) were instrumental in this process, even pressuring journalists to stop using the "d-word" because of its negative connotations ("securities," apparently, was more acceptable). Their efforts paid off; in the end, all of the bills to regulate derivatives activity that were introduced in 1994-95 died a quiet death.

The Decade of Rogue Traders

If the 1990s was the Decade of Derivatives, the use of those derivatives in the hands of some traders also marked it as the Decade of the Rogue Trader. Of course, there were rogue traders (those who operate beyond the bounds of acceptable behavior) before the 1990s, just as there were inside traders before the 1980s. But in the middle of the 1990s rogue traders suddenly became a phenomenon, a regular and increasingly worrisome feature of the markets, rather than shadowy operators on the fringes—just as Milken et al. had elevated insider trading and fraud to the very core of the investment bank itself.

Joseph Jett: The Million Dollar Lemonade Stand

When Joseph Jett arrived at Kidder Peabody in 1991, he badly needed to succeed. Despite his illustrious education, he had already lost two jobs on Wall Street and was keenly aware that this was probably his final shot at greatness. But his first year at Kidder was no more promising than his previous jobs; during his first five months, he made a paltry $417,000 for the firm and took home a humiliating "bonus" check of just $5000—a clear signal that his days were numbered.

His turnaround in 1992, therefore, was just short of astonishing. In the first ten months of that year, Jett's trading profits were a whopping $28 million, yielding a bonus of $2 million. And he kept getting better; in 1993, Jett earned at least $10 million in profits *every month*. His bonus for that year: $9 million (not to mention the glory of being named Kidder's Man of the Year in January 1994). As Jett wrote later in his autobiography, "our incredible profits [in 1993] meant our area was carrying Kidder Peabody."[15]

Jett's star trader status must have been all the more satisfying considering the ignominy of his early career. Indeed, he reveled in it, earning him the reputation of a difficult person who you crossed at your own peril. In a Harvard Business School case study, Jett is described as "…harsh and domineering with subordinates, many of whom were afraid of him… Jett had a well deserved reputation for firing anyone who questioned his trading methods."[16]

So when the sky fell in, Jett may not have had many allies. By early 1994, even his bosses—who had previously been admiring to the point of adoration towards their star earner—were getting dubious about the size of his trades and reported profits. During the first two months of the year, Jett had set another record: $66 billion in profits, an amount so astonishingly large that even his sleepy superiors were finally prodded into taking a closer look at his trades.

What they found was devastating: Jett's "trades," which in many cases were larger than the entire market size, were in fact largely paper, and his "profits" were the result of a computer glitch. They would never be realized in the form of cash.

How could this have happened? The explanation is pretty simple, so don't stop reading! Basically, Jett was trading government instruments that consisted of two parts: principal payment, and periodic interest payments. He would "strip" the instrument into its components and sell them off separately, then "reconstitute" the separate parts into the entire instrument again for repurchase at a future date—or vice versa.

One commentator explained this on *60 Minutes* as akin to trading four quarters for a dollar.

The profits in this activity are generally small but safe; if you trade in large enough volume you should be able to earn a decent profit, but Jett's reported profits were improbable to the point of absurdity. Financial observer Martin Mayer likened it to his daughter's lemonade stand. "If she comes in and says, 'Daddy, I earned ten dollars,' you say that's wonderful, honey," he explained. "If she comes in and says, 'Daddy, I earned a million dollars,' you say, WHAT???"[17]

Jett was running, in effect, a million-dollar lemonade stand, because Kidder's computers used different methods to value the same-day transactions and the future transactions.[18] This was a mistake, as any first-year finance student can tell you. But somehow the valuation methodology slipped in, so the numbers that flashed up on Jett's computer screen after he made a trade showed him that his profits were huge and growing. The more he traded, the more money he made.

The problem, of course, was that the money wasn't real—it was a figment of the computer's imagination. As a result, Kidder's profits and balance sheet were overstated by a staggering $350 million—Jett's false profits.

Who's To Blame?

Did Jett realize this? The question remains open. There is no doubt that he was shocked to his very core when he woke up on that April morning to learn that he was being accused of committing one of the largest securities scams in Wall Street history. To this day he maintains his innocence, arguing that his profits were based on a legitimate trading strategy and that his actions were open and aboveboard.

There's a great deal of truth to the latter argument, at least. As a *New York Times* reporter argued, "Can Jett be guilty of fraud if he hid nothing, falsified no records and was subject to several layers of oversight?"[19] Is it possible that Jett was simply an inexperienced trader, lulled to security by the ever-increasing profit numbers appearing on his computer screen? One Kidder executive observes: "It was like a lab rat in a cage. He pushed the lever, and food came out. The rat doesn't give much thought to why the food came out."[20]

It's also undeniably true that Jett hid nothing. After all, dozens of people at Kidder knew about his trading activities and had full access to his records. At various points during his glory days, superiors and colleagues at Kidder questioned how his "strategy" could yield such astonishing results. His books were audited on a number of occasions; everyone who examined his books came away satisfied.

But on the other hand, Jett's willingness to believe such wildly improbably computer printouts is worrisome even to his defenders. Former SEC official Gary Lynch, who was hired by Kidder to investigate the disaster, argues that it's like "receiving a hundred paychecks each week when you should get one. It's not adequate to say, 'I assumed the company meant to pay me one hundred times.'" Exploiting a dysfunctional system, Lynch concludes, is fraud.[21]

Jett was vilified in the press. He writes,

> I was straight from central casting—a black man on Wall Street, rare in itself, a conservative black man, hardworking, aggressive. Throughout the next few weeks, my story would fill talk shows, tabloid television, nightly newscasts and news magazines for hours each day. The reports shared one feature, from *The Wall Street Journal* to trash TV: The stories were breathtaking in their condemnation and unquestioning in their assumption of my guilt… The *Journal* found it newsworthy to report my interest in "the philosophy of Nietzsche to the symphonies of Mahler to the poetry of Lord Byron." Then it called me a "loner and a loser." Finally, the *Journal* wrote about a computer system at work—not the Kidder accounting program that made my trading possible, but rather reports that former coworkers at First Boston had found a list of women and their sexual habits on a computer of mine.[22]

Legal opinions, though, were less conclusive. The SEC eventually ruled that Jett did not commit any fraud, but had an "intent to defraud" (whatever that means); he was sanctioned for relatively minor "books and records violations," fined $200,000, and ordered to return $8.2 million in bonus money to Kidder. The split decision satisfied neither the SEC prosecutors nor Jett, though he was partially vindicated by NASD arbitrators who found him innocent of fraud and ordered Kidder to return $5 million that they had frozen in his brokerage account. But Jett spent years in legal purgatory, keeping body and soul together as a furniture mover, delivery man, personal trainer, and roofer. (Eventually he returned to Wall Street, where he now runs a hedge fund.)

The case against Jett's supervisors is perhaps slightly less ambiguous. As one observer notes, "At the least, the evidence adds up to an extraordinary chronicle of negligence by Kidder officials who were supposed to supervise Jett but missed one opportunity after another to halt his trading. Instead, they happily allowed his trading and generously rewarded it."[23] Management policy seemed to reflect that of Jack Welch, chief of Kidder's corporate parent General Electric: a hands-off approach combined with a relentless (some would say ruthless) focus on increasing profits. Jett's bosses were wildly anxious to impress Welch, which probably helps explain their disinclination to rein in Jett.

Nonetheless, Jett's management escaped with a slap on the hand. His supervisor, Ed Cerullo, left Kidder with a $10 million severance package, of which he eventually paid $50,000 to the SEC to settle the case against him. The damage to Kidder, though, was irreparable. GE sold Kidder for around $600 million (taking a huge loss; its investment in the firm was at least $1.4 billion). In doing so, it attributed the red ink in part to Joseph Jett—and the name of Kidder Peabody disappeared forever, as did the jobs of 2500 employees, who were left with a puny two weeks pay for every year of employment.

"Possibly the Worst Trader in History"

Toshihide Iguchi was not good at trading, but he was extraordinarily good at covering up his losses. A psychology major (and cheerleader) at Southwest Missouri State University, Iguchi joined Daiwa Bank's New York branch in 1977 and eventually came to run the back office operation of the bank's securities business, where trades are reconciled and recorded. In 1984 he made the great leap from back office to trading—but he retained his back office duties as well.

Iguchi started losing money almost immediately. Between 1984 and 1995, the hapless trader lost an average of almost $500,000 a day in the bond markets. But what he lacked in trading abilities (Frank Partnoy calls him "quite possibly the worst trader in history"[24]), he more than made up for in his cover-up ability. Exploiting his dual role as both trader and back office record keeper, Iguchi successfully hid his losses from the bank until mid-1995.

His methodology was straightforward: When he started losing money on his bond trades, he secretly sold off bonds from another account to cover his losses, which he simply failed to record. So that no one would notice the missing bonds, he maintained a parallel set of books—and neither Daiwa nor its auditors ever bothered to independently confirm his trades. During eleven years, he forged 30,000 trading slips.

Eventually Iguchi couldn't take it anymore. On July 13, 1995 he sent a thirty-page confession to the president of Daiwa in Tokyo, admitting that he had lost $1.1 billion of the bank's money in U.S. Treasury bond markets—one of the largest trading losses in banking history.

Like many a rogue trader before and after him, Iguchi was overwhelmed by the bank's hunger for his trading "profits." He noted that "the New York branch depended on me so heavily for profits"—which he was unable to produce. Daiwa was well-capitalized and able to handle the losses. But like so many before and after them, Iguchi and Daiwa were ultimately done in by the cover-up.

Daiwa's senior managers must have been devastated when they read Iguchi's confession letter. Yet their first impulse was to stonewall and cover up, much like Iguchi himself. At home, the Japanese economy was still struggling to recover from the collapse of the bubble economy in 1989-90, and business prospects in domestic markets were far from robust. A major setback in the bank's New York operation would be a blow at the wrong time, not just to Daiwa but to the Japanese economy as a whole.

So for two fateful months the bankers scurried frantically, trying to plug the losses and figure out how to avoid regulatory censure. Daiwa did not file a report with Japan's Ministry of Finance until August 8, and, in turn, the Japanese authorities failed to inform the U.S. Federal Reserve until September 18.

The Americans were incensed. Daiwa's attempt to cover up and delay reporting the loss was in direct violation of U.S. law, which requires a bank to report such events *immediately* to U.S. regulators. Worse, rumors swirled—fueled by Iguchi—that Daiwa officials had discussed the possibility of hiding the losses, perhaps in a Cayman Islands shell company or possibly in Japan, to escape U.S. scrutiny. In early September, for example, superiors ordered Iguchi to pretend to be on vacation so that a scheduled audit could be postponed, fueling eventual speculation that they were trying to transfer the losses to Japan to avoid having to deal with the much tougher U.S. regulators.

In any event, the die was cast when Iguchi agreed to cooperate with the FBI investigation into the two-month cover-up. That two-month delay eventually sparked criminal charges against both the bank and its officers. Iguchi was convicted and jailed in the U.S.; Daiwa itself pled guilty to conspiring to hide Iguchi's losses, paid $340 million in fines and, most shockingly, was forced to close its U.S. operations altogether by the infuriated American regulators. (Even more shocking, shareholders filed suit in Japan against a group of eleven Daiwa senior executives, who were ordered by a judge in 2000 to pay $750 million in compensation.)

Iguchi, who had requested solitary confinement because he was afraid of what other inmates would do to him when they learned he had cooperated with the FBI, spent fifteen months locked in a seven-by-eight-foot cell for twenty-three hours a day. For once, the punishment for a Wall Street crime seemed to fit—or even exceed—the transgression. Was a two-month cover-up worth the loss of a major bank's U.S. operation? Hell hath no fury, apparently, like that of dissed American bank regulators.

Rogue Trading Half a World Away

In mid-1992, an ambitious young man named Nick Leeson arrived at Barings Bank Singapore. His job was to arbitrage (make risk-free trades) to take advantage of tiny differences between the prices quoted for the same contracts on the Singapore and Japanese stock exchanges. This should have been a low-risk, low-profit operation. Since price differences between the two exchanges should generally be quite small, the trader does a high volume of low-margin deals; it's the Costco of the trading business. Leeson, however, took quite a different approach.

Making unauthorized trades on options and futures through a secret account, Number 88888, Leeson developed huge positions—one-way directional bets, not hedged by any matching or offsetting positions. Unfortunately for Barings, Leeson was no better a trader than Iguchi or Rusnak. His positions were losers almost from the very beginning. Then, like many unlucky gamblers, Leeson took bigger and bigger bets to try and reverse his losses. To bring in cash needed to finance his losing positions, he sold whopping big options contracts giving purchasers the right to cash in should the markets move in their favor (and, by definition, against Leeson).

Because he controlled both the trading operation and the back office, Leeson was able to hide these activities from his "supervisors." Indeed, he was viewed as a star trader back in London, one who single-handedly earned one-half of Barings Singapore's 1993 profits and one-half of the entire firm's 1994 profits. Apparently no one was even mildly curious about these fantastic profits generated from such a low-risk operation.

In the end, Leeson was saddled with liabilities of $1.3 billion, and Barings—banker to the British royal family—was suddenly insolvent. Leeson fled, leaving a handwritten note that said, simply, "I'm sorry." The Bank of England chose not to intervene, and eventually the Dutch bank ING agreed to assume most of Barings' liabilities for the princely sum of one pound. The venerable Barings name, sadly, disappeared from the world of banking.

From Hughes and MacDonald, *Carnival on Wall Street* (New York: John Wiley & Sons, 2004), p. 198.

An FX Trader in Baltimore

John Rusnak swaggered into Allfirst Bank, a sleepy subsidiary of Allied Irish Bank in Baltimore, with New York credentials and a determination to put the bank on the map in the world of currency trading. Rusnak had worked for Chemical Bank in New York (now part of the giant JP Morgan Chase), and was hired in 1993 to jumpstart Allfirst's proprietary (for profit) foreign exchange trading operations.

Until then, Allfirst had—like most small regional banks—limited its FX activity to transactions requested to service the needs of customers doing overseas business. But now, senior managers were looking to make some money by taking positions in the market, just like the big boys in New York. Rusnak seemed just the man to do it; he won the job by promising a low risk but aggressive strategy of trading options and futures to earn money on pricing discrepancies in the markets.

In fact, he never did this. From the beginning, Rusnak focused on low-tech trading, taking simple one-way bets on the euro and yen. Essentially, he bet that the yen would go up, and for a time he was lucky.

But his positions started to go sour (along with the yen) in 1997. Like the gambler that he was, Rusnak chose to hide his losses in the hopes that the next big bet—or the one after that—would pay off in spades. The more the yen dropped, the more determined he was to hang onto his losing position and wait for the inevitable, glorious rise. He was not a good trader—but he was "a star when it come to covering up his losses... If his trading was suicidal, his ability to cover up his losses was miraculous."[25]

Unluckily for Rusnak, the yen's recovery did not come soon enough. By February 2002 he had accumulated a deficit in his trading account of nearly $700 million, but no one knew; to cover up his losses, he had manufactured bogus trades with a series of Asian banks and even created false documents to confirm the trades. As in Iguchi's case, as long as the back office failed to contact the Asian bank counterparties to confirm the bogus trades, Rusnak was safe. To raise cash, he sold options to money-center banks like Citibank, Bank of America, Deutsche Bank, and Merrill Lynch. (The unlikelihood of a two-man trading operation in Baltimore being able to profit from trades with the market giants seems to have gone unnoticed.)

Rusnak's skills at cover up were exhausted by the end of 2001. A back office supervisor noticed missing confirmations on a couple of trades, and around the same time senior managers at Allfirst were becoming disturbed by the size of Rusnak's trading volume. He disappeared for a week to confer with lawyers and the FBI, eventually showing up in government custody.

The end of Rusnak's saga is also similar to Iguchi's. Neither man had profited very impressively from their wrongdoing: Rusnak earned around $850,000 in salary and bonus in 1997-2001, hardly a munificent sum by Wall Street standards. In October of 2002 he pled guilty to bank fraud, and received a reduced sentence in return for helping the government investigate other bank officials who may have been involved in the cover-up (in the end, it turned out that he had acted alone). Allied Irish eventually sold its troubled Allfirst unit for just over $3 billion to an American bank, which promptly laid off 20 percent of the bank's 5,500 employees.

Wherefore Art Thou a Rogue Trader?

Rogue traders have plagued the financial world since long before the 1990s, and they will continue to do so long after. But something in the environment of that decade seemed to foster an explosion in rogue trading both on Wall Street and around the world. Was it something in the air? Or something more profound?

During the 1990s, the path to magnificent wealth seemed smoother and more accessible than ever before. With Internet millionaires springing up by the, well, millions, new faith in the phenomenon abounded. The laws of risk and reward appeared to have been abolished, so that it was possible to earn excessive returns with minimal risk (witness Robert Citron and Joseph Jett).

At the same time, as financial markets soared ever upwards, belief in the "star trader" was magnified by his leaping successes on a Wall Street where both culture and compensation encouraged traders to take excessive risks, and to cover up losses. Joseph Jett's supervisor at Kidder, for example, reportedly believed in "Superman traders" who could best the market, and was actively seeking traders like that to impress his corporate parents.[26] The star trader was universally revered in the financial world, like the quarterback on the winning football team—Tom Wolfe called them "Masters of the Universe" in his bestseller *Bonfire of the Vanities*, and Michael Lewis called them "big swinging dicks" in his equally successful *Liar's Poker*.[27]

Their behavior reflected their status. Jett was famous for his tantrums, and for firing anyone who dared to question him; Rusnak, too, bullied back office workers and was universally considered difficult to work with.

Big egos seemed to accompany big traders at every step. Traders from Robert Citron to John Rusnak came to believe that they were smarter than the market—they could see the future as no one else could. So they clung stubbornly to losing positions no matter how high was the tide of red ink, and shot down any who dared to question the genius at work. (This is almost always a mistake, as finance expert Philippe Jorion says: "Good traders can almost be said to have *no ego* [italics mine]. They recognize their mistakes and cut their losses when necessary."[28])

At the same time, events conspired to make star traders much more difficult to manage than ever before. Increasingly, the MBA trader had given way to the rocket scientist trader, who was working with complex financial instruments that few really understood—especially his superiors. Senior bank officials tend to be men (and a few women) in their fifties and sixties, dinosaurs in the fast-moving financial markets of the 1990s. Few wanted to admit that they couldn't understand what their underlings were doing. Nick Leeson commented, for example, that Barings executives "never dared ask me any basic questions, since they were afraid of looking stupid about not understanding futures and options."[29]

Sophisticated computer programs exacerbated the problem, since few wanted to question them but even fewer really understood them. As the case of Joseph Jett proves, it takes a strong man indeed to question what your computer is telling you, even if it doesn't make any sense.

Ultimately, the collapse of Kidder Peabody suggests that it may be impossible to devise a system of controls that can foil a determined rogue trader. Obvious solutions abound—divorce traders from the back office, improve oversight—but even the most sophisticated financial institutions have fallen victim to the rogue trader. It is even possible that the more sophisticated the bank, the more danger it is in. After all, the scope for fraud may be limited in traditional commercial banking operations, where loans are generally granted after a fairly rigorous set of procedures. In securities trading though, especially when innovative financial instruments are involved, traders are able to take huge, highly leveraged positions in volatile markets where the opportunities for both risk and return are greatly magnified.

"A Hero Among Monkeys"

This reflects, to some extent, the blind faith in financial markets that dominated Wall Street during the 1990s. Market players from traders to CEOs came to believe that their ever-more sophisticated computer models and rocket scientists could conquer the markets as long as government kept its grubby little hands out of the game. Banks developed fancy risk management systems designed to help them reap the munificent rewards of the financial markets without excessive risk-taking.

The problem was, the bankers actually came to believe in these models. As Partnoy observes, "the names were fancy—VAR, RAROC 2020, CreditMetrics—but all these models really did was compare historical measures of risk and return."[30] The very presence of the models, though, gave an illusion of safety that may have prompted even greater risk-taking. It's like the skier who skis twice as fast when he wears a helmet, weaving in and out of the trees with reckless abandon based on a foolish faith in his flimsy headgear.

Long-Term Capital

The story of Long-Term Capital Management does not fit our parameters either, because it is not a scandal. There are no crooks, no rogue traders, no market manipulators, no inside traders. No one went to jail. In fact, the tale starts with a group of Nobel Laureates and financial whiz kids—with math degrees from the finest universities—who formed a hedge fund (an investment pool for well-heeled, sophisticated investors that generally operates beyond the realm of government regulators).

The whiz kids created a financial model that enabled them to take huge, highly leveraged risks in global financial markets. "Its intellectual supermen," writes Roger Lowenstein, "had apparently been able to reduce an uncertain world to rigorous, cold-blooded odds—on form, they were the very best that modern finance had to offer."[31]

Or were they? Unfortunately, the markets in 1997-98 took an unexpected and unprecedented turn, upsetting LTCM's models which were, of course, based on historical trading patterns. Remarkably, LTCM's brilliant models had not taken account of the correlations between markets, especially at times of crisis; when things go bad, all markets go down simultaneously. A lot of things went wrong at once, the markets crashed and burned, and LTCM stood on the verge of collapse. In effect, it was hit by the perfect financial storm; all of its bets went wrong at the same time.

In the end, U.S. banking authorities feared that the collapse of an investment firm with more than $1 *trillion* of outstanding positions would threaten the stability of the entire U.S. banking system, so they brokered an extraordinary rescue by fourteen of the nation's leading commercial and investment banks. But the LTCM story remains a cautionary tale for those who place excessive faith in their computer models and rocket scientists, and in the predictability and reasonableness of financial markets. On Wall Street, it seems, a little skepticism goes a long way.

From *Carnival on Wall Street*, p. 194.

The bankers also came to believe in themselves. In his fascinating book, *Fooled by Randomness*, Nassim Nicholas Taleb warns that aggressive traders are victims of delusion, which leads them into overconfidence and ever more foolish risks. They are essentially "lucky fools," who don't have the slightest suspicion that they belong in this category—they attribute their success to skill, rather than luck, and come to believe in their ability to outperform the markets.

This is a dangerous belief, according to Taleb. Market fools, he believes, tend to:

- overestimate the accuracy of their beliefs;
- get married to their positions (even losing ones); and
- engage in denial when things go bad.

"One can make money in the financial markets totally out of randomness," Taleb warns, especially during the great bull market of the 1990s (one dollar invested in an average stock in 1982 would have shot up twenty times by 1998). To illustrate his point, he says,

If one puts an infinite number of monkeys in front of (strongly built) typewriters, and lets them clap away, there is a certainty that one of them would come out with an exact version of the Iliad. Upon examination, this may be less interesting a concept than it appears at first: Such probability is very low. But let us carry the reasoning one step beyond. Now that we have found that hero among monkeys, would any reader invest his life's savings on a bet that the monkey would write the Odyssey next?[32]

And yet, that is exactly what traders did. They lucked out on the greatest bull market of all time and thought themselves financial geniuses. (One lesson of the Orange County disaster, writes Professor Jorion, "is that Robert Citron's great performance in the years before 1994 was due mostly to luck, not to investment skills."[33]) It was a painful journey back to reality.

The Seeds of Enron

At the time, these bumps in the road seemed to be just that—hiccups that briefly disturbed the surface of a great bull market, but left no lasting impact. Market participants were complacent, even celebrating the apparent ability of the market to transcend these hiccups and move on to ever greater heights. Partnoy observes, "It didn't seem that anything serious was wrong, and their ability to shake off a scandal made markets seem even more under control."[34]

But with the ability of hindsight (unfair, but awfully convenient), it is easy to see the seeds of Enron being sown in these years. Many of the so-called "minor" scandals of the 1990s reflected the same exact aspects of Wall Street that would be so painfully revealed just a few years later:

- blind faith in the power of the markets;
- blind faith in the power of rocket scientist traders, who could gleefully and painlessly spin wheat into gold;
- blind faith in the power of technology to "manage" risk and magnify opportunities;
- disdain and inattention towards government supervisors, many of whom agreed that their most important job was to step aside so the markets could work their magic (especially since this was the message from their political masters in Washington);
- weak internal controls over all-powerful managers and traders (a 1998 survey of CFOs at major firms found that more than two-thirds had been asked to misrepresent corporate results); and
- the triumph of well-nigh incomprehensible financial derivatives, which were designed to evade scrutiny and befuddle even the most determined observer.

So what appeared to be a few bad apples in the 1990s, in hindsight, was in fact the rot at the core of Wall Street itself—a rot that was to be painfully and messily exposed in the early years of the next decade.

Notes

1.   Joseph Jett with Sabra Chartrard, *Black and White on Wall Street: The Untold Story of the Man Wrongly Accused of Bringing Down Kidder Peabody* (New York: William Morrow & Company, 1999), p. 24.
2.   Jane E. Hughes, "A Dangerous Globalization Arrogance," *Providence Journal*, February 13, 2002.
3.   The most sophisticated investors could, more or less, follow the machinations of the Quants. But beyond this core group of highly sophisticated investors, most did not get the fine points of the financial products; they could read the forest, but not see the trees. Therein lay the danger.

4.   Statement attributed to Felix Rohatyn, senior partner at Lazard Freres & Co., as reported by Jonathan R. Laing, "The Next Meltdown," *Barron's*, June 7, 1993.

5.   Frank Partnoy, *Infectious Greed: How Deceit and Risk Corrupted the Financial Markets* (New York: Henry Holt & Company, 2003), p. 116.

6.   Philippe Jorion, "Orange County Case: Using Value at Risk to Control Financial Risk," available at www.gsm.uci.edu.

7.   Philippe Jorion, *Big Bets Gone Bad: Derivatives and Bankruptcy in Orange County* (San Diego: Academic Press, 1995), p. 86.

8.   Ibid., p. 18.

9.   Ibid., p. 7.

10.   Ibid., p. 94.

11.   Partnoy, *Infectious Greed*, p. 73.

12.   Ibid., p. 53.

13.   Ibid., p. 115.

14.   Ibid., p. 137.

15.   Joseph Jett, *Black and White on Wall Street*, p. 5.

16.   Robert L. Simons and Antonio Davila, "Kidder, Peabody & Co.: Creating Elusive Profits," Harvard Business School Case #9-197-038, 1996, p. 10.

17.   *60 Minutes*, "Did He or Didn't He," February 19, 1995; available on CBS Video.

18.   For those who are interested, here are the details. For forward transactions, Kidder's Government Trader System correctly assigned the same value to strips and recons on settlement date. However, at the transaction date the system valued the strips at their discounted cash flow value (market price), while the bonds were valued at their settlement date value. This had the effect of attributing a profit for the recon as of transaction date—a profit equal to the difference between the value of the strips at transaction date and their value on settlement date. This profit would disappear over time, of course, as settlement date approached and the values neared equality, but Jett could deal with this problem by juggling the length of his trades. In effect, it was a present value problem: The system was valuing one instrument at its present value and one at its future value, yielding a false, unrealizable profit when the two values are compared.

19.   Saul Hansell, "Joseph Jett: A Scoundrel or a Scapegoat?" *New York Times*, April 6, 1997, section 3, p. 1.

20.   Ibid.

21.   Ibid.

22.   Jett, *Black and White on Wall Street*, p. 254.

23.   Hansell, "Joseph Jett."

24.   Partnoy, *Infectious Greed*, p. 245.

25.   William Leith, "How to Lose a Billion," *Guardian*, October 26, 2002, http://www.guardian.co.uk/print/0,3858,4531019-103425,00.html.

26.   Hansell, "Joseph Jett."

27.   Leith, "How to Lose a Billion."

28.   Jorion, *Big Bets Gone Bad*, p. 96.

29.   Leith, "How to Lose a Billion."

30.   Partnoy, *Infectious Greed*, p. 264.

31.   Roger Lowenstein, *When Genius Failed: The Rise and Fall of Long-Term Capital Management* (New York: Random House, 2000), p. xix.

32.   Nassim Nicholas Taleb, *Fooled by Randomness: The Hidden Role of Chance in Life and in the Markets* (New York: Texere, 2004), p. 125.

33.   Jorion, *Big Bets Gone Bad*, p. 89.

34.   Partnoy, *Infectious Greed*, p. 2.

10

Enron Etc. Vol. I:
Crooks, Liars, and Envelope-Pushers

"People think that I'm a greedy guy; that I was overcompensated. Greed, I think is the key word. I firmly believed that I never did or intended to do anything wrong... I cannot believe they say words like larceny."—Dennis Kozlowski, quoted in Andrew Ross Sorkin, New York Times, *January 16, 2005*

In June 2001, Tyco chief Dennis Kozlowski wanted to throw an unforgettable party for his wife Karen's fortieth birthday. So he invited seventy-five of his dearest and closest friends to celebrate with the happy couple on the Mediterranean island of Sardinia, where they would be entertained by singer Jimmy Buffett, as well as a vodka-spouting statue of David and a cake with exploding, uh, mammary glands. Half of the $2 million cost of Karen's party ($26,000 per guest) was billed directly to Tyco.

This email, sent two months before the great event by a Tyco employee to the party planners, says it all:

> Guests arrive at the club starting at 7:15pm. The van pulls up to the main entrance. Two gladiators are standing next to the door, one opens the door, the other helps the guests. We have a lion or horse with a chariot for the shock value... The guests come into the pool area, the band is playing, they are dressed in elegant chic. Big ice sculpture of David, lots of shellfish and caviar at his feet. A waiter is pouring stoli vodka into his back so it comes out his penis into a crystal glass. Waiters are passing cocktails in chalices. They are dressed in linen togas with fig wreath on head...
>
> Everyone is jumping from table to table... We start the show of pictures on the screen, great background music in sync with the slides. At the end Elvis is on the screen wishing K a Happy Birthday and apologizing that he could not make it. It starts to fade and Elvis is on stage and starts singing happy birthday with the Swing-dogs. A huge cake is brought out with the waiters in togas singing and holding the cake up for all to see. The tits explode, Elvis kicks it in full throttle...[1]

In the end, the Sardinia bash was unforgettable all right—as a symbol of the era of excess that the birthday girl's husband came to exemplify, much like Michael Milken's Predators' Balls and the gilded "cottages" of the robber barons in Newport, Rhode Island came to symbolize those eras. Indeed, the implosion of U.S. capital markets as the twentieth century gave way to the twenty-first contains a set of themes and characters that are all too familiar to readers of this history.

Just as in previous scandal-ridden eras, the crooks, liars, and envelope-pushers of the late 1990s operated along a spectrum of sleaze. At one end were the downright, down-and-dirty crooks, who gleefully plundered their own companies and ran roughshod over the hapless shareholders they were supposed to be serving. At the other end were the envelope-pushers, who were arguably *serving* the needs of those very same shareholders by dressing up financial statements to impress creditors and investors, in the time-honored tradition of U.S. corporate accounting.

When does an envelope-pusher become a crook? That, of course, is the unanswerable question at the heart of the accounting scandals that rocked the U.S. business world in 2000-2002.

Scattered throughout this world is the usual cast of characters in what one commentator has called the "Kabuki play" of scandal:

- The crooks,
- The liars,
- The envelope-pushers,
- The enablers, and
- The scapegoats.

Where everyone fits into this cast of characters will be the subject of this chapter.

In Defense of GAAP

It is the U.S. accounting system that makes this spectrum of sleaze possible. To understand how this works, let's suppose that Joe Schmo, a college senior, is preparing his resume for the first time. His work experience to date consists of dogsitting, counter work at a neighborhood pizzeria, and mowing lawns. How does he present this on his resume?

Option One:

Work Experience

Summer 2004	Fed and walked dogs while owners were on vacation
Summer 2003	Counter boy at Dino's Pizza
Summer 2002	Mowed lawns

Or, consider Option Two:

Work Experience

Summer 2004	Launched small business to care for property of vacationing homeowners
Summer 2003	Managed operations and customer service for bustling food service establishment
Summer 2002	Operated small landscaping enterprise

Which option is more likely to get Joe a job? Option Two, obviously. But is Option Two fraudulent? Or fiendishly clever? Which should Joe choose?

This, in a nutshell, is the puzzlement of U.S. accounting standards. When the CFO at a public corporation in the U.S. sits down to prepare his financial statements at the end of the year, he bases them on a set of principles called GAAP (Generally Accepted Accounting Principles). But GAAP, in turn, is approximately as rigid as a ball of Silly Putty. It is based on a set of "thou shalt not" rules, letting the CFO know what is absolutely not permissible but leaving him a broad range of judgment within the huge universe of what is permissible.

For example, consider a landscaping business with a fleet of trucks. Every year the trucks are serviced at a neighborhood gas station, which does a thorough tune-up and replaces aging parts. How does the business record this expenditure in its financial statements?

GAAP tells us that ordinary and routine maintenance expenses should be expensed as incurred—that is, they appear on the income statement as an expense that is subtracted from revenue for that year. But GAAP also says that expenditures that increase the useful life or enhance the productivity of the asset should be capitalized—that is, they should be added to the value of the asset itself on the balance sheet, rather than appearing on the income statement.

So what do we do with the trucks? Well, it seems pretty clear that oil changes and tune-ups are ordinary maintenance costs, and should appear on the income statement as expenses. So far, so good. But what if we replaced the transmission on one truck, and replaced the tires on two more? What if we install air-conditioning? And what if we paint the trucks? Does it matter if we paint an advertising slogan on them or just repaint them a dull white?

All of these questions fall into the gray area of GAAP. Complicating the matter further, most rational business owners would prefer the second option—capitalizing the expenditure—because that way they avoid adding an expense to the income statement for the year and thus show a higher revenue to their shareholders.

In fact, GAAP allows business managers to make hundreds, perhaps thousands, of such judgments every time they sit down to prepare a financial statement. Accounting in the United States is an art, not a science; give ten highly qualified accountants the same set of data, and they will prepare ten different—but all legal—sets of financial statements.

Why? The funny thing is, most accounting experts would agree that, for the most part, the flexibility of GAAP is one of the great strengths of the U.S. business system. Set against the more rigid accounting systems favored in Western Europe and Japan, GAAP has enabled U.S. business to be more entrepreneurial, daring, and innovative; it has enabled U.S. capital markets to become the largest and most dynamic in the world. GAAP has proven malleable enough to survive the shift from a manufacturing-based economy to a service-based economy, and has even been able to handle the oddities of Internet winners like eBay and Google.

So while GAAP has lent itself to ever more aggressive envelope-pushing, it is not at all clear that this is a bad thing. Indeed, it is in the shareholders' best interests for management to put the best possible light on a company's financial results for the year. Strong financial statements enable the firm to attract more buyers for its stock, thus pushing up the stock price and enriching existing stockholders, and they encourage lenders to advance more capital to the firm. As a result, the company has ample funds to grow and prosper.

The problem, of course, is that the envelope can be pushed too far. When does window-dressing cross the line into fraud? Experts disagree mightily, since every incident of accounting wrongdoing carries its own individual set of judgments and gray matter. But this problem—which is a central element in an accounting system as flexible as GAAP—is at the core of the scandals that came to rock the corporate world around the time of the new millennium.

Crooks and Rogues

Piggy Bank Companies

If there is a spectrum of sleaze within which U.S. managers may operate, the top (or bottom) of the spectrum is occupied by those who fed at the corporate trough, turning their companies into virtual piggy banks for the personal use of senior managers and their kin. To some extent, of course, everyone fed from the corporate trough (see Sardinia party, above). Like everything else in this saga, it is really a continuum of greed along which everyone may be positioned.

Certainly it was business as usual to extract quite amazing perks from the corporate coffers. Enron's top managers—especially chief Ken Lay—used its fleet of corporate jets as a personal limo service, transporting family members (and, on one notable occasion, daughter Robin Lay's bed) around the world, from the playgrounds of southern France to car races in Canada and vacations in Mexican resorts. Author Robert Bryce remarks,

> No other part of Enron's business reflected the company's out-of-control egos and out-of-control spending more than the aviation department. While other parts of the company were burning through cash at record rates, Enron executives were cruising five miles high in ultra-luxe style...
>
> "The biggest abuser of the planes was Ken Lay and his family," said one long-time Enron pilot, who lost over $2 million in retirement and deferred compensation after the company's bankruptcy. Whether the destination was the Lays' chalet in Aspen or a quick trip to Cabo San Lucas, Ken and Linda Lay always flew in the newest Falcon 900 in the Enron fleet. It didn't matter whether a smaller, cheaper plane was available. Nor did it matter whether the Lays were using the plane for personal use. Aviation department officials understood that a Falcon 900 should be available for the Lays at a moment's notice. Sometimes, the Lays needed two jets: a His and a Hers.[2]

Outrageous corporate perks like this certainly don't pass the sniff test, but neither are they, for the most part, illegal. However, the widespread and ever-more-lavish use of such perks during the late 1990s illustrated a worrisome phenomenon: the growing power of corporate managers. None of the players who should have been keeping an eye on management—the auditors, outside directors, or outside shareholders—could, in fact, exert any power over senior managers.

Tyco and Adelphia

This lack of control over management enabled all types of shenanigans, from the irritating but relatively harmless use of corporate perks described above, to much more disastrous incidents of theft and looting. At the top of the list, though, are Tyco and Adelphia.

Tyco was a classic conglomerate, making everything from fire alarms to health care products. When Dennis Kozlowski took over as CEO in 1992, he had already been with the company for more than two decades, and he was expected to provide a steady, experienced hand on the helm. In 1999, though, he first ran into trouble. An analyst charged that Tyco had hyped its financial results, and the SEC launched an investigation.

By year-end, the controversy had halved the company's stock price, and Kozlowski's future looked gloomy.

The next year, though, he came roaring back. In mid-2000 the SEC ended its probe, giving the company a clean bill of health, and Kozlowski went on a buying spree. He snapped up forty companies in 2000 alone for around $9 billion. The markets practically canonized him, as profits soared and Tyco's market capitalization topped $90 billion, more than General Motors, Ford, and Sears combined. *Business Week*, naming him one of the "top 25 managers to watch" in January 2001, wrote, "This Midas touch in deal after deal has transformed Tyco from an obscure manufacturer into a powerhouse worth fifty times more than when Kozlowski took charge eight years ago. It's an achievement that has led some to compare Kozlowski with General Electric Company's Jack Welch."[3]

An unfortunate comparison for Jack Welch, as it turned out. Barely eighteen months after that fawning article appeared, Dennis Kozlowski, along with CFO Mark Swartz and one other Tyco executive, were indicted on charges that they looted their own company of more than $600 million. Amazingly, Kozlowski actually got caught for a penny-ante scheme: conspiring to evade sales taxes on paintings that he purchased with Tyco's money for his Manhattan apartment.

The Sardinia party, it turned out, was just the tip of the iceberg. Kozlowski and his confederates had been skimming company profits to buy swanky apartments and vacation homes, and then to fill them with expensive trinkets—like equipping Kozlowski's $18 million Fifth Avenue duplex with its infamous $6,000 shower curtain, $2,900 coat hangers, and $15,000 umbrella stand. Among other things, Kozlowski billed Tyco for:

    $72,042 for jewelry
    $155,067 for clothing
    $96,943 for flowers
    $60,427 for club memberships
    $52,334 for wine
    $110,000 for corporate use of his personal yacht
    $7,000,000 to buy his first wife a Park Avenue pad

At the same time, Kozlowski's acquisition spree was looking less brilliant. His mid-2001 purchase of financial services firm CIT for $10 billion was a disaster; barely a year later he was shopping it around to resell at a huge loss. So in the end investors lost many billions more in value than Kozlowski had looted.

But Dennis Kozlowski's credentials as poster boy for corporate theft were easily rivaled by those of John Rigas, CEO and chairman of Adelphia.

One of the pioneers of the cable business, Rigas was worth billions by the dawn of the twenty-first century. He owned the Buffalo Sabres hockey team and was well known for his local philanthropies: He sent busloads of kids to Sabres games, and used Adelphia's corporate jet to fly sick people to faith healers and cancer treatment centers. Rigas was famous in the cable industry for taking huge risks, and leveraging Adelphia to the hilt. In the early days, he was often just one step ahead of the creditors. He told his secretary, "I'm either going to become a millionaire, or I'm going to go bankrupt."

He became a millionaire. The company expanded rapidly through the 1980s and 1990s to become the nation's sixth largest cable TV provider, with $3.6 billion in annual revenues. The problem was, management never matured along with the company. Even as Adelphia grew and modernized, Rigas and his family continued to operate it like a "mom and pop business," in which "decisions were made at the dinner table rather than [in] a boardroom," according to one executive.

The results were predictable. In March 2002 Adelphia disclosed that it had made $2.3 *billion* in off-balance sheet loans to the Rigas family, which were unlikely to ever be repaid. Rigas resigned, along with his three sons, who all held executive positions and board seats (Tim Rigas, who was responsible for the financial side of the business, reportedly ran it "like a Saudi prince.") Eventually it turned out that Adelphia had inflated revenue and capitalized routine expenses (remember the truck example), and the once-proud company filed for bankruptcy in June. But most of all, the Rigases had looted shareholders' money.

Adelphia, it emerged, had paid for the Rigas family's $150 million purchase of the Buffalo Sabres, and had paid $12.8 million in 2001 for office furniture and design services provided by—wait for it—Doris Rigas.[4] All in all, Rigas used more than $310 million of Adelphia shareholders' money for personal purposes, treating the company like his "personal piggy bank" according to the indictment.

The Tyco and Adelphia stories, while reprehensible, are pretty straightforward. Both companies are probably strong enough to survive the blows—they have profitable products and loyal customers—once their crooked management is out of the picture. Neither Kozlowski nor Rigas are rocket scientists, and their nefarious activities were pretty simple; it doesn't take much brain power or financial finagling to loot a company.

They are routine examples of old-fashioned fraud, rooted in poor supervision and ethically challenged managers; the results are predictable.

Enron, on the other hand…

Enron: A Rogue Company

There is nothing simple about Enron. Just understanding what they did and how they made their living is absurdly difficult; forget about untangling their financial statements. The only thing that's simple about Enron is the end: It self-destructed. Reporters Bethany McLean and Peter Elkind, who were instrumental in the unraveling of this once-great company, wrote:

> Enron, which once aspired to be known as "the world's greatest company," became a different kind of symbol—shorthand for all that was wrong with corporate America. Its bankruptcy marked not merely the death of a company but the end of an era. Enron's failure resonated powerfully because the entire company stood revealed as a sort of wonderland, where little was as it seemed. Rarely has there ever been such a chasm between corporate illusion and reality. The public scrutiny Enron triggered exposed more epic business scandals—tales of cooked books and excess at companies like Tyco, WorldCom, and Adelphia. Enron's wash swamped the entire U.S. energy industry, wiping out hundreds of billions in stock value. It destroyed the nation's most venerable accounting firm, Arthur Andersen. And it exposed holes in our patchwork system of business oversight—shocking lapses by government regulators, auditors, banks, lawyers, Wall Street analysts, and credit agencies—shaking faith in U.S. financial markets.[5]

And yet, a lot of brainpower went into both making and breaking Enron. The saga really begins in the early 1990s, when one of Enron's new hires, the brash and ambitious Jeff Skilling, realized something about natural gas—it was a commodity, just like pork bellies and oil, and could be traded in the same manner. So he created a market, pretty much single-handedly, much as Michael Milken had done with junk bonds a decade earlier. A natural gas contract, he used to say, "was a little like a cow… A cow doesn't just have one kind of meat; it has all sorts of different meats, from sirloin to hamburger. And people are willing to pay different prices for the part that they want. In the same way you could divide a gas contract into many different parts and sell them to people with different needs."[6]

Skilling's idea of trading natural gas contracts was a huge triumph, both for Enron and for the industry. Not surprisingly, Enron easily dominated the market that it had created—much like Milken in his junk bond market—and soon graduated to much more complicated trades in derivatives stemming from natural gas contracts. (Skilling worked with Bankers Trust—remember them?—to learn how to price and manage the risks associated with these derivatives.) Skilling had spotted a market opportunity, and he had the vision to turn it into a reality.

The world would be a better place if Skilling, who became president and chief operating officer in 1996, had continued to use his skills for good. But as Enron grew and (presumably) prospered through the 1990s, something went wrong. For one thing, Skilling and other senior managers were under enormous pressure to deliver profits. Enron aimed at becoming the world's biggest company; it was promising investors 15 percent growth in earnings *every year*, an ambitious target for any company but especially challenging for Enron.

You see, by the mid-1990s Enron's profits stemmed largely from its trading activities. Even though the company dated back to the early days of the gas pipeline business and still had substantial hard assets, under Skilling's control it had morphed into an enormous trading operation. Essentially, the company revolved around its trading room. Skilling saw Enron's future as its brainpower, not its physical assets.

Why is this a problem? Because trading, by its very nature, is risky and capricious. Wall Street expected Enron to deliver earnings growth of 15 percent or more year after year—but trading operations don't work that way. Reporters McLean and Elkind explain, "Enron's dirty little secret: [It was] a company built around trading and dealmaking, [which] cannot possibly count on steadily increasing earnings." Enron was in the business of speculation, which does not naturally generate steady EPS growth.[7]

So it had to improvise. At first, the company employed the usual window dressing tactics at the end of each quarter—delaying losses, accelerating revenues, playing with the numbers on some assets. These tactics may be morally gray, but under the rules of GAAP they are generally legal and widely accepted by U.S. financial players. A few journalists questioned whether Enron was managing its earnings through aggressive accounting (one omniscient Morgan Stanley analyst wrote in early 1997: "[O]ne of the biggest concerns consistently voiced about Enron is the complexity of its operations and how those interrelationships affect the quality of its earnings"), but most were lulled by the company's swashbuckling finance team and glorious earnings reports.

But gradually even the usual tactics were not enough. In the latter part of the 1990s Skilling decided to replicate his natural gas trading with other commodities, to push Enron into the trading of electric power and broadband. But Enron had a natural advantage in the gas market—it was a major gas producer itself—that it lacked in these other markets. So as real profits turned south, managers were under increasing pressure to manufacture profits.

Andrew Fastow, who became CFO in early 1998, did just that. It was his job to help Lay and Skilling present what they wanted the world to see, not Enron's reality. Fastow created a series of off-balance sheet special purpose companies and mind-numbingly complex financing structures, partnerships, and deals to conceal Enron's real financial position and present a rosy, entirely false picture instead. One former employee explained the process as follows:

> "Say you have a dog, but you need to create a duck on the financial statements. Fortunately, there are specific accounting rules for what constitutes a duck: yellow feet, white covering, orange beak. So you take the dog and paint its feet yellow and its fur white and you paste an orange plastic beak on its nose, and then you say to your accountants, 'This is a duck! Don't you agree that it's a duck?' And the accountants say, "Yes, according to the rules, this is a duck.' Everybody knows that it's a dog, not a duck, but that doesn't matter, because you've met the rules for calling it a duck."[8]

While Fastow was spinning dogs into ducks, he was also spinning wheat into gold—for himself, that is. By mid-2001 Andrew Fastow was worth $60 million, the bulk of which had come not from his work as CFO of Enron but from his private partnerships' dealings with Enron. And Fastow wasn't alone. Between 1998 and 2001, twenty-four Enron executives and board members sold company stock worth more than $1 billion—while investors ultimately lost around $70 billion in value.

But Enron itself was sinking fast under the weight of its new electricity and broadband ventures. Fastow spun desperately in the waning years of the decade, driving his staff of over 100 finance specialists to create literally hundreds of special-purpose entities (with names like Chewco and LJM1) to hide company debt. As a result, an investigative committee later concluded, "the transactions between Enron and the LJM partnerships resulted in Enron increasing its reported financial results by more than a billion dollars, and enriching Fastow and his co-investors by tens of millions of dollars at Enron's expense." But even this wasn't enough, as the house of cards tottered and eventually collapsed, thanks in part to one unhappy employee.

Sherron Watkins (who became *Time* magazine's person of the year in 2002) was an unlikely hero. The second cousin of singer Lyle Lovett, she had worked the cash register at her family's grocery store before getting her accounting degree and going to work for, of all firms, Arthur Andersen, then ultimately moving over to Enron. By mid-2001, though, her job had turned to ashes. Desperately worried about the company's numbers, she wrote to chairman Ken Lay, "I am incredibly nervous that we will implode in a wave of accounting scandals," and she quoted another employee as saying, "I know it would be devastating to all of us, but I wish we'd get caught. We're such a crooked company."

We will probably never know Lay's thoughts upon reading Watkins' missive. He engaged a team of lawyers to review her charges—but he hired Vinson & Elkins, the same law firm that had done the legal work on the very transactions that so worried Watkins. (Enron was the law firm's largest client, generating annual billings of $35 million.) Not surprisingly, the lawyers reported back that the deals were fine.

But other problems were brewing, as the bull stock market ended in spring 2000 and Enron's stock price headed south. By early 2001 the investment community was turning against the company, noting its lack of cash flow, high debt, and overpriced stock. Most important, analysts belatedly realized that they couldn't figure out just how Enron made its money. When Jeff Skilling called one questioner an "asshole" in a widely publicized conference call in March 2001, the stock slide accelerated.

From that point on, the company's days were probably numbered. Skilling resigned abruptly in August, barely six months after he received the long-coveted CEO title, but Lay soldiered on, reassuring employees and investors alike. (On September 26, 2001, he told employees that "our financial liquidity has never been stronger.") But even as Lay and other senior executives quietly dumped their stock, employees were told that they couldn't move their own assets in Enron stock into other securities in the company's 401(K) plan because the plan was switching administrators.

On October 16, Enron announced a $618 million loss in the third quarter, and the stock price plummeted. But even as the house of cards was collapsing, the players were still scheming. In the days just before its historic bankruptcy filing on December 2, 2001, Enron quietly paid $55.7 million to 500 lucky employees who agreed to stay on for ninety days. Remarkably, the team of six Enron people who went to New York to handle the bankruptcy filing flew aboard the $45 million corporate jet and stayed at the Four Seasons, proving that it is possible to continue feeding at the corporate trough even after it's empty.

And the rest of the employees? Well, by the time the 401(K) asset freeze ended on November 19, Enron's stock price had plunged from $32/share to $9. Thousands had lost everything—not only their jobs, but their retirement savings as well. And people with the Crooked E on their resumes were not readily employable. And Enron helped play its part in sinking the accounting firm of Arthur Andersen (employees of which gave their blessings to the energy company's elaborate off-balance sheet activities) and it certainly tarnished the reputations of many Wall Street research analysts.[9]

The Lays, too, pleaded financial distress. In what has to be one of the worst public relations ideas of all time, Linda Lay—who still owns about $9 million worth of real estate in Houston alone—appeared on the *Today* show in a bid for sympathy. McLean and Elkind describe her appearance:

> The Lay family had "gone down with the ship," had "lost everything," and was "battling for liquidity," she said tearfully. Her appearance was widely ridiculed, for good reason. The Lays still owned millions in real estate, much of it not even on the market. Ken and Linda also continued to live in their exclusive condominium, and Lay still enjoyed his private office on the top floor of a building in River Oaks, where he was attended to by a small personal staff. He still owes $7 million on his Enron line of credit.[10]

Needless to say, the ensuing lawsuits will keep a small army of lawyers employed over the next decade or so. CFO Andy Fastow pled guilty to two conspiracy charges and agreed to cooperate with prosecutors; a number of mid-level executives have also agreed to cooperate. Nonetheless, the prosecution's job will not be easy. The courts decided to stage a "mega-trial" (starting in early 2006) in which Ken Lay, Jeff Skilling, and chief accountant Richard Causey would stand trial together on dozens of counts of fraud and insider trading. Causey's last-minute decision to cooperate with prosecutors helped their case. Lay and Skilling were found guilty, but the former CEO avoided jail as he died of heart complications in July 2006.

Liars and Envelope-Pushers

Moving along the spectrum from the crooks and rogues, next in line are the liars, fibbers, and envelope-pushers. As Enron's implosion cast a spotlight on accounting practices, particularly in the tottering telecoms industry, many, many more irregularities came to light. Were they the result of outright liars, or well-intentioned envelope-pushers? You can be the judge.

WorldCom

When WorldCom eclipsed Enron to become the country's largest bankruptcy in July 2002, probably no one was more surprised than Bernie Ebbers. A former milkman, bartender, car salesman, motel manager, and high school basketball coach from Alberta, Canada, Ebbers took over a struggling telecommunications company in 1985 and turned it into a $180 billion behemoth by the end of the 1990s.

Ebbers was an interesting character. A devout Christian, he started every board and shareholders meeting with a prayer. Clad in his trademark alligator boots, he swaggered into the industry and managed to increase WorldCom's value *seven thousand times* during the 1990s. With Ebbers' crowning triumph, the much-ballyhooed takeover of MCI in late 1997, WorldCom moved into second place in the long-distance business. And by the end of the decade, the company had 20 million customers and 60,000 employees worldwide.

But all was not as it seemed. Ebbers' aggressive acquisitions spree had not turned out well; some of the companies he snapped up were a poor fit, and bad management resulted in a growing reputation for lousy customer service. Then Ebbers overreached. In October 1999 WorldCom announced that it would be buying Sprint for a whopping $129 billion, and from then on the end was probably inevitable.

Unfortunately for Ebbers, his timing couldn't have been worse. Right around the same time that he announced his gargantuan purchase, Internet growth began to slow and the telecoms industry went into meltdown. Over the course of one year, the cost of a long distance telephone call in North America plunged from fifteen cents to two cents a minute—good news for consumers, but devastating for huge long distance providers like WorldCom.

And then the second shoe dropped: Regulators blocked the deal with Sprint, and WorldCom's stock went into free-fall. So WorldCom, much as Enron had done, turned to accounting sleights of hand to keep anxious shareholders satisfied. But unlike Enron, WorldCom used tricks that any Accounting 101 student could pick up. Essentially, WorldCom's CFO, Scott Sullivan, used an amazingly simple (but time-honored) formula: He converted routine expenses, like the truck tune-up described at the beginning of this chapter, into capital investments. This had the effect of reducing expenses for the current period and thus inflating revenue—to the tune of up to $9 billion.

But even more unfortunately for Ebbers, the Enron implosion had the effect of immediately turning the spotlight on accounting trickery—and the WorldCom schemes quickly unraveled. (The free online encyclopedia *Wikipedia* lists one entry for 2000 under "accounting scandals"—Xerox—and one for 2001, Enron. But for 2002 it shows twenty-eight entries, listed alphabetically from AOL to WorldCom.) In April 2002 the board fired Ebbers, but it was many months too late; the June disclosure of huge accounting misdeeds was followed by bankruptcy in July, at which point the company was worth just $280 million. Up to one-quarter of its workforce was being laid off, and the stock was trading at just nine cents a share, down from a peak of $65 per share.

While WorldCom is often likened to Enron (*Time* magazine lumped Enron whistleblower Sherron Watkins with WorldCom whistleblower Cynthia Cooper for its person of the year in 2002), in fact the cases are quite different. For one thing, on a dollar-for-dollar basis the WorldCom debacle was much larger than that at Enron. At the time of its filing, WorldCom's total assets were close to $104 billion (and debt was $41 billion), compared to Enron's $63.4 billion in total assets. Needless to say, WorldCom's demise cost investors billions of dollars. Also, as noted above, the WorldCom fraud was astonishingly primitive, very unlike the astonishingly complex financial shenanigans that Enron pioneered. Perhaps most important, WorldCom (like Tyco and Adelphia) provided vital services, as author Lynne Jeter explains:

> What would become of the WorldCom Group, which provided network services for the U.S. government's critical applications? These included communications services for customer support to 80 million Social Security beneficiaries, air traffic control applications for the Federal Aviation Administration, network management for the Department of Defense, and critical data network services for the United States Postal Service. WorldCom Group also provided long-distance voice and data communications services for the U.S. House of Representatives, Senate, General Accounting Office, and other government agencies.[11]

This stands in stark contrast to Enron, which by the mid-1990s earned its money by trading complex financial instruments, while heaping scorn on the old-fashioned notion of selling goods and services to actually create value. As a result, WorldCom's operations will probably continue in some form, while Enron's will not.

But what the two do share is a lingering and frustrating ambiguity about the foundations of the fraud itself. Fraud it was—there's no lingering doubt about that. But did Scott Sullivan or Jeff Skilling or Andy Fastow know it was fraud? What did chiefs Ken Lay and Bernie Ebbers know, and when did they know it? Were they envelope pushers who, perhaps unknowingly, crossed that invisible line, or did they set out, deliberately and maliciously, to commit a fraud?

We will never know. But it's impossible to escape the suspicion that these very able and talented financial minds did not—and do not—believe that they did anything wrong. Or at least, nothing wronger than what senior managers all over the United States do every day, every accounting period, without fail. After all, the 1990s were a time when corporate values exalted those who managed to hit earnings targets, no matter how they did it. Enron and WorldCom went over the line, but were they really behaving much differently from the rest of the gang? Isn't it the American way to take full advantage of flexible accounting rules to reflect the highest income possible? Hadn't that become more important than giving a full and fair representation of the company's underlying financial position?

The Rest: Global Crossing, Qwest, Lucent, and Xerox

Nothing illustrates this ambiguity better than the other, subsidiary cases of accounting trickery that came to light in the wake of the Enron and WorldCom debacles.

The first, Global Crossing, was a late bloomer, having been formed in 1999 by a merger between a Bermuda-based fiber optics specialist and a U.S. telecom firm. Founder Gary Winnick was a former junk bond salesman and close associate of Michael Milken (remember him?). At first, the company was considered a promising newcomer to the field, and its stock market valuation soared as high as $75 billion in its heady first year. But Global Crossing (GC) was saddled with huge debts, and was hard-hit by the telecoms meltdown of 1999-2001.

The company went under quickly. By January 2002 it was bankrupt, in what was then the country's fourth biggest corporate failure; its stock was down to just 51 cents per share. Following the familiar pattern, a whistleblower emerged to charge that management had used accounting techniques to inflate profits and deceive shareholders. Basically, GC had swapped capacity on its network with other carriers in transactions that produced no real value (or cash), but were nonetheless booked as revenues.

No criminal charges were filed, though creditors and shareholders may file lawsuits in an effort to chip away at Winnick's massive personal assets. (Top managers sold hundreds of millions of dollars worth of stock well before the bankruptcy.) Incompetent or crooked? Eventually, perhaps some juries will decide.

One of the firms with which Global Crossing had swapped fiber optic capacity was Qwest. Qwest employees called these deals the company's "heroin" according to the eventual SEC complaint, which held that managers had fraudulently falsified their books to the tune of over $4 billion, largely as a result of these swaps.

Like Global Crossing, Qwest turned to swaps when its core business turned sour. In 1999 the company's sales fell short of projections, increasing pressure on managers to generate "revenues" somehow, and the notion of swapping capacity was born. (Arthur Andersen, which audited both companies, had no objection.) In the end, the stock tumbled from $60 per share to under $1 per share by mid-2002, costing investors billions—but Qwest's executives and board members had netted a cumulative profit of $640 million by cannily selling off their company stock in 1997-2001. Qwest eventually settled the SEC charges for $250 million in late 2002 without admitting any wrongdoing.

And then there's Lucent. The giant maker of telecom equipment was reeling from the industry collapse by 2000, having lost $12 billion in the past year alone and laid off almost 40 percent of its workforce. Predictably, in early 2001 the SEC launched an investigation into allegations of—guess what—improper accounting. For many investors this was a major shock as Lucent had been one of the highfliers of the New Economy.[12] This time the charge was that managers had improperly booked revenues of $679 million in the 2000 fiscal year.

Lucent's outcome, though, did not follow the now-familiar path. In fact, it turned out, Lucent itself had uncovered the problem after an internal investigation and restated the income, then reported the matter to the SEC. And in the end, the probe was settled with no fines or financial restatements required, just a promise by Lucent to avoid any future violation of securities laws. Lucent, it seemed, was more of a victim of the times than a perpetrator.

But then things took a curious twist. Barely a year after the settlement, regulators turned around and fined Lucent $25 million for *lack of cooperation.* They accused managers of failing to provide proper documents, withholding evidence, and failing to disclose key issues. So did Lucent commit accounting fraud after all? Was it just easier to prove lack of cooperation than outright fraud? Or is it worse to annoy the SEC than to commit accounting fraud?

Just as ambiguous was the case of Xerox. In June 2002 the venerable company announced that it would restate earnings for 1997-2001 due to accounting irregularities over that period, which would slash pretax income by $1.4 billion. The SEC, finding that senior management had "orchestrated" a four-year scheme to disguise operating results, levied a fine of $10 million, which the company agreed to while admitting no wrongdoing.

But Xerox's former auditors, KPMG, stand by their work. They insist that the restatement makes no sense, and that there were no phony revenues—the issue is the timing of revenue recognition, an issue that respectable accountants may legitimately disagree over, rather than fraud. Some experts even agree with this argument.

So the Lucent and Xerox cases are, at the very least, at the opposite end of the sleaze spectrum from WorldCom. Almost certainly they were not instances of deliberate fraud; more likely, they were cases of aggressive envelope-pushing that would probably never have been questioned in another time and place. GAAP accounting is, after all, an art rather than a science. But by the turn of the century, a witch hunt was well underway to catch *all* perpetrators of aggressive accounting—malevolent or not.

Conclusion

Dennis Kozlowski, whose exploits began this chapter, was destined to spend the better part of his years after Tyco in the courtroom. In June 2005, he and former Chief Financial Officer Mark H. Swartz were convicted on twenty-two of twenty-three counts of grand larceny, conspiracy, securities fraud, and falsifying business records. Prosecutors accused the two men of conspiring to defraud Tyco of millions of dollars to fund extravagant lifestyles.[13] And what about Ebbers? In July 2005 the former CEO who oversaw the largest corporate fraud in U.S. history was sentenced to twenty-five years of prison. His reaction was to hunch forward in a courtroom chair, quietly crying. As one reporter on the scene noted, this was "essentially a life term for a man 63 years old and with a history of heart trouble."[14] As for Enron's Ken Lay, he was convicted of fraud and conspiracy in May 2006, but died of a heart attack on July 5, before sentencing. While the wheels of justice turn ever so slowly, a frustrating process for anyone seeking some sense of fair play from the scandals that rocked the U.S. economy, the corporate heads were hardly alone in their misdeeds as we shall see in the next chapter.

Notes

1.   Full text of memo is available at www.thesmokinggun.com.
2.   Robert Bryce, *Pipe Dreams: Greed, Ego, and the Death of Enron* (New York: Public Affairs, 2002), pp. 258-9.
3.   Ibid., p. 11.
4.   Bryce, *Pipe Dreams*, p. 13.
5.   Bethany McLean and Peter Elkind, *The Smartest Guys in the Room: The Amazing Rise and Scandalous Fall of Enron* (New York: Penguin, 2003), pp. xxiv.
6.   Ibid., p. 38.
7.   Ibid., p 126.
8.   Ibid., pp. 142-3.
9.   See Rebecca Smith and John Emschwiller, "Fancy Finances Were the Key to Enron's Success and Now to Its Distress," *Wall Street Journal*, November 8, 2001 and Joshua Chaffin and Stephen Fidler, "CSFB Team Played Key Role in Setting Up Enron Partnerships," *Financial Times*, March 4, 2002.

10.   McClean and Elkind, *The Smartest Guys in the Room*, p. 413.
11.   Lynne Jeter, *Disconnected: Deceit & Betrayal at WorldCom* (New Jersey: John Wiley & Sons, 2003), pp. 195-196.
12.   Based on extensive conversations with U.S. and Japanese investors in 2001 and 2002, Lucent's downfall was a major shock and its survival was a worry. Questions over the company's accounting practices also forced attention on its major rival, Nortel, based in Canada. Both Lucent and Nortel spent the next several years seeking to clean up their books and regain profitability. As of 2006 both companies are still in business, but the accounting scandals left a clear taint over the companies and their stock prices have languished well below the previous highs.
13.   Associated Press, "Status of High-Profile Corporate Scandals," *Houston Chronicle*, http://www.chron.com/disp/story.mpl/ap/business/3537909.html.
14.   Erin McClam, "A Year of Reckoning for Scandal-Tainted CEOs in the United States," *CBC Business News*, December 18, 2005, http://www.cbc.ca/cp/business/05128/b21830.html.

11

Enron Etc. Vol. II:
Enablers, Symbols, and Scapegoats

Both the accounting tricks described in the previous chapter and the ensuing witch hunt could never have taken place without a host of supporting characters. Just as an alcoholic is enabled by willing suppliers of drinks, managers were enabled by their auditors, bankers, lawyers, directors, and regulators—in fact, the very people who were supposed to be overseeing operations rather than underpinning them. At the same time, the pendulum of public opinion swung against the tide of greed and many of the former symbols of the new economy and wealth became scapegoats. In this sense, history was repeated.

The Enablers

The Auditors: Arthur Andersen

The poster child for enablers, though, has to be Arthur Andersen. Andersen "audited" the financial statements of Enron, WorldCom, Qwest, and others involved in the accounting scandals (the quotes are well-advised). Sadly, the eighty-nine-year-old firm had been known for much of its history as the most steadfast of all accounting firms in its adherence to integrity. Founder Arthur Andersen himself had famously lost a major client for refusing to alter its financial statements: "There's not enough money in the city of Chicago," he proclaimed, "to induce me to change that report!" The firm's motto was "Think straight, talk straight."[1]

But something went terribly awry at Arthur Andersen (AA) by the 1990s. It was the smallest of the Big 5 audit firms, and pressure to retain/gain corporate clients was intense. Moreover, as competition intensified in the auditing business, AA increasingly turned to consulting to generate profits—which meant that it was soliciting its auditing clients for the much more lucrative consulting services. The pressure to deliver pleasing audits must have been overwhelming. Indeed, the drive to be both accountant and consultant upped the level of tensions within the firm, finally resulting in it being split into two separate subsidiaries under the corporate flag of Andersen Worldwide.

Enter David Duncan. Duncan was the partner in charge of the Enron audit team—an exalted position indeed, considering Enron's importance to AA. Enron was one of AA's top four clients and enjoyed an extraordinarily close relationship with the firm (Enron had hired no fewer than eighty-six AA accountants). In 2000, Enron paid AA $52 million, half of which went for consulting services.

As Enron's auditor, Duncan was responsible for ensuring that its financial statements were in accordance with GAAP—that they fully and fairly disclosed the true financial condition of the company. Obviously, Enron's glowing financial reports had not. So as Enron plummeted into oblivion, attention (quite understandably) focused on the auditors who had signed off on these financial statements. AA desperately sought to distance itself from its flailing client at first, firing Duncan and claiming that he had "without any consultation with others in the firm" organized the destruction of Enron's documents.

But that strategy failed when it was revealed that officials at AA's Chicago headquarters had been concerned about Enron's questionable accounting as early as February 2001. (Earlier, one partner who had raised questions about Enron's accounting for its complex partnership schemes had been quickly removed from the account after Enron complained.) Partners at that time had considered the extreme step of dropping Enron as a client—but Enron was by then generating around $50 million per year in auditing and consulting fees, and AA hoped to double that amount in the coming years. The matter was dropped.

So in June 2002 a jury found AA guilty of obstructing justice by shredding documents related to Enron, sounding the final death knell for the firm. Probably the most damaging evidence came from one AA executive stating on a training video that if documents were shredded and then the investigators arrived, that would be good.[2] Interestingly enough, it was the company that was convicted, not individuals (unlike other cases to follow). AA had already lost much of its business, and two-thirds of its 28,000-strong U.S. workforce. Facing multimillion dollar lawsuits by Enron investors and shareholders and forbidden from auditing publicly traded companies after August 2002, the firm collapsed. It was a sad ending for the once-proud firm founded by Arthur Andersen himself, the man who had once proclaimed that there was not enough "money in Chicago" to get him to falsify financial reports.

In an interesting footnote, the U.S. Supreme Court later overturned the 2002 criminal conviction of Andersen. In 2005, the Supreme Court ruled that the Houston jury that found Andersen guilty of obstruction of justice was given overly broad instructions by the federal judge who presided at the trial. Because of these "faulty" instructions, the justices ruled the firm was convicted without proof that its shredding of documents was deliberately intended to undermine a looming Securities Exchange Commission inquiry in fall 2001. As William B. Mateja, a former official of the Justice Department's corporate fraud task force commented: "To lose a case like this is huge. Arthur Andersen was the poster-child case of all the corporate fraud cases."[3]

Enablers: The Board of Directors

Perhaps one of the most striking examples of an enabler to financial fraud was the gross negligence of Enron's board of directors, a well-connected and highly educated group of people charged with the responsibility of making certain that the company was run in a prudent and lawful fashion. In the aftermath of the company's collapse, a congressional hearing investigation found the Enron board had failed in a number of areas, in particular, in terms of its fiduciary responsibility. As the Congressional report stated: "The Enron Board of Directors failed to safeguard Enron shareholders and contributed to the collapse of the seventh largest public company in the United States, by allowing Enron to engage in high risk accounting, inappropriate conflict of interest transactions, extensive undisclosed off-the-books activities, and excessive executive compensation." Probably the most condemning line in the report was the following: "The Board witnessed numerous indications of questionable practices by Enron management over several years, but chose to ignore them to the detriment of Enron shareholders, employees and business associates."[4]

Although the Congressional investigation found no evidence of self-dealing, corruption, or fraud by the board, it did condemn the group's "see-no-evil, hear-no-evil" approach. Indeed, as the rash of corporate scandals rocked U.S. financial markets in 2002 and 2003, it was revealed that many boards were not living up to their responsibilities. This resulted in a reexamination of the role of directors throughout corporate America, with a greater clarification of their role and authority.

Enablers: The Bankers

If Enron et al. could not have perpetrated their accounting games without the eager assistance of an army of accountants, equally could they not have stayed in business without the bankers. The boom years for Enron and the Internet/telecoms industry coincided, conveniently, with the cult of the star investment banker—and with huge conflicts of interest at the big financial institutions that had come to bestride the petty world.

In fact, the Master of the Universe trader was, by the boom years of the late 1990s, rivaled by the Master of the Universe analyst at the leading investment banks. Analysts like Jack Grubman at Salomon Smith Barney (SSB) and Henry Blodget at Merrill Lynch were lauded and rewarded for their work on the hero stocks of the day—Enron, WorldCom, and their like.

The Star Analyst. What exactly was the analysts' responsibility with respect to those stocks? Well, in a perfect world their job, of course, was to analyze the prospects of these companies and report fairly and objectively to prospective investors on their findings. But this is where the conflicts of interest came to the forefront. Grubman, Blodget, and their compatriots, it turned out, were rewarded for their ability to win *investment banking business* from the companies being analyzed—from the very subject of the reports themselves—rather than for the accuracy of those reports. As one Goldman Sachs executive wrote in a memo, "Bringing in the big bucks is primary to an analyst's success and actually being able to pick a stock takes second."

A very distant second, it seemed. Analysts who hyped Enron up to the bitter end, for example, later claimed that they had been deceived by the company. But journalists McLean and Elkind note that "if they were indeed victims, they were willing ones." And independent analyst Howard Schilit told Congress, "For any analyst to say there were no warning signs in the public filings, they could not have read the same public filings that I did."[5] The incentive to please Enron was enormous: Between 1986 and 2001, the biggest Wall Street firms earned a whopping $323 million for underwriting Enron's stocks and bonds. And by the late 1990s, Enron was one of the largest payers of investment banking fees in the world. (Enron also had a very nasty side: It would threaten to cut any investment bank out of its business if the banker annoyed Enron in any way.)

Examples abound. Former Merrill Lynch CEO David Komansky, for instance, discussed with Tyco's Dennis Kozlowski the hiring of an analyst who Tyco liked to handle research coverage of the company. Kozlowski, it seemed, was not happy with the Merrill analyst who had been covering Tyco—so Merrill's CEO carefully consulted Kozlowski before hiring analyst Phua Young. Eventually, Merrill would agree to pay $200 million to resolve an investigation by pesky New York Attorney General Eliot Spitzer into conflicts of interest in research and allocations of IPO stock (more on that later). (Phua Young was later fired from Merrill Lynch and in 2004 was fined $225,000 by the National Association of Securities Dealers [NASD] and suspended from the industry for one year.)[6]

WorldCom, too, figures prominently in this picture. Financial institutions close to the company knew much more than they let on about WorldCom's woes (even internally downgrading the firm), and acted to protect themselves while eagerly selling WorldCom securities to unwitting investors. One bank analyst recommended that his own bank stop lending money to WorldCom, but the bank continued selling its bonds to investors. Three big banks—J. P. Morgan, Deutsche Bank, and Bank of America—expressed serious concerns internally about WorldCom's financial soundness in early 2001, just months before they helped the company sell $12 billion in debt (in the third biggest debt offering in history). These doubts, needless to say, were never conveyed to the investors who bought the debt just fourteen months before the company went under. As of early 2004, these bonds were worth just $350, down from an initial purchase price of $1000.

Illegal? Perhaps not. After all, argue the lawyers, securities laws do not require the banks that helped WorldCom to disclose cautions by their credit analysts about the company's condition. Buyer beware. And remember: The analyst's job was to win investment banking business from WorldCom, not to provide retail investors with the best possible advice. One Goldman analyst listed his three most important goals for 2000 as follows:

1)   Get more investment banking revenue.
2)   Get more investment banking revenue.
3)   Get more investment banking revenue.

Or there's the example of Bear Stearns and CAIS Internet. In 1999 Bear handled the IPO (initial public offering) of CAIS, a Washington company that was going to get rich by installing high-speed Internet connections in hotels, apartments, and office buildings. Shares were initially priced at $19/share, peaked at $43/share, and were down to 12 cents/share by the time the company filed by bankruptcy two and a half years later. The

Bear Stearns analyst who recommended the stock to investors called it a "piece of shit" in an internal email to a coworker. Investors lost $1 billion in value, and Bear paid $80 million to the government in penalties.

Investors lost $2.4 billion on LifeMinders.com Inc., too, a business plan based on the notion that people would voluntarily sign up to get email advertisements. The analyst at Merrill Lynch also, coincidentally, called this stock "a piece of shit" in an internal email. The company was eventually sold for $1.95/share, down from a peak of $91/share at its height.[7]

IPO Allocations. Nothing upset the notion of Wall Street as a level playing field as much as the revelations about how IPO shares were allocated in the late 1990s. IPO shares can be pure gold. When a company issues stock for the first time in an IPO, or initial public offering, the investment bank that underwrites the stock often underprices it. Why? Well, it's smart business to allow some room for the stock price to rise on its first day of trading—that creates a positive buzz about the stock—and to leave investors with the sense that this is a stock on its way up.

There's nothing wrong with this practice, although it got out of hand in the 1990s; underpricing averaged less than 5 percent early in the decade, and amounted to fully 30 percent in 1999 according to one study. (Another study put the first day gains in new telecom stock issues between 1999 and 2003 at $9.6 billion.) But it does create a guaranteed profit for those lucky folks who get hold of the first shares issued, since they're pretty much guaranteed to rise—perhaps soar—in price on the first day or so of trading. So who gets these precious shares? Ah, that's the rub.

Investment bankers, it turns out, allocated these shares very carefully. It would make sense for them to favor their best clients, and they did—but not in the manner that one might expect. Instead of allocating the shares to those individuals who were top banking clients, they allocated this free money to those individuals who were *senior managers of companies that were investment banking clients.*

The difference is critical. It suggests that executives, who are supposed to be acting in their company's best interests, would instead be awarding its investment banking business to the financial institution that lavished the largest amounts of risk-free, guaranteed profits on the executives themselves. It also explodes the myth, that Wall Street is a level playing field. Millions of investors rushed into the stock market in the 1990s and grabbed up shares of the hottest stocks, little knowing that the system was already rigged to favor top executives who got in early because their companies were paying huge investment banking fees to the underwriters.

Among the biggest winners in this game were Bernie Ebbers of WorldCom, who picked up 869,000 shares in hot IPOs between 1996 and 2000. Ebbers, in turn, awarded Salomon Smith Barney (SSB) investment banking business worth $80 million in fees over the same period. Scott Sullivan, WorldCom's CFO, got 32,000 IPO shares from SSB, which allocated one million IPO shares in all to WorldCom executives.

WorldCom was hardly alone. One memo dated March 31, 1999 detailed the requests for shares of a hot net issue by twenty-six top-drawer clients of SSB. The list was dominated by executives of companies that were investment banking clients of SSB—twenty of the twenty-six, in fact. (The story of this "hot issue," Rhythm New Connections, is itself a cautionary tale. The stock opened at $21/share on April 7, 1999; goosed by buy recommendations by SSB's star analyst Jack Grubman, it soared to more than $93/share in one week. Two years later it was bankrupt.)

Symbols: Jack Grubman & Salomon. No one epitomized the era of the star analyst more than Jack Grubman. As SSB's telecoms analyst, he rarely met a stock he didn't love. During the height of the telecoms boom, 1999-2000, he maintained buy recommendations on thirty out of thirty-six companies in the sector; sixteen of those eventually went bankrupt. But if Grubman's batting average on stock picks wasn't great, he was awfully good at helping to generate investment banking business for SSB from the subjects of his analysis. In 1997-2001 SSB earned more investment banking fees from telecom companies than any other Wall Street firm—$809 million from underwriting telecom stocks and bonds, and $178 million more for giving advice on mergers and acquisitions.[8]

Grubman was especially close to Bernie Ebbers of WorldCom. The two men shared a common background: "We both come from the wrong side of the tracks vis-à-vis the financial community," Grubman later commented. Author Om Malik explains,

> The story goes that once during a WorldCom quarterly conference call, Bernie and Grubman discussed the golf game they had played a week earlier. It was Grubman's way of flexing his muscles and letting the rest of the world know who was the ax on WorldCom. "Ax" is an insider term for an analyst who can make or break a stock with thumbs up or down. WorldCom, through Ebbers, was attached at the hip to Salomon Smith Barney, through Grubman. Salomon's parent company, Citigroup, had loaned Ebbers $679 million. It's speculated that Grubman got a finder's fee—about 10 to 15 percent of the profits made by the Citigroup on the loan—for arranging this deal.[9]

SSB helped Ebbers raise billions of dollars by selling its stocks and bonds, partly thanks to the vociferous advocacy of analyst Jack Grubman. So when WorldCom crashed, Grubman pretty much fell to earth along with it. He resigned on August 18, 2002 with $32 million in cash and stock compensation, and a promise from SSB that they would pay his legal fees. He left a great many failed companies and sadder but wiser investors in his wake—but not without providing some tabloid fodder as well. Grubman, it seems, may have changed his ratings on AT&T to please his boss, Sandy Weill, so that Weill could get Grubman's twins into an elite Manhattan nursery school—the 92nd Street Y, where the tots played on a rooftop playground with a retractable roof, and mingled with the offspring of Woody Allen, Katie Couric, and Michael J. Fox (Madonna's daughter Lourdes was rejected). The tabloids had a field day with "Nursery Gate," and the twins ended up in the Manhattan public schools.

Jack Grubman in His Own Words: Playing the Fiddle

A math major with a master's degree in probability theory from Columbia, Grubman was not unaware of what was happening. The email trail that he left tells an interesting story.

In early 2001, he sent the following email to his boss:

> Most of our banking clients are going to zero and you know I wanted to downgrade them months ago but got huge pushback from banking. I wonder what use bankers are if all they can depend on to get business is analysts who recommend their banking clients.

In February he issued a bullish report on Focal Communications, but the company apparently complained about some of the report's content. Grubman fired off an email to two SSB bankers:

> [If] I so much as hear one more f——— peep out of them [Focal] we will put the proper rating (i.e., 4 not even 3) on this stock which every single smart buy sider [institutional investor] feels is going to zero. We lost credibility...because we support pigs like Focal.

And in April, he admitted in an email to his assistant that he had failed to perform his due diligence on the now-bankrupt Winstar. "If anything, the record shows we support our banking clients too well for too loe.

Grubman's own words in the Nursery Gate fracas are even more revealing. He sent the following memo entitled "AT&T and the 92nd Street Y" to Citigroup CEO Sandy Weill in November 1999:

... On another matter, as I alluded to you the other day, we are going through the ridiculous but necessary process of pre-school applications in Manhattan. For someone who grew up in a household with a father making $8,000 a year and for someone who attended public schools, I do find this process a bit strange, but there are no bounds for what you do for your children.

To give you some details, our children—Davis and Elizabeth Grubman—are currently 2 years, 5 months-old, boy and girl twins and they will be 3 years, 3 months-old when they enter nursery school in September 2000 (which is the admissions date that we are applying for). Of the schools we've looked at, the 92nd Street Y is, without question, the one we'd love our children to attend. To us, it has the right mix of educational and developmental programs and it has a healthy Jewish culture without being over the top on the religious scale. Given that it's statistically easier to get into the Harvard Freshman Class than it is to get into pre-school at the 92nd Street Y (by the way, this is a correct statement), it comes down to "who you know."

Attached is the list of the Board of Directors from the 92nd Street Y. Fred Salerno is helping me with Patricia Cayne, who I think is Jimmy Cayne's wife from Bear Stearns, and Fred is on the Board of Bear Stearns or at least was. However, if you feel comfortable and know some of these board members well enough, I would greatly appreciate it if you could ask them to use any influence they feel comfortable in using to help us as well. I noticed Bill Heyman is on the board and I think he works somewhere in the Citigroup corporate structure but I don't really know Bill.

Anyway, anything you could do Sandy would be greatly appreciated. As I mentioned, I will keep you posted on the progress with AT&T which I think is going well. Thank you.

Note the reference to AT&T in the final paragraph. In January 2002 Grubman sent the following, damning email to a friend:

You know everyone thinks I upgraded [AT&T] to get lead for [AT&T Wireless]. Nope. I used Sandy to get my kids in 92nd ST Y pre-school (which is harder than Harvard) and Sandy needed Armstrong's vote on our board to nuke Reed in showdown. Once coast was clear for both of us (ie Sandy clear victor and my kids confirmed) I went back to my normal negative self on [AT&T]. Armstrong never knew that we both (Sandy and I) played him like a fiddle.

Jack Grubman's emails can be found at www.sec.gov/litigation/complaints/comp18111.htm.

The Lawyers Go to Work. SSB's promise of legal fees to Grubman was far from trivial. Mountains of lawsuits have been filed, and armies of lawyers are busily at work preparing briefs, settlements, and pleadings. Some of the suits have already been settled. In late 2004 top Silicon Valley banker Frank Quattrone of CSFB, for instance, was found guilty of impeding the government investigation into IPO allocations, (though in 2006 a federal appeals court overturned his earlier conviction. In the same year Citigroup made one of the largest out-of-court settlements in history, paying out $2.65 billion to investors in WorldCom to settle claims that Citi had taken part in its accounting fraud. While admitting no wrongdoing, Citi also quadrupled its reserves for other pending lawsuits—including the Enron mess—to $6.7 billion. Grubman was fined $15 million and his compatriot Henry Blodget at Merrill Lynch $4 million; both were barred from the securities industry for life.

Pressed by the indefatigable New York attorney general Eliot Spitzer, Wall Street's leading banks agreed in spring 2003 to cut the ties between analysts and bankers, and to stop reserving shares in IPOs for executives of client companies. The settlement produced $1.4 billion in fines, mostly ponied up by SSB ($400 million), CSFB ($200 million), and Merrill Lynch ($200 million). As usual, the banks admitted no wrongdoing, but agreed to stop doing whatever had gotten them in trouble in the first place. At the very least, the settlements will provide ample ammunition for the legion of lawsuits filed in civil courts by irate shareholders.

Just as predictably, the settlements have satisfied no one. Critics charge that they provide no compensation for the real victims; only $399 million of the $1.4 billion fine, for instance, is earmarked for restitution. Set against the billions lost on bad investments, this does seem to be a puny figure. Moreover, shareholders—rather than the senior managers—will actually bear the burden of the fines. Of Wall Street's $1.4 billion, just the $19 million paid by Blodget and Grubman will come out of executives' pockets; the rest will be paid by the shareholders themselves.

Enablers: The Political Connection

As in every previous instance of gross financial scandal that we've chronicled, the wrongdoers had very close—and very necessary—government connections. Friends in high places enabled the shenanigans, while politicians in turn fed from the corporate trough, and everyone was happy. Except, perhaps, for the shareholders and employees who the pols were supposed to be serving.

As usual, Enron is the most egregious example. Enron's ties with the government were extensive, prodigious, and lavish, starting at the top with Ken Lay. Lay—dubbed Kenny Boy by none other than Bush 43 himself—was seriously considered for a Cabinet post in 2000, and was both a close friend of the Bush family and an important cheerleader for the Republican Party. In a 1997 video—which must have embarrassed the Bushes no end when it turned up on MSNBC in late 2002—George Bush senior tells Enron's president, "You have been fantastic to the Bush family. I don't think anybody did more than you did to support George." (Lay was one of Bush 43's "pioneers," raising $100,000 for the 2000 campaign. He also made Enron's fleet of aircraft available to the Bush campaign as well; it was used eight times.)

But it did not stop with Lay or Bush. Enron enjoyed extensive ties with government on all levels, as chronicled below:

- Three-quarters of all congressmen received campaign contributions from Enron.
- Enron donated more than a million dollars to the Republican Party.
- Bush 43 received more than $800,000 from Enron in his runs for both governor and president.
- Secretary of the Army Thomas White was a former Enron vice president, and owned $50-100 million in shares.
- U.S Trade Representative Robert Zoellick served on Enron's advisory council.
- Lawrence Lindsey, Bush 43's top economic adviser, was a former paid consultant to Enron.
- Vice President Dick Cheney met with Enron executives at least six times in 2001 alone. Lay advised the White House on energy policy.
- Energy Secretary Spencer Abraham discussed energy policy with Enron, and took campaign contributions from Enron as a senator.

Enron benefited handsomely from its connections. In 1998, for example, a minor diplomatic flap arose when former British Ambassador Sir Christopher Meyer twisted arms in a reluctant UK government to ensure that Lay was received at the ministerial level during a trip to London. Top officials in both the Clinton and Bush administrations served as bill collectors for Enron, pressuring the Indian government to pay up for an electricity project that was widely regarded as corrupt.

It did not stop with Enron, either. Global Crossing's Gary Winnick played golf with President Clinton and enjoyed a personal friendship with California Governor Gray Davis; he entertained Presidents Nixon, Reagan, and Bush at his legendary Bel Air mansion. Bush 41 made speeches at various Global Crossing events and, rather than taking $80,000 in cash, opted to be paid in Global Crossing shares that were worth $14 million at their peak. And Bernie Ebbers of WorldCom had longtime Mississippi House Speaker Tim Ford on his speed-dial.

Enablers: The Media

As always, a fickle and fawning media was a willing handmaiden as well. Media coverage of the various players followed a familiar pattern—first adoration, then vilification (shades of Samuel Insull in the 1920s and 1930s). During the adoration phase, it seemed, no honor was too lofty for the corporate magicians who were spinning paper into gold.

Ken Lay, for example, was a public figure by the mid-1990s. He was a fixture on the charity circuit, and appeared regularly on corporate boards and at political functions. His frequent visits to Washington reflected the high esteem in which policymakers held him (and his lavish contributions as well). Lay was widely seen as a business visionary, following in the hallowed footsteps of none other than GE's Jack Welch himself.

As noted earlier, *CFO* magazine bestowed its CFO Excellence Award on Enron's Andrew Fastow in 1999 (WorldCom's Scott Sullivan had gotten it the year before). Harvard Business School wrote no fewer than five case studies touting the miracle of the Enron model; *Fortune* named Enron America's Most Innovative Company for six consecutive years; and *CEO* magazine picked Enron's board of directors as one of the top five in corporate America.

Others basked in the light of adulation as well. In 1996, the *Wall Street Journal* ranked WorldCom at the top of its list of 1000 corporations in return to shareholders over the past decade, and chief Bernie Ebbers was feted as the Bill Gates of the telecom industry. Bill Clinton spoke at WorldCom's offices in March 2000 and told employees, "I came here today because you are a symbol of twenty-first-century America. You are an embodiment of what I want for the future." Star analyst Jack Grubman, interviewed by adoring reporters, told them, "What used to be a conflict is now synergy"—and no one even blinked.

Enablers: Lawyers, Directors, and More

Finally, the financial wrongdoings of the boom were underwritten by a small army of supporting characters who benefited handsomely from corporate largesse and turned a blind eye to its excesses. Lawyers fall into this category (remember Vinson & Elkins, the legal firm that okayed Enron's off-balance sheet partnerships, not once but twice?). So do complacent boards, which are supposed to oversee management but ended up entirely at the mercy of all-powerful executives. As one commentator pointed out, by the late 1990s the typical American board of directors consisted of "ten friends of the chairman, a token woman, and a token representative of a minority group."

Even the business cycle did its part. The booming economy enabled overseers to ignore the conflicts of interest that littered and ultimately crippled the market. "Why fix what ain't broke" became the refrain, until the business cycle turned—exposing all the weaknesses of a crony-driven system in the harsh light of a market downturn. It is no coincidence that the accounting games emerged after the Nasdaq crashed in April 2000. To this day, it is unclear how many financial irregularities would ever have come to light if the boom in the Internet and telecoms market had not turned into a bust.

Symbols and Scapegoats

As in previous scandal-prone eras, a culture of greed and excess overtook Wall Street in the heady days of the Internet/telecom boom. Enron's Jeff Skilling, clearly a spiritual descendant of Ivan (Greed-Is-Good) Boesky, held a Darwinian view of the business world, often proclaiming that greed was the best motivator on earth. Nothing was grandiose enough, no pay package munificent enough, no party lavish enough, to satisfy the grandiose appetites that had taken hold of corporate America. Former Fed Chairman Paul Volcker commented in disgust, "Corporate greed exploded beyond anything that could be imagined in 1990. Traditional norms didn't exist. You had this whole culture where the only sign of worth was how much money you made."

Money flowed like water. WorldCom's Scott Sullivan, who was one of the highest paid CFOs in the country in 1998, was blessed with a total compensation for that year of $19.25 *million*. He went right out and put down $2 million for four acres in Boca Raton, Florida, where he planned to build his dream mansion (which was only partially finished when he was led away in handcuffs in July 2002). Author Lynne Jeter describes Sullivan's new digs:

> The 16,410 square foot Mediterranean Revival style home—white with a red tiled roof—had eight bedrooms. It featured 117 windows and 87 doors, nine refrigerators, four microwave ovens, a wine room and separate cellar, a half dozen Jacuzzis, a six-car garage, a library with adjoining galleries, a soundproof 18-seat movie theater, a game room, and a domed exercise facility. The massive master suite featured a "mini pool"—an oversized garden tub measuring six feet wide and eight feet long—matching showers and toilets, and trailer-size closets. A storage room was created just for furs... Unless the Justice Department or SEC won a case against Sullivan, it would remain his property, as long as he could pay for it.

But Sullivan's mansion couldn't compete with that of Global Crossing's Gary Winnick in the ostentatious sweepstakes. Malik reports, "In 2000, [Winnick] bought a 15-bedroom 23,000 square foot mansion in Los

Angeles' tony Bel-Air neighborhood for a whopping $65 million—the highest price ever paid for a single-family home in the United States. And he was going to spend $30 million on renovations!"

All of this grandeur, of course, was fueled by the stock options frenzy. Executives' generous pay packets were not enough, generous as they had become (in 1973, the average CEO earned 45 times the average pay of his workers; by 2001, the multiple had leaped to 500 times). So in the 1990s their paychecks were padded by increasingly more munificent stock options grants—which spiraled ever-upwards as the bull market exploded. Stock options for senior managers have always been around, and are widely viewed by management experts as an important incentive, but the size and value of the grants in the 1990s were unprecedented.

In 1980, barely one-third of CEO's at public companies had stock options. By 1994, 70 percent received option grants, and in the latter years of the decade "mega-options"—grants worth at least $10 million—became the norm. The cult of mega-options, according to one writer, "revolutionized the culture of corporate America." Option grants had gone way beyond the realm of simple incentives; now, they gave senior managers a huge vested interest in engineering a steady and strong increase in the stock price. So the incentive morphed from that of managing the company well, to managing the stock price well—perhaps even misleading investors as to its true financial condition, if necessary. Enron, not coincidentally, was one of Wall Street's most aggressive grantor of stock options; by the end of 2000, over 13 percent of its outstanding stock was held in options.

The culture of greed was accompanied by a sense of complacency. With no one overseeing the actions of senior managers, they were secure in the knowledge that no senior Wall Streeter had done serious time for financial fraud since 1990, with the single exception of Nick Leeson in Singapore. Penalties were light, and supervisors were relaxed. And Michael Milken's emergence from prison as a wealthy man with his fingers still well into the Wall Street pie didn't hurt, either.

But eventually the day of reckoning would come, of course. As the market crash unfolded, a fickle media turned on those it had adored just a few short years (even months) before, and the public clamored for their heads. A few unlucky souls emerged as symbols—scapegoats?—of everything that had gone wrong in the late 1990s, and they suffered accordingly.

Jack Welch

GE's celebrated leader, Jack Welch, became the first scapegoat to capture public attention. Dubbed "Neutron Jack" by his detractors, he was known for his ruthless cost-cutting as well as his ability to push GE's market value up from $13 billion when he took over as CEO in 1981, to fully $400 billion when he retired in 2001. Welch, who was widely viewed as the most admired CEO in the world, had enjoyed "two decades of uninterrupted fawning" by an adoring media. He was hotly pursued as a motivational speaker for audiences worldwide, and had received an unprecedented $7 million advance for his autobiography, *Jack: Straight from the Gut*.

Ironically, Welch's troubles began with a typically adoring article in the well-respected *Harvard Business Review* (HBR). He fell in love with HBR editor Suzy Wetlaufer (who was forced to resign as a result of the affair), and filed for divorce from longtime wife Jane (number 2). But Jane was not content to go quietly into the darkness. She filed divorce papers that outlined Welch's munificent retirement package from a grateful GE, and the hatefest began.

According to these papers, Welch got:

- a $9 million annual pension;
- 24-hour access to GE's Boeing 737;
- a Central Park apartment complete with flowers and food;
- a limited edition Mercedes Benz;
- court side tickets for the Knicks and the U.S. Open, seating at Wimbledon, box seats for the Red Sox and Yankees;
- cell phones for five cars; and
- satellite TV for his four homes.

The tabloids were overjoyed, and even the legitimate press piled on. The perks were certainly legal, but Welch eventually announced in a *Wall Street Journal* column that he would relinquish many of them in a sop to public opinion.

Was this a fair outcome? Welch's supporters argued that the perks represented money that Welch earned fair and square in his two decades at the helm of GE, decades in which he delivered tremendous value for shareholders and employees. But it is equally true that Welch, a man whose personal net worth hovered around $900 million, could probably have managed to afford box seats on his own (or, at the very least, find a major corporation willing to squeeze him into their playbox).

Richard Grasso

The next target for an angry public was Dick Grasso, the NYSE chairman who had been hailed as a hero for his handling of the market in the dark days following 9/11. By 2003, the bloom was off the rose. Revelations of Grasso's $140 million pay package outraged even jaded Wall Street veterans, who wondered aloud why America's chief markets regulator should be earning such an amazing sum. A besieged Grasso—who had, after all, committed no illegality, fraud, or con—eventually agreed to give up $48 million in future pay to quiet the uproar, but he has steadfastly refused to give up any of the money he had already received.

Martha Stewart

But Grasso and Welch were just tiny hiccups compared to the huge explosion that was Martha Stewart. Stewart was founder and CEO of a publicly traded company, Martha Stewart Living Omnimedia; she also ran a magazine, penned bestselling books, produced and starred in a TV show, and wrote a syndicated newspaper column. She was an entire industry in and of herself.

But Stewart could also be tone-deaf. Her troubles began with a phone message from stockbroker Peter Bacanovic, on December 27, 2002. Bacanovic left a message for Stewart, who was on her way to a Mexican vacation, telling her that ImClone shares were trending down. As soon as Stewart's plane touched down, she returned Bacanovic's call and told his assistant to dump her stock. But she had another source as well: ImClone, a biotech company that was working on a promising new anti-cancer drug, was run by a close friend of Stewart's named Sam Waksal. So, in a move that would come to haunt her, she also called Waksal and left a message asking him what was going on with ImClone.

Waksal never returned the call—perhaps because he was caught up in his own troubles. Waksal and other family members had apparently been dumping their own shares, based on their knowledge that the FDA was about to announce negative results on ImClone's new anti-cancer drug. When Waksal and his broker were indicted for insider trading, those fateful phone calls of Stewart's came to the center of the stage, and Stewart's carefully cultivated life began to come apart at the seams.

After a lengthy public nightmare, Stewart went to jail for obstructing justice (note that, like Arthur Andersen, Lucent, and many others, she was never found guilty of fraud—just for covering something up. In fact, a judge threw out the fraud charge, saying that "no jury could feasibly find it to be accurate"). The problem was a story that she told prosecutors, claiming that she had a preexisting sell order at $60/share that triggered the selloff. But the story didn't pass the sniff test: If she had such an order on file, then why did Bacanovic have to call her at all? Why weren't the shares just sold automatically when the stock fell through $60?

But Stewart was decidedly not guilty of fraud or insider trading—so she was found guilty for covering up an underlying action that apparently was not illegal. By the time she went to jail in late 2004, her personal fortune had plunged from $1 billion to $335 million and ever-fickle public sympathy was swinging back her way. Even the most avid Martha-haters were disturbed by the notion of her in prison stripes—while the true crooks and criminals of the Enron Etc. era continued to fence with the lawyers and live their lavish, jet-setting lives.

It was Stewart's misfortune that she had become a symbol and a scapegoat, and it was on those grounds that she was convicted. One of the jurors at her trial, a computer technician from the Bronx named Chappell Hartridge, triumphantly told reporters that the verdict sent a message to the "bigwigs" that no one's above the law. "Maybe it's a victory for the little guys," he proclaimed proudly, "who lose money in the markets thanks to these kinds of transactions."

Maybe Hartridge should go back to his computers. Which "little guys," precisely, did Stewart's actions hurt? The sale of her ImClone stock grossed $240,000, certainly not enough to influence the markets or to do any damage to anyone except, of course, Stewart herself. The only "little guys" who suffered were holders of Martha Stewart Living shares, who saw their value plunge as the media took hold of the Stewart story and elevated it into a full-fledged phenomenon.

In fact, it is hard to escape the sense that all of these very public figures—Jack Welch, Dick Grasso, and Martha Stewart—had done very little to deserve their fates, other than being in the wrong place at the very wrong time. All were public faces of a scandal-ridden era, easy to identify and easy to hate (many of the anti-Martha diatribes were astonishingly personal) at a time when the public needed a scapegoat. Much like Michael Milken a decade earlier, they became the poster children for an era of greed and excess. They were undoubtedly greedy, undoubtedly to an excessive level. But greed—while extremely unattractive—is not a crime.

All the same, David Kelley, the U.S. attorney for the Southern District of New York who prosecuted Stewart, later commented, "I have heard anecdotally stories of folks coming into regulatory agencies and saying, 'I'm going to tell you the truth because I do not want to end up like Martha Stewart.' If that is one of the impacts of this case, great."

It's the Character, Stupid

The great financier J. P. Morgan once famously told a congressional hearing that in banking decisions, "the first thing is character." "Before money or property?" he was asked. "Before money or property or anything else," Morgan replied. "Money cannot buy it."

Warren Buffett would agree. Buffett, widely viewed as the greatest investor of all time, wrote in 2002 that "for many years, I've had little confidence in the earnings numbers reported by most corporations." The problem, he says, is not just the outright crooks like Enron and WorldCom, but the "legal but improper" accounting methods that are routinely used by corporate chiefs to inflate earnings. And reforms like adding more independent directors, beefing up oversight, and policing the auditors won't help, in an environment where surveys show that two-thirds of CEOs have asked their CFOs to juggle the numbers.

Buffett's solution, like the man himself, is simple but elegant: CEOs just need to "do what's right." In other words, it's the character, stupid. But what does this mean in a world where the best defense appears to be the nincompoop argument? Enron's Ken Lay, for instance, claimed that he was unaware of his subordinates' shenanigans—he was a victim of fraud, much like his hapless shareholders. WorldCom's Bernie Ebbers also claims to be a victim, as did Arthur Andersen. This means that those who are supposed to be in charge are either crooked or incompetent. It will be difficult to regain trust in a system where our choice is between crooks and idiots.

This is why many dismayed observers have come to view the failings of the Enron Etc. era as systemic failures. A scathing op-ed piece in the *Washington Post* entitled "A tsunami of scandal" charges that "the most well-run casino in the world suddenly looks like a shoddy set-up for suckers." Author Jim Hoagland concludes despairingly, "This is not just about a few bad apples…this is about the system."

Certainly it is true that Enron et al. needed lots of help to keep their schemes alive—the enablers, as we call them. Enron needed:

- accountants to bless their financial statements;
- lawyers to approve the deal structures;
- bankers and investment bankers to provide capital;

- rating agencies to remain bullish despite Enron's huge off-balance sheet debt burden; and
- directors to remain asleep.

Everyone cooperated enthusiastically. All of these enablers were smart enough and had enough information to raise some pretty big red flags, but no one did. (Ken Lay, for instance, was a Ph.D. economist and the friend of presidents—it's hard to fit him into the innocent victim slot.)

So it's easy to see why economist Paul Krugman has called Enron "a cancer on capitalism," and it's easy to echo Hoagland's despairing conclusion that the entire system stinks. Sometimes it seems that we are caught in the famous definition of the village idiot: someone who keeps doing things the same way, but expects a different result.

Enter Eliot Spitzer. His anti-sleaze crusade at the end of the Enron Etc. era is widely viewed on Wall Street as just another swing of the pendulum to appease public anger, fueled by Spitzer's own, very evident, political ambitions. His reforms are useless at best, obstructive to capitalism at worst, and in the long run will have no more impact than other reforms cobbled together at the end of similar, scandal-ridden eras.

But the view from Main Street is somewhat different. There Spitzer is viewed as a modern-day Eliot Ness, taking aim against the organized mob that has taken over Wall Street and taking a lawful, righteous position to stamp out the corruption.

Which Spitzer will it be, and what does this mean for the future? That is the subject of our concluding chapter.

Notes

1. Barbara Ley Toffler and Jennifer Reingold, *Final Accounting: Ambition, Greed, and the Fall of Arthur Andersen* (New York: Broadway Books, 2003), p. 12.
2. "Andersen Guilty in Enron Case," *BBC News*, June 15, 2002, http://news.bbc.co.uk/1/hi/business/2047122.stm.
3. Charles Lane, "Justices Overturn Andersen Conviction," *Washington Post*, June 1, 2005, p. A1.
4. Permanent Subcommittee on Investigations of the Committee on Governmental Affairs United States Senate, "The Role of the Board of Directors in Enron's Collapse" (Washington, D.C.), July 8, 2002, p. 3.
5. Bethany McLean and Peter Elkind, *The Smartest Guys in the Room: The Amazing Rise and Scandalous Fall of Enron* (New York: Penguin, 2003), p. 231.
6. National Association of Securities Dealers, News Release, "NASD Fines and Suspends Phua Young, Former Merrill Lynch Research Analyst," May 25, 2004.
7. Jerry Knight, "Puny Penalty, Given Damage to Investors," *Washington Post*, May 5, 2003.
8. Jane Hughes and Scott MacDonald, *Carnival on Wall Street: Global Financial Markets in the 1990s* (Hoboken, NJ: John Wiley & Sons, 2004) pp. 195-196.

9. Om Malik, *Broadbandits: Inside the $750 Billion Telecom Heist* (Hoboken, NJ: John Wiley & Sons, 2002), p. 198.
10. Julie Creswell, "S.E.C. Overturns Investment Banker's Lifetime Ban from the Industry," *New York Times*, March 25, 2006, p. A3. The 2nd U.S. Circuit Court of Appeals in Manhattan said the evidence was sufficient to sustain a conviction but that the May 2004 verdict must be thrown out because the jury was improperly instructed on how to interpret the law. At the end of the 2004 trial Quattrone was sentenced to eighteen months in jail, but was allowed to remain free while appealing his conviction.
11. John Cassidy, "The Greed Cycle," *New Yorker*, September 23, 2002, p. 64.
12. Ibid.
13. Lynne Jeter, *Disconnected: Deceit and Betrayal at WorldCom* (Hoboken, NJ: John Wiley & Sons, 2003), p. 144.
14. Malik, *Broadbandits*, pp. 76-77.
15. John Cassidy, "The Greed Cycle."
16. "Neutron Jack and his Electric Affair," *Guardian*, March 17, 2002, http://observer.guardian.co.uk/focus/story/0,6903,668839,00.html.
17. Stephanie Kirchgaessner, "The Confessions of a Corporate Crime-Fighter," *Financial Times*, September 6, 2005, p. 10.
18. Warren Buffett, "Who Really Cooks the Books," *New York Times*, July 24, 2002, http://www.nytimes.com/2002/07/24/opinion/24BUFF.html?ex=1148702400&en=efe7de3228a810f2&ei=5070.
19. Jim Hoagland, "A Tsunami of Scandal," *Washington Post*, July 7, 2002, p. B7

12

Eliot the Untouchable (Spitzer, not Ness)

When legendary lawman Eliot Ness heard that the trucks and other vehicles seized during raids on Al Capone's breweries and warehouses were headed for the auction block, he "gleefully made plans for one of the most bizarre public displays downtown Chicago had ever seen." Biographer Paul W. Heimel writes:

[Ness] summoned the Capone Squad to a federal government warehouse to help wash and wax each of the vehicles. Early the next morning, he telephoned the Lexington Hotel, talked his way through a desk clerk, and spoke directly to Capone.

"Whad'ya want?" Capone grumbled.

"Well, Mr. Capone, I just wanted to tell you that, if you look out your front windows down on Michigan Avenue at exactly eleven o'clock, you'll see something that will interest you."

Ness hung up before Capone could respond.

At the designated time, Ness and his team, joined by about three dozen recruits from the Prohibition Bureau, arrived at the garage and took their positions aboard the shiny trucks. They fell in behind a police escort and formed a line that covered three city blocks. With sirens wailing and lights flashing, the caravan lumbered forward on Michigan Avenue.

Forty-five vehicles seized during Prohibition Bureau raids paraded steadily toward the Lexington. Ness rode in the lead car, armed with a sawed-off shotgun, more for show than security.

Capone appeared at an upstairs window with his bodyguards and flew into a violent rage when he realized what was happening. He allegedly lifted two chairs and smashed them over a table, screaming, "I'll kill 'im! I'll kill 'im with my own bare hands." Ness, in his memoirs, called the parade "a brilliant psychological counter-stroke."

"What we had done this day was enrage the bloodiest mob in criminal history," Ness explained. "We had hurled the defiance of the Untouchables into their teeth; they surely knew by now that we were prepared to fight to the finish."

According to Ness's account, two nights later, he was relaxing at his apartment, listening to an opera on the phonograph, a cat sleeping on Eliot's lap, when the phone rang. The raspy voice at the other end warned the federal agent that his days were numbered. "You won't know when, and you won't know where," said the caller. "The next time I see you will be at your funeral."[1]

Eliot Spitzer, too, likes to challenge his adversaries head-on—and let them know that he, too, is prepared to "fight to the finish." On November 12, 2002, the New York State attorney general was invited to give a speech at the Institutional Investors dinner, held every year to honor the magazine's "All Star Research Team" award winners. The honorees may have regretted their invitation. Spitzer began by thanking the group for inviting him, joking that it was nice to put faces to all those emails. The joke fell flat. He then went on to excoriate the profession and denigrate its value. The room fell silent; some muttered expletives and some walked out. Spitzer told the analysts,

> Some in the industry offer investor greed, wide-eyed optimism and a herd mentality rather than misleading research to explain the losses investors have experienced. These apologists might admit to distortions, but never dishonesty. But to be frank about it, the advice provided to investors *was* often dishonest. It was dishonest because small investors were advised to buy stocks that the analyst believed they never should have owned, and told to hold stocks that they long ago should have sold.

He went on to tell his stonyfaced listeners that he had hired an independent firm, Investars, to evaluate the analysts' research.

> Investars measured the performance of the recommendations made in the twelve months prior to an analyst being named to the all-star team. They also measured the performance of competing analysts not named to the team. In all, 110,000 analyst recommendations were reviewed.
>   The results are in, and they're telling. In many instances, those named to the all-star team are turning in lackluster performances. The advice of analysts not chosen would very often have been more profitable to individual investors than the advice of all-star team members.

In other words, the emperor has no clothes.

Any Google search of "Eliot Spitzer + Eliot Ness" turns up no fewer than 879 hits, most of them adoring. The temptation to liken Wall Street's fearless crusader Eliot to Chicago's fearless crimebuster Eliot seems to be irresistible, and almost entirely to the benefit of Eliot Spitzer. Ness, after all, was an American treasury agent famous for both his incorruptibility and for his determined effort to bring down the gangsters who had taken over Chicago. Leader of a legendary team known as the Untouchables, Ness was single-handedly responsible for putting Al Capone behind bars.

Or so the myth goes. In December 2002 *Time* magazine named Spitzer its "Crusader of the Year," noting that he has been called the Enforcer or the Sheriff of Wall Street. Other press monikers included "the peoples' lawyer," "the patron saint of small investors," and "an unlikely champion of the little guy." In 2004, *New York* magazine went even further, naming this "modern-day Eliot Ness" one of the fifty sexiest men in New York. *Time* gushed, "The new ethics [Spitzer] championed are touching in their simplicity: analysts' ratings should reflect what they actually believe. There has not been such an affirmation of what's right since Moses and the Ten Commandments."[2]

Pretty big shoes to fill. If Spitzer sometimes seems to be larger than life, then he is only following in the footsteps of his namesake. Eventually, so the legend goes, both should ride off into the sunset like John Wayne at the end of a movie—Ness to his just rewards, Spitzer to the statehouse or beyond.

The Myth

Most modern-day Americans know Eliot Ness from TV or the movies, where he was played by no less a tight-jawed, alpha male actor than Kevin Costner. But everyone knows three things about Ness: He got Al Capone and defeated the Chicago mob; he was a publicity hound with political ambitions; but above all, he was incorruptible. Indeed, as one commentator notes, Americans have fallen in love with Eliot Ness, "this authentic American hero." He was a brave and honest lawman who took on the brutal gangster and won. After he put Capone away, he spent another decade challenging the mob, broadening his crusade to include labor racketeers, crooked cops, and even serial killers—and he chronicled his exploits in a bestselling book about his adventures called *The Untouchables*. (It was eventually made into a popular television series, not once, but twice, and into the abovementioned movie.)[3]

Add this to the myth of Eliot Spitzer and you have…well, you practically get Moses. The *Boston Globe* commented that "Eliot Spitzer's first name could be an homage to Eliot Ness, the G-man who cleaned up Chicago in the 1930s."[4] Everyone knows three things about Spitzer, too: He got Jack Grubman et al. and he cleaned up Wall Street; he is a publicity hound with political ambitions; but still, he's probably incorruptible. (As Alan Dershowitz, the Harvard Law School professor for whom Spitzer once worked, observed, "He's always been accused of being ambitious, but I don't believe he would ever put his ambition before justice."[5])

Now it's time to look at the reality.

The Reality: Eliot Ness

It would be impossible for the myth to exaggerate the brutality and power of Ness's nemesis. When Eliot Ness descended upon the Chicago mob, Al Capone was at the top of his game. He was one of the most flamboyant and successful criminals in U.S. history, with a well-deserved reputation for mind-numbing cruelty. By the mid-1920s, Capone had defeated or co-opted various rivals to become the undisputed king of both the Chicago underworld and the Chicago government. Biographer John Kobler recounts a famous story in his *Capone: The Life and World of Al Capone.* Capone had invited three Sicilian gangsters to a lavish feast. He was the most exuberant and genial of hosts until the enormous meal had been consumed. Then, suddenly, he accused them of disloyalty—an offense he could not tolerate:

> Capone's bodyguards fell upon them, lashing them to their chairs with wire and gagging them. Capone got up, holding a baseball bat. Slowly, he walked the length of the table and halted behind the first guest of honor. With both hands, he lifted the bat and slammed it down full force. Slowly, methodically, he struck again and again, breaking bones in the man's shoulders, arms and chest. He moved to the next man and, when he had reduced him to mangled flesh and bone, to the third. One of the bodyguards then fetched his revolver from the checkroom and shot each man in the back of the head.[6]

Capone, in fact, had killed hundreds; he was behind the slaughter of rival gangsters in the infamous St. Valentine's Day massacre (from which Bugsy Moran escaped unharmed because he was running late), as well as the death of journalists and law enforcement officials. Above all else, Capone had a genius for taking what was a very fragmented business—crime—and consolidating the various criminal enterprises into one empire under his domination. And crime was very, very good for Capone, who earned an estimated $100 million per year in 1925-1930 from his gambling, prostitution, and bootlegging operations. Thanks to a judicious mix of intimidation (see above) and bribery, he had nothing to fear from the law.

An enormous swath of official Chicago, up to and including His Honor the Mayor, was in Capone's pocket. But public anger was swelling, prodded by the influential publisher of the *Chicago Daily News*, Frank Knox. So with the local authorities unwilling to take any action, the feds stepped in (presaging Spitzer, who would later say that he and other local authorities had to step in because the feds wouldn't). They took a two-pronged approach: building a tax evasion case against Capone, and disrupting his bootlegging operations. Ness was appointed to head the bootlegging side.[7]

Ness and his team led a series of daring and largely successful raids on Capone's breweries and hard liquor operations. In their first six months, Ness's team closed down nineteen distilleries and breweries, costing the infuriated Capone over $1 million. But in the end, it was the tax evasion side that put Capone in jail; on June 5, 1931, a grand jury indicted Capone on twenty-two counts of tax evasion.

Wily as ever, Capone played on the government's concerns about the life expectancy of its witnesses, and cut a plea bargain deal that gave him a light sentence. But the judge shocked everyone by refusing to accept the plea, and Capone's case went to a jury. A still-complacent Capone managed to bribe the jury, only to be thwarted once again when the still-vigilant judge switched jurors at the last minute. On October 17, 1931 Capone was found guilty on enough counts to send him to prison for eleven years.[8]

Ness was the hero of the hour, and he reveled in his role. There is no doubt that he enjoyed media attention, cultivating his relationships with reporters and giving public accounts of his team's daring raids. But there is also no doubt that he risked his life on those raids, and it was not all for publicity. Mobsters followed Ness and the other Untouchables day and night; he survived several nerve-shattering attempts on his life, and saw a close friend brutally murdered. Yes, Eliot Ness was a publicity hound who craved excitement and danger—but he was also a man of strong ideals, sincerely determined to clean up the corrupt mess that Chicago had become. Indeed, public humiliation was one of the many weapons he employed against Capone, in an effort to counter the crime boss's celebrity status. Capone is no Robin Hood, nor even a Butch Cassidy, Ness wanted to proclaim.

And he was also, genuinely, incorruptible. When Ness put together his team, it was difficult to find honest men to fight Capone among the corruption-ridden ranks of Chicago's law enforcement officials. Once Ness began his crusade, Capone's first move, not surprisingly, was an attempt to buy Ness off. He offered the young man $2,000 per year—a princely sum, considering that Ness's salary at the time was only $2,800 per year—but Ness refused. (Actually, he announced his refusal loudly and publicly, humiliating Capone and leading reporters to dub him "the Untouchable.")

But in the end, it is the man and not the movie that matters. And on this basis, Ness's legacy is uncertain. We must judge him on the measuring stick of his own goals—not just to put Capone away, but to wrest Chicago away from the grip of organized gangsters, once and for all.

Did Ness achieve this goal? Capone entered the U.S. penitentiary in Atlanta in October 1931, around the same time that fellow gangster Frank Nitti was released. Nitti returned to Chicago and undertook the task of rebuilding the structure that had been disrupted by Ness's raids and Capone's conviction. It was not an easy task. Business was hard hit by the end of Prohibition, the advent of the Great Depression, and by the jailing of not only Capone but other top gangsters on tax charges.

But Nitti and his compatriots were creative, and they diversified quickly into new markets, such as labor racketeering and gambling. Having learned a lesson from Capone's mistakes, they were careful to fly under the radar, shunning publicity and flamboyant flaunting of their wealth and power. Moreover, the feds were distracted by other activities; increasingly, they occupied themselves by chasing bank robbers, kidnappers, communists, and spies. Top feds believed that with Capone in jail, his gang was finished—in fact, the FBI thought that organized crime was inactive in Chicago until the mid-1940s![9]

These developments, obviously, cast doubt on the lasting impact of Ness's actions. Ness himself was in a downward spiral. He went on to become Cleveland's chief of police at just thirty-three years old, but his early successes were tarnished by his inability to capture a serial killer, and he resigned in 1942 following a drunken car accident. He suffered a humiliating defeat in the Cleveland mayoral election in 1947 and ended up in Pennsylvania working for a failed company called Guaranty Paper. He was just fifty-four when he died of a heart attack.

The Reality: Eliot Spitzer

Mythologists, of course, prefer to focus on Ness's early accomplishments rather than his later failures. Much like Ness's early days in Chicago, when Eliot Spitzer first surveyed the Wall Street scene in the late 1990s (he was elected New York attorney general in 1998), he found widespread contempt for the law in an industry that was bloated with outrageous salaries and egos, and was increasingly obsessed with pushing the envelope to greater and greater excesses. Cronyism was rampant, respect for the law at a new low. Accounting standards were being twisted and perverted to accommodate the whims of chief executives; investment bankers were playing fast and loose with the public trust; and "independent" directors were about as plentiful as honest Chicago cops. The system cried out for a crusade.

Like Ness, Spitzer rushed in where others feared to tread. The federal regulators, most notably the SEC—whose purview Wall Street really was—were ineffectively slow, so he stepped in to fill the breach as news of Wall Street wrongdoing started to emerge. From his perch as attorney general of the State of New York, Spitzer was actually in an enviable position: New York's Martin Law, passed in the wake of the Great Depression, gave its attorney general extraordinary powers of subpoena and prosecution in the arena of financial fraud.

Spitzer's crusade began as a fishing expedition at Merrill Lynch. In early 2002, an aide showed him some emails that suggested Merrill had downgraded Internet company GoTo.com because it had not given Merrill its investment banking business. Spitzer must have felt quite a surge of adrenaline. He subpoenaed everything in sight (and a lot that was out of sight, too!), bringing him a windfall of thirty boxes of emails. Merrill eventually paid a $100 million fine and agreed to apologize and reform the way it paid its analysts.

Nobody was pleased with the deal, in what would become a hallmark of Spitzer's career. Critics on one side charged that it was too lenient on Merrill—no one went to jail, and the fine was peanuts for a firm with average profits of $3.25 billion per year. On the other side, detractors said that it was too harsh, especially since Spitzer did not really have jurisdiction over financial institutions anyway; that was the SEC's role.

But for Spitzer it was just the beginning. His subpoenas rapidly multiplied, and federal regulators were finally galvanized to jump into the fray as well. Damning email after damning email turned up, and the public was revolted by the evidence of cronyism and corruption in the ranks of Wall Street's most august financial institutions. In April 2003 Spitzer and the feds settled with ten leading investment banks on the following terms:

- The investment banks would pay $1.4 billion in penalties and fines;
- They would supply independent research to investors for five years;
- They would implement structural reforms to separate research analysts from investment bankers (especially painful because of the pay packet implications for star analysts, accustomed to pulling in anywhere from $1 million to over $10 million a year based on the I-banking business they helped to generate); and
- Jack Grubman of Salomon Smith Barney and Henry Blodget of Merrill Lynch would be forever barred from the securities business. (Blodget had famously dismissed one stock as a "piece of shit" only weeks before Merrill Lynch touted it as an "attractive investment.")

Once again, critics clamored that the deal was either too harsh or too lenient, depending on their political leanings. (It was not the end of the road for the banks, though, which expected to pay out billions more to settle private lawsuits brought by outraged investors.) Unabashed, Spitzer charged on ahead, branching out into investigations of excessive executive pay, mutual funds, and the insurance industry.

Regarded as dull and boring, the insurance sector was also highly profitable and clubby. Perhaps too clubby from Spitzer's point of view. His first cast of the net into the deep waters of the insurance sector came in 2004 and was against the nation's largest insurance broker, Marsh & McLennan. It soon spread to other insurance brokers, such as Aon and Willis and eventually to American International Group (AIG). Insurance brokers are limited in number and help companies buy insurance, much like a realtor does real estate. Spitzer's allegations were that the industry was bid-rigging, an informal agreement on prices between the brokers and insurance providers to submit higher bids (at the cost of the companies looking for insurance). Actually the insurer agreed to put in higher bids to let the incumbent stay in place while they would have been willing to bid lower. This way the brokers controlled both ends of the business.

Spitzer's raid on the insurance sector brought him into a head-to-head battle with one of the industry's giants, Maurice (Hank) Greenberg, long-time head of AIG. Greenberg in 2005 was ranked by Forbes as the 132nd wealthiest man in the world, exceedingly well connected in Washington's political circles, and the father of two sons heading their own major insurance-related companies. He was also known to be highly autocratic in running his company and abrasive to those who ran afoul of him. As one journalist noted: "While Greenberg also had a famous wit, it often appeared in public when he was using it against someone. He loved to deride analysts for what he felt were stupid questions, and managers for what he thought were lackluster results."[10] Greenberg also took great pride in AIG, a company that he had largely built up as an insurance powerhouse. The company is the largest underwriter of commercial and industrial insurance in the United States, as well as the top underwriter of director and officer insurance, professional liability insurance, and environmental and aviation insurance. If that were not enough, AIG is also the top life insurer in Japan (the world's second largest economy), a major player in the emerging Chinese insurance market, and the biggest corporate investor in U.S. Treasury bonds. Used to getting his way on most things, he did not suffer fools. Unfortunately, Greenberg appears to have regarded most regulators as fools.

As Spitzer's pressure on the insurance sector mounted, Greenberg, as the well-identified head of AIG, came under pressure. In addition to participating in bid-rigging, Spitzer eventually accused Greenberg of manipulating AIG's financial results and misleading investors. Questions were also raised over payments made by AIG to C.V. Starr & Company, a private group of insurance agencies controlled and run by Starr and other AIG executives. Indeed, a lawsuit was launched against AIG by shareholders in 2002, based on the view that the payments made to C.V. Starr were illegal.

Greenberg pushed back both publicly and allegedly behind the scenes, seeking to use his political contacts to force Spitzer to back off. Spitzer, however, was undeterred and AIG's board grew increasingly nervous about the cost of picking a fight with the New York attorney general, especially as it appeared to be an increasingly personalized affair. Although Greenberg maintained that he had done nothing wrong, he was pushed out of his company in March 2005 and AIG admitted to $1.7 billion in improper accounting. This gave grist to the media mill, which published with titles like "A Top Insurance Company as the New Enron?"[11] Certainly, if AIG, a major force in insurance had failed, there would be ripples in the economy. However, AIG and other insurance companies ultimately bowed to Spitzer's pressure and eliminated bid-rigging and other objectionable practices, fired wrongdoing employees, and otherwise cleaned house. Greenberg was not alone in leaving the CEO's suite—Marsh & McLennan's chairman and others were ousted as well.

In Spitzer's view, the absence of legal and regulatory restraints had fostered the grossly distorted climate that defined Wall Street by the late 1990s. The overwhelming message was one of huge egos and huge greed, exemplified by the excessive compensation packages of top CEOs. (The ratio of CEO compensation to that of the average worker soared from 41:1 in 1980 to 531:1 in 2002, according to *Vanity Fair.*) Although not necessarily illegal, the rubberstamping of gargantuan pay packages by compliant boards smacked of a downward spiral in business ethics, at the very least.

Worse, it seemed downright un-American. The message from top managers like GE's Jack Welch, Tyco's Dennis Kozlowski, and the New York Stock Exchange's Dick Grasso was that hard work did pay—but just for those willing and able to grab the prize, and not for the little guy. Spitzer's mission was not to wreck the system, but to put the shareholder back in control.

His crusades won him some public acclaim, but pure and unadulterated hatred on Wall Street (see above Institutional Investor dinner). He was widely viewed as Public Enemy Number One, with much of the criticism centering on his penchant for publicity. (Since his causes were, at least in some cases, obviously with merit, this was the second best line of attack.) Indeed, a Google search of "Eliot Spitzer + publicity hound" turns up 216 hits, and the Google results for "Eliot Spitzer" are topped by www.spitzer2006.com.

The financial press led the charge. Rob Norton wrote in *Fortune*: "[It's] pretty obvious that Spitzer went after Merrill primarily to boost his own political career rather than to seek justice for the small investor."[12] Wall Street commentator (and a longtime friend of Spitzer's) James Cramer said flatly, "Everyone on Wall Street hates this guy." Seizing on Spitzer's plans to run for governor, the august *Wall Street Journal* sniped about his "politically opportune campaign against Wall Street." And *Slate* observed that Spitzer was "temperamentally unable to stay out of the headlines for more than 72 hours."

Like Ness, it is undoubtedly true that Spitzer craves the headlines. But it's also true that Spitzer, like Ness, is a true believer who is determined to shake up business-as-usual on Wall Street and prod the Street into genuine, lasting reform. In all fairness, it should be noted that public-ity—while furthering Spitzer's political ambitions—is also an important tool in his drive to clean up the investment banking business. Financial institutions rest on their reputations, and Spitzer's ability to name-and-shame the biggest offenders is probably a much more powerful weapon than all of his prosecutorial tricks put together.

Thus even the *Wall Street Journal*'s editorial page has applauded Spitzer's drive to clean up the mutual funds industry, which was hard hit by revelations of shady practices that rigged the business in favor of the big, in-and-out investors at the expense of—guess who?—the little guys. Mutual funds, it turned out, were granting special privileges to favored big clients that included both illegal after-hours trading and very questionable (but legal) market timing practices. If it smelled a lot like IPO "spinning,"[13] that's because it was very similar, and Spitzer's role in probing and exposing these practices—not to mention the $3 billion in penalties that he extracted—can only be welcomed.

Even so, Spitzer's detractors in the financial and business world are too many to count. In early 2005 the president of the U.S. Chamber of Commerce launched a broadside against Spitzer, denouncing him for employing "the most egregious and unacceptable form of intimidation that we have ever seen in this country in modern times." For the most part, critics like this content themselves with attacking Spitzer's meth-odology (intimidation, publicity, overreaching) rather than his actual goals. But Spitzer, like Ness, should be judged first and foremost on his own goals and beliefs.

Spitzer decided early on that he would not focus on putting the wrongdoers in prison. He must have observed that his predecessors, like Rudolph Giuliani, were effective in throwing some high-profile offenders (like Michael Milken and Ivan Boesky) in jail, but the system chugged on unabated (and many of Giuliani's biggest cases were ultimately reversed or dismissed). Spitzer's former boss in the Manhattan district attorney's racketeering unit, Michael Cherkasky (now CEO of Marsh & McLennan), commented, "Prosecutors have classically done a very good job of putting people in jail, but it doesn't change anything."[14]

So Spitzer's goals were much loftier: to effect reform of the financial industry's fundamental structure, not just to rid the system of a few bad apples. (It could be argued that Ness, by contrast, focused on the biggest, baddst apple of all—Al Capone.) Spitzer aimed to achieve "real and rapid reform of American business," not just a few perp walks.[15] In pursuit of this goal, he worked methodically to:

1.   uncover a system-wide problem;
2.   apply pressure on the system with a few high-profile cases and publicity; and
3.   then use that leverage to effect system-wide reform, usually through a negotiated settlement.

In that sense, Spitzer probably views himself more as a policymaker than as a prosecutor. Certainly he did succeed in becoming an agent of change. Prodded and embarrassed by Spitzer's energetic anti-sleaze campaign, the once-somnolent SEC has become more aggressive in pursuing its own actions (though the SEC still does not inspire the fear that Spitzer does on Wall Street; insiders know that it takes forever to conclude an investigation, and that its penalties are relatively mild in the end). And stunned by the excesses that Spitzer helped to expose, Congress passed the Sarbanes-Oxley Act in 2002, the most far-reaching piece of financial legislation since the 1930s. (Sarb-Ox actually penalizes small businesses with *additional* costs, but more on that later.)

So did Spitzer succeed in his goal of using the law to change industry structure? In naming Spitzer its "Crusader of the Year" in 2002, *Time* proclaimed that "Wall Street would never be the same" again; Spitzer himself said, after the $1.4 billion banking settlement, that "this agreement will permanently change the way Wall Street operates." But is that hyperbole, or truth?

Early signs are not encouraging. In the end, the reins of regulatory power rest in Washington, not in New York, and it is hard to believe that Spitzer has changed any minds there, where it really matters. The Bush administration is firmly in the pro-business camp and indeed has very little understanding of (or interest in) the inner workings of Wall Street.

Bush has drawn his treasury secretaries from big business in a marked departure from the Clinton years—perhaps the best example of the ABC (Anything But Clinton) mentality that occasionally triumphs over common sense in the Bush White House. (This is not a political statement, by the way; many of the Wall Street excesses of the late 1990s took place on Clinton's watch.)

The crowning achievement of federal lawmakers on this issue, of course, is the Sarbanes-Oxley Act (SOX). This landmark legislation, ballyhooed as the most sweeping reform of the financial industry since the 1930s, aims to improve corporate governance and level the playing field. It requires public companies to:

- increase their level of financial statement disclosure;
- have a lawyer-approved internal code of ethics;
- restrict share trading by, and loans to, corporate officers; and
- ensure that the CEO and CFO personally attest to the accuracy of the financial statements.

In addition, SOX sets up a new accounting oversight board, and prohibits audit firms from performing consulting services and audit operations for the same client.

In its early years, SOX has proven to be, above all, a boon for lawyers and accountants (wags dub it the Consultants & Lawyers Full Employment Act, or the Accountants Relief Act). Costs of SOX compliance have gone through the roof, thanks to the higher costs of audits, legal opinions, insurance premiums for directors' and officers' liability insurance, and salaries of independent directors. Smaller public companies are among the hardest hit, with one survey finding that the average cost of being public for a company with annual revenues of under $1 billion has jumped 30 percent since 2002. Giant General Electric says that it has spent $30 million on updating and documenting its internal control system alone; total SOX costs for Fortune 1000 companies have probably exceeded $5 billion.

But is all this money being spent wisely? Most observers now agree that SOX was constructed in haste, following the public clamor that erupted after the Enron and WorldCom debacles, and that it is accordingly flawed (budding lawyers learn in their first year of law school that bad cases make bad laws). But Washington, both Republican and Democratic, and including the nominally pro-business Bush White House, leaped on the bandwagon and signed SOX into law in record time. The costs of compliance, and the unforeseen consequences of the law, are only now becoming apparent.

One unforeseen consequence, for example, is the likelihood that fewer companies will choose to go public—keeping their accounts shrouded in secrecy as a result. (This is akin to more people choosing to drive rather than fly because of new rules mandating that small children must be strapped into a car seat on an airplane; unfortunately, this decision endangers many more children than an airplane flight would.) A 2004 survey finds that more than 20 percent of public companies in the United States are thinking of going private because of the increased cost of government regulations, and a growing number of European companies are openly questioning the worth of a New York listing in the post-SOX environment. The finance director of a top European company recently told the *Financial Times*, "If we knew Sarbanes was coming, we never would have listed there."

To be fair, SOX is not the only spice in this mix. Auditors and lawyers are also taking a tougher stance on their clients, terrified of being the next Arthur Andersen; credit rating agencies have become more careful; and investors are demanding more transparent financial statements from their managers. But, inevitably, the post-SOX righteousness has spawned a growing backlash against the excess of regulation and oversight that it created.

Indeed, the Bush II administration has already indicated its intention of supporting the business lobby in its hostility to greater oversight. Governments are considering ways to protect auditors from huge legal claims in both the United States and UK (partly in response to furious lobbying by the remaining Big Four accounting firms). And the Financial Accounting Standards Board (FASB) reported in early 2005 that companies and auditors are "afraid of the new regime," unable to exercise their judgment because of fears that they will be challenged by overzealous regulators, plaintiffs' attorneys, and/or the media. Respected observer John Plender wrote in the *Financial Times*, "the watchdogs are out of control." The next act in the Kabuki play is getting underway, as too much reform and regulation inevitably gives way to deregulation and a return of the wild times.

Conclusion: Riding Off Into the Sunset?

Revisiting the Eliot Ness/Eliot Spitzer analogy, it still seems remarkably valid in many ways. In Ness's day, the feds got Capone on tax evasion; Spitzer, too, uses sideshows like tax evasion and obstruction of justice to bring down the wrongdoers. In the name of the public good, both men waded into messes that others have carefully avoided. Both have used and enjoyed publicity, partly for the public good and partly to further their own personal ambitions—but both are also true believers.

In the end, though, Eliot Ness probably accomplished little of lasting value. In the first place, it was not Ness but the dogged efforts of Treasury and Justice Department investigators that put Capone away; and in the second place, Capone was promptly replaced by a new generation of gangsters who continued and expanded his empire. So Ness got the headlines, but others got the job done—for what it was worth.

It is an unfortunate analogy for Spitzer, and for Wall Street on the whole. When Representative Michael Oxley (R-Ohio) charged angrily "the truth is that Eliot Spitzer is no Eliot Ness. As hard as he may be trying, it takes more than slapping on a hat to become untouchable," he may have been paying Spitzer a compliment. Indeed, what distinguishes Spitzer from other would-be reformers—and from Ness himself—is Spitzer's ability to identify the big issues that affect all of Wall Street, and his willingness to take on long-accepted business practices, no matter how deeply entrenched they have become. Ness went for the perp walks, but Spitzer is going for the system itself.

In the long term, though, their legacies may be the same. Spitzer was fortunate in that he, like Ness, emerged on the scene at a moment when public outrage was coming to the boil. The scandal cycle was at a point when reform was both welcome and overdue, and Spitzer was in the ideal position to jump into the fray—partly because the Bush administration only belatedly (and halfheartedly) caught on to the wave of public outrage. But several years after the fall of Enron, a popular backlash against regulation is, predictably, coming to the fore. Spitzer's eyes are now fixed on a higher prize—governor or perhaps even president—and industry lobbyists will take advantage of his distraction, public disinterest, and Washington's support, to swing the pendulum back again towards deregulation.

Indeed, there are already indications that the pendulum has swung. In early 2005, the *New York Times* reported that a leading portfolio manager had analyzed IPO financial statements since 1991, and found that 51 percent of companies that went public in 2004 had poor to very poor corporate governance practices. This was actually *up* from 37 percent during the wild stock market year of 1999 (though down from 63 percent in 2002). The manager observed that despite the plethora of new regulations, "the quality of governance has deteriorated in IPOs." The biggest problem: a dearth of truly independent directors—especially dismaying after the uproar on this issue that erupted in the post-Enron era.[16]

In another example, Tyco—remember them?—announced in early 2005 that its post-Kozlowski CEO, Edward Breen, was poised to earn at least $200 million from his unrestricted shares and stock options, which he received as part of his incentive compensation package for taking on the task of turning around Tyco. Considering that Tyco's core business was actually quite solid, making for a less-than-Herculean turnaround task, this seemed a throwback to the excessive comp days of the late 1990s.

These stories, while anecdotal, seem to confirm the suspicions of securities industry executives interviewed by the *Wall Street Journal* in 2002, who agreed that any changes in the industry as a result of Spitzer, SOX, et al. would be "minimal and short-lived." In a sense, Spitzer is two souls: a reformer, whose mark may be ephemeral; and the politician, whose odyssey is just beginning.

In the end, the myth of Eliot Ness was much more powerful than the man. Perhaps that will be the ultimate truth of the Eliot Ness/Eliot Spitzer analogy.

Notes

1.   Paul Heimel notes that this story, while widely circulated, may be apocryphal. It was detailed by Ness in his autobiography *The Untouchables* and passed along by word of mouth, but never documented by historians. Paul Heimel, *Eliot Ness: The True Story* (Nashville, TN: Cumberland House, 2nd edition, 2000), pp. 116-117.
2.   Adi Ignatius, "Crusader of the Year," *Time*, December 21, 2002, p. 18.
3.   Marilyn Bardsley, "Eliot Ness: The Man Behind the Myth," www.crimelibrary.com.
4.   Peter Canellos, "Enforcing Public Interest Can Be Bad Political Move," *Boston Globe*, December 21, 2004, p. 19.
5.   Quoted from Holly Brubach, "Spitzer's Justice," *Vanity Fair,* January 2005, p. 119.
6.   www.crimelibrary.com.
7.   Ibid.; Heimel, *Eliot Ness*, pp. 74-75.
8.   Capone, who had already been infected with syphilis, deteriorated both physically and mentally in prison. He was suffering from severe dementia by the time of his release, and died quietly in Florida in 1947.
9.   www.americanmafia.com.
10.   Jenny Anderson, "AIG Chief Cheerfully Carts Steady Course," *International Herald Tribune*, December 20, 2005. Originally in the *New York Times*. http://www.iht.com/bin/print_ipub.php?file=/articles/2005/12/20/business/aig.php.
11.   Ron Scherer, "A Top Insurance Company as the New Enron?" *Christian Science Monitor*, April 1, 2005, p. 20.
12.   Rob Norton, "The Problem with Eliot Spitzer," *Fortune*, July 8, 2002.
13.   Spinning was the practice, discussed in chapter 10, of allocating precious and scarce shares in hot IPOs to preferred investment banking clients.

14.   Mark Gimein, "Eliot Spitzer: The Enforcer," *Fortune,* September 16, 2002, p. 55.
15.   Ibid.
16.   Gretchen Morgenson, "New Stocks, Same Old Problems," *New York Times*, January 23, 2005, section 3, p. 1.

13

Conclusion

"History will be kind for me for I intend to write it."—Winston Churchill

The United States has a long history of financial scandals, rich in intriguingly complex individuals, angry and righteous reformers, a fickle media, indignant investors, and a dash of sex and violence. In this the United States is hardly unique. During the 1990s, for example, pyramid schemes created havoc in countries as diverse as Albania, Russia, and Suriname. Indeed, the eventual failure of Albania's pyramid schemes resulted in the collapse of law and order, leaving the country in a state of civil war ended only by the intervention of concerned neighbors. Italy is still cleaning up after exposing the shady dealings of food producer Parmalat, and questions have been raised about President Jacques Chirac's use of so-called "secret funds" while he was the mayor of Paris. China's creaky financial system has seen its own set of scandals, involving some high-ranking officials. Japan, the United Kingdom, and Germany too have seen their own fair share of financial scandals. All of this points to the universal tension in capitalism between what is legal, what is ethical, and what serves the community good.

What is unique about Wall Street is its role at the very core of global capitalism. For better or for worse, the dominant strand of U.S. business culture accepts and promotes risk taking. Fundamentally, finance is a game of high risk, high reward. As one New York bond trader once stated: "It is like being asked to put your manhood up on the table for a bet and daring anyone to chop it off. If they don't, you walk off with a pile of cash. If they do, well…" While this description may be a bit of a graphic overstatement, it does underscore the central issue of risk-reward. (Fortunately most "bets" in financial markets are made on stocks, bonds, and derivatives and do not involve body parts.)

The nature of the business of finance promotes risk-taking. The risk-reward element is usually restrained on the risk side by credit research, quantitative modeling, and compliance officers. Greed is a motivating force, but the system of checks and balances is meant to keep people from being "too greedy." This returns us to the image of the film *Wall Street* and one of its main characters, Gordon Gekko, who is increasingly driven by the excitement of the deal and winning, as opposed to the accumulation of wealth. Where this system runs into contradictions is with the promotion of risk (and greed) within reasonable bounds. Yet when business cultures shift as the result of technological and financial production innovations, the goalposts have a tendency to be moved—at least until they are realigned by events and regulators. And while the goalposts are on the move, the "too greedy" impulse becomes a problem, especially when it becomes the house business culture fronted by investment bankers and traders and supported by lawyers and accountants, a fawning media, compliant authorities, and a bedazzled public. When the denouement comes, it is often rapid, brutal, and disorienting, leaving behind a societal and economic disequilibrium that takes years to recover.

This was certainly the case with Refco Inc., in October 2005. Refco was an independent provider of execution and clearing services for exchange-traded derivatives, and a major provider of prime brokerage services in the fixed income and foreign exchange markets. The company had operations in fourteen countries, some 200,000 customer accounts, and a well-respected management team under Cambridge University graduate Philip Bennett. Or so it seemed. On October 10, 2005, the company disclosed that Bennett had concealed debt from investors and auditors—some $430 million—and that financial statements for the years 2002-2005 should not be relied upon. Seven days later, Refco filed for bankruptcy, one of the most rapid such descents from the corporate heights in years. What made the Refco scandal all the more embarrassing was that the company had only ten weeks earlier sold shares to the public for the first time, raising $670 million at $22 a share. This meant that both investment banks and accountants failed in their due diligence to discover a significant financial fraud. The ensuing allegations that the company's CEO was personally involved in fraud sparked a terminal crisis of confidence that was rapid, brutal, and disorienting.

Having looked back over more than 200 years of U.S. history, it is clear that the drama of American kabuki has been played and replayed. As U.S. historian Kevin Phillips noted in 2002: "Near the peak of the great booms, old economic cautions are dismissed, financial and managerial operators sidestep increasingly inadequate regulations and ethics surrender to greed. Then, after the collapse, the dirty linen falls out of the closet. Public muttering usually swells into a powerful chorus for reform—deep, systemic changes designed to catch up with a whole new range and capacity for frauds and finagles and bring them under regulatory control."[1]

Although booms may provide an impetus for scandals, financial fraud can occur wherever the money goes. In many regards, financial scandals are much like a balloon. Squeeze one part of the balloon and the air is forced into another part of the balloon, often in a distorted way. In this sense, the supposedly deep, systemic changes designed to catch up with the market and prevent frauds and bring them under regulatory control are limited. There are no foolproof safeguards.

Nonetheless, the reformers keep fighting. In the early twenty-first century, the well-publicized, hard-charging New York Attorney General Eliot Spitzer and anti-corruption legislation of the Sarbanes-Oxley Act and the USA Patriot Act aimed to clean up the vast sweep of Wall Street as investment banks, insurance companies, mutual funds, and insurance brokerages all fell under increased regulatory scrutiny. Fines were paid, people went to prison, and new measures were adopted to insure financial probity. Financial reporting is conducted with better disclosure and transparency.

Many of the companies hit by corruption problems have worked hard to steer away from past practices. As *USA Today* commented of Tyco International post-Kozlowski (in January 2005): "The plush Park Avenue headquarters is gone. So is the liquidity crisis. So are the million-dollar birthday bashes, the eight digit bonuses for the senior executives and the acquisition binge that pushed Tyco's debt load to the breaking point."[2] Tyco International is hardly alone in seeking to move away from bad practices that led to scandals and corporate upheaval.

Even the media, once a source of much uncritical praise of corporate chiefs, turned a corner and became more critical. Along these lines, *Barron's*, the long established premier publication of Wall Street, dared to question the legacy of General Electric's former CEO, Jack Welch, in late 2005. *Barron's* Jonathan Laing asked: "Wonder why GE's profit growth isn't what it used to be? One reason: a $9.4 billion insurance-reserve deficit former CEO Jack Welch bequeathed to his successor."[3] What the journalist suggested was that Welch intentionally under-reserved GE's reinsurance unit to pump up short-term profits, at the expense of the longer term. According to Laing: "During the last five years of the Welch era, ended in 2001, GE's reported earnings jumped from 72 cents a share to $1.37, a rise of 65 cents a share, or 90.2%—spectacular for a behemoth like GE. But without a massive under-reserving at its reinsurance unit, the company would have shown a cumulative earnings gain of just four cents, or 5.6%." Although not necessarily "illegal," someone had to pay for the deficit in later years. In this case it has been Welch's successor, Jeff Immelt, whose tenure at the helm of GE has been marked by relatively lackluster earnings, partially caused by a build-up of reserves (necessary to help GE sell off the reinsurance unit).

Welch responded to Laing's article, arguing that the article was "one of the oldest tricks in the book—to isolate one factor in a large, complex company and twist it to make a point about an entire enterprise."[4] *Barron's*, however, couldn't let the manner rest, adding to a rebuttal from Laing the comments of one Bonnie A. Hughes: "Corporate chiefs like Jack Welch have left the 'little people' in their wake as they close plants and make other life-altering decisions for workers, while taking more gold for themselves." Over-hyped and probably over-compensated, Welch can hardly be put in the same gang as the fallen corporate gods of Enron, WorldCom, or Adelphia. Yet the moral tone of *Barron's* comes close to doing just that, leaving a lingering wisp of a thought projected at the reader: Welch is a modern-day robber baron.

Despite the change in moral environment, the end of the boom, and subsequent regulatory clampdown, the balloon was only squeezed rather than popped, leaving money and talent to flow elsewhere. Part of the problem is that over the last fifteen years (1990-2005), financial instruments became increasingly complex as more parties used financial engineers to manipulate earnings and avoid regulation.[5] One consequence of this is that control and ownership of companies moved (and continues to move) further apart, as even sophisticated investors could not monitor increasingly aggressive managers. Consequently, when it came to reform, the full scope of the problem was not addressed. As one former participant in U.S. capital markets noted of the passage of such legislation as Sarbanes-Oxley and the USA Patriot Act: "But the reforms were largely cosmetic and did not address the profound changes in financial markets."[6]

The Tension Issue

Capitalism represents an ongoing tension between profit maximization and the good of the community, sometimes not the same thing. As Raymond Baker, author of *Capitalism's Achilles Heel: Dirty Money and How to Renew the Free-Market System*, and Jennifer Nordin, a director of economic studies at the Center for International Policy, noted: "This tension points to a fundamental question: which should come first for the global industry—maximizing profits or pursuing lawful and just business transactions?"[7] In many cases, capitalists are tempted to cut corners in order to make money and this is where the scandals occur.

With an economy increasingly dominated by financial services, anything that roils the financial markets, like a major scandal, has a greater possibility of rippling through the rest of the economy. The combination of Enron, WorldCom, and Tyco International was bruising for the U.S. economy, in particular, as the downfall of these behemoths killed business confidence and sent investors out of the market with substantial losses. The words "wealth destruction" meant the loss of billions of dollars of retirement money and squeezed the economy. Management in the business sector was not focused on productivity and profits, but on survival, by cleaning up balance sheets and making certain that accounting practices were more conservative and transparent. It can easily be said that what was best for the community was not on the minds of those who led Enron, Adelphia, and Tyco.

There is another aspect of this in terms of placing an overemphasis on profits and that is short-term thinking, which is leading to an erosion of U.S. competitiveness. Although the emphasis on short-term profitability is not a fraudulent act, it is part of the "too much greed" dynamic. When companies focus on quarter-by-quarter profitability (often in order to fatten the bonuses of the top managers), they do so at the risk of not investing in sufficient longer-term research and development.

In testimony to the U.S. Congress in 2005, William R. Brody, president of Johns Hopkins University, raised concerns about the drying up of the U.S. innovation pipeline, something that is essential to the nation's long-term productivity and economic well-being. A decline in innovation would mean that U.S. competitiveness in important high-tech areas would fall behind that of China, India, and Western Europe. He noted that about one-third of all jobs in the United States require science or technology competency, but only 17 percent of Americans graduate with science or technology majors. Brody added that U.S. federal research and development spending as a percentage of GDP peaked in 1965, at just under 2 percent. In 2005, it stands around 0.8 percent. By 2010, it is anticipated that the emerging economies of Asia will produce more patents and spend more on R&D than the United States.[8]

Moreover, the United States has already made the shift from being the leader in global high-tech exports (at 31 percent in 1980), to being a net importer. Rounding out the picture, the U.S. Council of Competitiveness research shows that the real income of many Americans did not improve during the economic boom of the last decades of the twentieth century. This was the same period when outrageous salaries were advanced to the management teams of major U.S. companies, including Enron, Tyco, and WorldCom. Accordingly, Brody notes that the overwhelming "drumbeat of quarterly results are driving business decisions and drowning out long-term management, investment and innovation strategies." This relates back to impatient investors with short-term horizons. It should come as no shock that shareholder return is the number one priority of most CEOs (and their compensation) and that "innovation" ranks far behind.

Although the criticism of an overemphasis on short-term thinking does not immediately equate to financial scandals, there is a relationship. Americans place a massive level of importance on the financial sector. More Americans than ever before are linked to the stock market, either by directly holding stocks and bonds, or through pension programs, or through their dealings with an insurance company or bank. Thanks to the dominance of financial services in the U.S. economy, the pressure to accumulate large profits combines with the promotion of risk taking and—in some cases—with too much greed, ending up in a financial scandal. The simple math is that as financial services dominate the economy, any major ripples in the system caused by fraud in this sector are all the more damaging to the rest of U.S. economy. Despite the tighter regulatory environment created by Eliot Spitzer, other state attorneys general, Sarbanes-Oxley, and the Patriot Act, the next scandal is already lurking not far from the light of regulatory scrutiny.

Certainly areas where problems could occur include derivatives and hedge funds, two areas where financial innovation has run well ahead of the regulatory regime. According to the International Swaps and Derivatives Association, the global market for credit derivatives stood at $12.43 trillion as of the end of June 2005, up 128 percent from the same period in 2004. Hedge funds and the assets they have under management have also mushroomed. From relatively small numbers in 2000, the hedge fund industry has more than doubled by 2005 to 8000 funds, managing $1.37 trillion in assets. Credit derivatives and hedge funds are likely to see further growth as both represent ways that investors can have their investment objectives and the management of risk tailored for their specific needs. Indeed, in a recent survey of finance professors at the top fifty business schools worldwide conducted by the International Swaps and Derivatives Association, respondents overwhelmingly agreed that credit derivatives help companies manage financial risk more effectively and that the impact on the global financial system is beneficial.[9]

At the same time, these areas are not without risk. As financial journalist Roger Lowenstein noted in 2005: "So forget hedge funds; if you're searching for the next financial storm try derivatives. (Nothing much you can do about them either.).Come to think about it, most of the sudden financial disasters of the previous decade—Orange County, L.T.C.M., Enron—involved derivatives, too."[10] Concerns have been raised about the efficiency of back office operations (i.e., documentation backlogs) for those institutions trading credit derivatives, settlement of credit derivative trades, and the danger of the wrong people (i.e., the financially unsophisticated) getting their hands on them (think Orange County). As one former Moody's analyst quipped about trading in credit derivatives: "This is something that should not be tried at home, i.e. better leave it to the experts."

The danger with credit derivatives is the potential for a rogue trader, especially in light of concerns about documentation backlogs. This was certainly the problem at Barings, where a rogue trader exploited inadequate back office operations when conducting complex straddle trades. In response to these concerns there has been a major push coming from international regulators. As the Bank for International Settlements understated in November 2005: "While work is under way in the financial industry to improve the market infrastructure for these transactions, further progress is required to enhance market stability."[11] Indeed.

As for hedge funds, the need for tougher regulation (after a rising number of scandals as with Bayou Management and Wood River Partners) is forcing the industry to improve on self-regulation. Local regulators are also more focused. For many hedge fund managers, however, the intense pressure to make profits in what has become an increasingly crowded field makes the need for better compliance all that more compelling. As one hedge fund manager explained: "No one wants to cut that corner and have the regulators show up. It is bad for business. With so many new funds cropping up every day, any whiff of trouble and the money walks out the door."

Is Regulation the Answer?

It appears that every time a major financial scandal occurs and the reverberations ripple through society, there is a clamor for more regulation. This was observable with the Progressive movement, the Pecora investigations, FDR's 100 days, the S&L crisis, and the aftermath of the last great boom and ensuing scandals. Each round of scandal seems to produce new agencies and regulations. The public is left looking at a sometimes bewildering universe of an alphabet stew of acronyms. Yet, for all the regulation, scandals still occur. As a Standard & Poor's report in November 2005 noted of Sarbanes-Oxley: "[I]t is becoming clear that it will take more than beefed up internal financial controls to guarantee sterling corporate performance. The financial fraud at Refco Inc. in the U.S. is a recent example of the limited ability of enhanced regulation and financial controls to eliminate corporate wrongdoing."[12]

Because of past scandals in the United States and elsewhere, there is now an extensive system of committees, organizations, rules, and guidelines that seek to govern and manage the international financial system. Among those institutions are the International Monetary Fund, the Bank for International Settlements, the Basel committees on banking, and the International Swaps and Derivatives Association. The idea behind this sweeping patchwork of institutions, committees, and guidelines is to create a more homogenous financial system, capable of reducing disruptions caused by financial crisis (including scandals as depicted in this book).

Despite all the efforts to regulate the nooks and crannies of the financial world, innovation and greed run counter to control. This means that the existing framework (bolstered in the United States by Sarbanes-Oxley and other measures) ultimately fails to fully take into account the danger posed by a financial scandal in a major institution. Technology, innovation, and globalization have augmented the danger of contagion. Indeed, it can be argued that efforts to create a more homogeneous financial system could actually increase systemic fragility.[13]

Conclusion

Whenever there is a whiff of scandal in the air, we think of apples. Are the scandals the result of a few bad apples or is the entire orchard afflicted with blight? The historical record suggests that there are a few bad apples, but they keep coming back. Then again, without the bad apples, American financial history would be that much more boring, the ups and downs that much less giddy, and the drama that much more insipid. And without some degree of creative destruction, there would be no major advances.

Financial scandals are part of the landscape of American history. Although this is not a source a pride, it reflects the Darwinian aspect of business, the pressure to maximize profits and to fulfill individual greed. Short of completely overhauling the U.S. socioeconomic system, it is difficult to see how this could change, despite the growing inequalities evident in the country. This leaves the words of Mark Twain to be most apt: "If you pick up a starving dog and make him prosperous, he will not bite you. This is the principal difference between a dog and a man." Looking at the likes of Jay Gould, Daniel Drew, and Kenneth Lay, Twain's words have a historical echo that just will not go away.

Notes

1.   Kevin Phillips, "The Cycles of Financial Scandal," *New York Times*, July 17, 2002, p. A22.
2.   Leslie Cauley, "CEO Leads Troubled Tyco Into Turnaround," *USA Today*, January 24, 2005, Special Reprint edition, available on Tyco International website, http://ytyco.com/www/Documents/pdf/usatoday_jan_05.pdf.
3.   Jonathan R. Laing, "Jack's Magic: Revising a Legacy," *Barron's*, December 26, 2005, p. 17.
4.   "That Old Jack Magic: Jack Welch's Response to Jonathan Laing," *Barron's*, January 2, 2006, p. 34.
5.   Frank Partnoy, *Infectious Greed: How Deceit and Risk Corrupted the Financial Markets* (New York: Times Books, 2003), p. 3.
6.   Ibid., p. 393.
7.   Raymond Baker and Jennifer Nordin, "How Dirty Money Thwarts Capitalism's True Course," *Financial Times*, October 11, 2005, p. 19.
8.   Remarks by William R. Brody, president of The Johns Hopkins University, "U.S. Competitiveness: The Innovation Challenge," Testimony to the House Committee on Science, July 21, 2005. Most of the data in this paragraph and the following one are culled from Brody's testimony.
9.   See International Swaps and Derivatives Association, *A Survey of Finance Professors' Views on Derivatives*, Survey Conducted by The International Swaps and Derivatives Association, March 2004, 19th Annual General Meeting, Chicago, p. 4.
10.   Roger Lowenstein, "See a Bubble?" *New York Times Magazine*, June 5, 2005, p. 21.
11.   Bank for International Settlements, "FSF Meets with the Hedge Fund Community and Their Counterparts," November 29, 2005.
12.   George Dallas and Neri Bukspan, "Corporate Governance: A New Era Goes Beyond Regulation," *Standard & Poor's CreditWeek*, November 30, 2005, p. 12.
13.   This argument is taken up by Hern Alexander, Rahul Dhumale, and John Eatwell, *Global Governance of Financial Systems: The International Regulation of Systemic Risk* (New York: Oxford University Press, 2005).

Selected Bibliography

Primary Sources

Bank for International Settlements, "FSF Meets with the Hedge Fund Community and Their Counterparts," Press Release, November 29, 2005.

Brody, William R., President of the Johns Hopkins University, "U.S. Competitiveness: The Innovation Challenge," Testimony to the House Committee on Science, July 21, 2005. Washington, D.C.

Grafton, John, editor, *Great Speeches: Franklin Delano Roosevelt* (Mineola, New York: Dover Publications, Inc., 1999).

Insull, Samuel, *The Memoirs of Samuel Insull: An Autobiography* (Polo, Illinois: Transportation Trails, 1992).

International Monetary Fund, *Global Financial Stability Report: Market Developments and Issues, April 2005* (Washington, D.C.: International Monetary Fund, 2005).

International Swaps and Derivatives Association, *A Survey of Finance Professors' Views on Derivatives*, Survey Conducted by the International Swaps and Derivatives Association, March 2004. Prepared for the 19th Annual General Meeting, Chicago.

McCain, Senator John, "Speech on Corporate Governance Reform," National Press Club, July 11, 2002, http://mccain.senate.gov./index.cfm?fuseaction=Newscenter.ViewPressRelease&Content_…

National Association of Securities Dealers (NASD), News Release, "NASD Fines and Suspends Phua Young, Former Merrill Lynch Research Analyst," May 25, 2004.

Roosevelt, Franklin Delano, "Commonwealth Club Address," September 23, 1932, San Francisco, California, quoted from http://www.americanrhetoric.com/speecjes/fdrcommonwealth.htm.

United States Senate, Permanent Subcommittee on Investigations of the Committee on Governmental Affairs, "The Role of the Board of Directors in Enron's Collapse" (Washington, D.C.), July 8, 2002.

Articles

Anderson, Jenny, "AIG Chief Cheerfully Charts Steady Course," *International Herald Tribune*, December 20, 2005. Originally published in *New York Times*. http://www.iht.com/bin/print_ipub.php?file=articles/2005/12/20/business/aig.php.

Baker, Raymond and Jennifer Nordin, "How Dirty Money Thwarts Capitalism's True Course," *Financial Times*, October 11, 2005: 19.

Bartlett, Sarah, "Curbing Excess on Wall Street," *New York Times*, December 25, 1988: C1.

Beales, Richard, "Derivatives: Popular Credit Market Still Too Opaque," *Financial Times*, January 6, 2006: 15.

Beales, Richard, "Sequel Could Contain Many Plot Twists," *Financial Times*, January 6, 2006: 18.

Buffett, Warren, "Who Really Cooks the Books," *New York Times*, July 24, 2002.

BusinessWeek, "The Top 25 Managers—Managers to Watch," *Business Week Online,* January 8, 2001.

Cahan, Vicky, Douglas A. Harbrecht, and Richard Fly, "What Washington Can Do To Clean Up the Street," *Business Week*, March 2, 1987: 35.

"Case Study: Daiwa," available at www.erisks.com.

"Case Study: Orange County," available at www.erisks.com.

Cassidy, John, "The Greed Cycle," *New Yorker*, September 23, 2002.

Dallas, George and Neri Bukspan, "Corporate Governance: A New Era Goes Beyond Regulation," *Standard & Poor's CreditWeek*, November 30, 2005: 12-17.

De Long, J. Bradford, "Robber Barons," University of California at Berkeley, January 1, 1998, http://econ161berkeley.edu/Econ_Articles/carnegie/delong_moscow.paper2.html.

Dowell, William, "I Didn't Set Out To Rob A Bank," *Time*, February 10, 1997.

Duffy, Michael, "By the Sign of the Crooked E," *Time.com*, January 19, 2002.

Economist, "Italian Banking: Year-end Accounts," *Economist*, December 24, 2005: 98.

Economist Editorial, "Enron a year on," *Economist*, November 28, 2002.

Eichenwald, Kurt, "After a Boom, There Will Be Scandal," *New York Times*, December 16, 2002: C3.

Eichenwald, Kurt, "Wages Even Wall Street Can't Stomach," *New York Times*, April 3, 1989: D1.

Gerth, Jeff, "The Savings Debacle," *New York Times*, July 3, 1990: D5.

Glater, Jonathan D., "Caught Between Doing Well and Doing Good," *New York Times*, November 18, 2005.

Gullapalli, Diya, "Living with Sarbanes-Oxley," *Wall Street Journal*, October 17, 2005: R1-R3.

Hansell, Saul, "Joseph Jett: A Scoundrel or a Scapegoat?" *New York Times*, April 6, 1997.

Hitt, Jack, "American Kabuki: The Ritual of Scandal," *New York Times* (The Week in Review), July 18, 2004: 1-3.

Hoagland, Jim, "A Tsunami of Scandal," *Washington Post*, July 7, 2002.

Jahnke, Art, "Did Michael Milken Deserve a Pardon?" *Darwin*, January 22, 2001, available at www.darwinmag.com.

Jorion, Philippe, "Orange County Case: Using Value at Risk to Control Financial Risk," available at www.gsm.uci.edu.

Kay, John, "Business Leaders Have No Natural Authority," *Financial Times*, April 15, 2005: 17.

Kelleher, Ellen and Andrea Felsted, "A Year On, Spitzer Keeps Up the Pressure," *Financial Times*, October 14, 2005: 20.

Kinsley, Michael, "Wall Street's Other Scandal," *Washington Post*, March 5, 1987: A27.

Knight, Jerry, "The S&L—Junk Bond Link," *Washington Post*, February 18, 1990: H1.

Knight, Jerry, "Puny Penalty, Given Damage to Investors," *Washington Post*, May 4, 2003.

Labaton, Stephen, "Crime and Consequences Still Weigh on Corporate World," *New York Times*, January 5, 2006: C1, C4.

Lagone, Ken, "Boondoggle of a Case," *Wall Street Journal*, September 30, 2005: A10.

Laing, Jonathan R., "Jack's Magic: Revising a Legacy," *Barron's*, December 26, 2005: 17-18.

Leith, William, "How to Lose a Billion," *Guardian*, October 26, 2002.

Leonard, Devin, "The Adelphia Story," *Fortune*, August 12, 2002.

Lowenstein, Roger, "See A Bubble?" *New York Times Magazine*, June 5, 2005: 19-22.

MacDonald, Scott B., "Are Derivatives a Threat to U.S. Banks?" *KWR International Advisor #10*, August 2001.

———, "Life Among the Ruins—The U.S. Economy Post-9/11," *KWR International Advisor*, November 2001.

———, "The Rise and Fall of the Glass-Steagall Act," *Financial History* (Publication of the Museum of American Financial History), Issue 83, 2005.

———, "U.S. Markets—Is the Paradigm Changing?" *Financial Sense Online*, May 7, 2004.

McCartney, Robert J., "Michael Milken's Trail of Injured Parties," *Washington Post*, April 29, 1990: H1.

McGeehan, Patrick, "Masters of the Universe, Leached (for Now)," *New York Times*, July 18, 2004: WK3.

Michaels, J. W., "History Lesson," *Forbes*, December 24, 1990: 38.

Michaels, "My Story—Michael Milken," *Forbes*, March 16, 1992: 78.

Mock, Sanford J., "The Credit Mobilier: Financial Scandal of the 1860s," *Financial History* (Publication of the Museum of American Financial History) (Winter 2004): 30-34.

Moel, Alberto and Robert C. Merton, "Savings and Loans and the Mortgage Markets" (Boston: Harvard Business School Publishing, 1997).

Morgenson, Gretchen, "Same Old Greed, Different Scoundrels in 2005," *International Herald Tribune*, January 1, 2006. Originally published in *New York Times*. http://www.iht.com/bin/print_ipub.php?file=articles2006/01/01/yourmoney/morgenson.php.

———, "Another Slap at Democracy on Wall Street," *New York Times*, August 23, 2002.

———, "Salomon Memo Hints at Favor on New Stock," *New York Times*, August 28, 2002.

————, "Three Banks Had Early Concerns on WorldCom," *New York Times*, March 16, 2004.

Mumma, Christopher, "Case Against Greenberg Would Proceed Under AIG Suit Settlement," *Bloomberg.com*, January 10, 2006. http://www.bloomberg.com/apps/news?pid=71000001&refer=news_index&sid=aJDNxua.

"Neutron Jack and His Electric Affair," *Guardian*, March 17, 2002.

Norris, Floyd, "S.E.C. Agrees on Set of Principles For Fining Companies for Fraud," *New York Times*, January 5, 2006: C1, C5.

Peltz, Michael, "Riding the Hedge Fund Boom," *Bloomberg Markets*, May 2005: 56-65.

Peltz, Michael, "Paradigm Lost: Bankers Trust Chairman Charles Sanford Jr.'s 'Particle Finance' Theory," *Institutional Investor*, April 1, 1995.

Phillips, Kevin, "The Cycles of Financial Scandal," *New York Times*, July 17, 2002.

Richter, Paul, "Ranking Milken Among the Rogues," *New York Times*, April 29, 1990: D1.

Roberts, Russell, "Jim Fisk, Wall Street Scoundrel, Con Artist and Schemer," *Financial History* (Winter 2002): 2-5.

Robinson, Edward, "Behind the Rot at Refco," *Bloomberg Markets*, February 2006: 36-49.

Rowe, James L. Jr., "S&L's Junk Bond Investments Arouse Concerns," *Washington Post*, December 21, 1986: K1.

Rudolph, Barbara and John Greenwald, "Where's the Limit?" *Time*, December 5, 1988: 66.

Saporito, Bill, "How Fastow Helped Enron Fall," *Time* (Online Edition), February 10, 2002, http://www.time.com/time/business/article/0,8599,201871,00.html.

Scanell, Kara, Ian McDonald and Ianthe Jeanne Dugan, "Bayou Duo Plead Guilty to Fraud," *Wall Street Journal*, September 30, 2005: C1, C4.

Schack, Justin, "Settling for Nothing," *Institutional Investor*, October 2005: 26-36.

Schrage, Michael, "Drexel's Demise Should Be a Warning about Financial Innovation," *Washington Post*, February 16, 1990: C3.

Simpson, Glenn R., "Drexel-Hill Connection," *Washington Post*, February 26, 1990: D1.

Taub, Stephen, "Labor of Love," *Institutional Investor*, March 2005: 24-28.

Teitelbaum, Richard, "AIG Takes the Heat," *Bloomberg Markets*, May 2005: 32-46.

Thomas, Landon, Jr., "On Wall Street: A Rise in Dismissals Over Ethics," *New York Times*, March 29, 2005: C9.

Time, "Damnation of Mitchell," *Time* Archive, March 6, 1933, http://www.time.com/time/archive/preview/0,10987,745272,00.html.

————, "Dome Comes Home," October 24, 1927, *Time* Archive, http:www.time.com/time/archive/preview/0,10987,736904,00.html.

————, "Judge for Bankers," *Time* Archive, April 20, 1936, http://www.time.com/time/archive/preview/0,10987,848540,00.html.

————, "Long, Long Trial," April 9, 1928, *Time* Archive, http://www.time. com/time/archive/preview/0,10987,787077,00.html.

————, "Teapot Dome," October 11, 1926: *Time* Archive http://www.time. com/time/archive/preview/0,10987,729532,00.html.

————, "Wealth on Trial," *Time* Archive, June 12, 1933, http://www.time/archive/preview/0,10987,745668,00.html.

Ulick, Jake, "Year of the Scandal," *money.cnn.com*, December 17, 2002.

Vise, David A., "Fallen Wall Street Banker Wanted To Be the Best," *Washington Post*, February 17, 1987: A1.

Vise, David A. and Steve Coll, "Drexel Study Says Junk Bonds Make Companies Grow," *Washington Post*, May 20, 1987: 64.

Wall Street Journal Editorial, "CEOs in Handcuffs," *Wall Street Journal*, July 26, 2002.

Wall Street Journal Editorial, "The $500 Million Scapegoat," *Wall Street Journal*, March 10, 1992: A18.

Walsh, Sharon Warren and Jerry Knight, "Junk Bonds Lobby Fights Ban on Investment," *Washington Post*, July 25, 1989: D1.

Wood, David, "Red Flags in Management Culture, Strategies, and Practices," *Standard & Poor's CreditWeek*, November 30, 2005: 21-24.

Yago, Glenn, "The Regulatory Reign of Terror," *Wall Street Journal*, March 4, 1992.

Books

Ackerman, Kenneth D., *The Gold Ring: Jim Fisk, Jay Gould, and Black Friday, 1869* (New York: Carroll and Graf Publishers, 1988, 2005).

Adams, William Howard, *Gouverneur Morris: An Independent Life* (New Haven: Yale University Press, 2003).

Albion, Robert Greenhalgh, *Rise of New York Port, 1815-1860* (New York: Charles Scriber & Sons, 1939).

Allen, Frederick Lewis, *Only Yesterday: An Informal History of the 1920s* (New York: John Wiley & Sons, Inc., 1997). Originally published in 1931.

Bain, David Howard, *Empire Express: Building the First Transcontinental Railroad* (New York: Penguin Books, 1999).

Bates, J. Leonard, *The Origins of Teapot Dome: Progressives, Parties and Petroleum* (Urbana: University of Illinois Press, 1963).

Beard, Patricia, *After the Bell: Gilded Age Secrets, Boardroom Betrayals, and the Party That Ignited the Great Wall Street Scandal of 1905* (New York: Perennial, 2003).

Bergreen, Laurence, *Capone: The Man and His Era* (New York: Simon & Schuster, 1994).

Bonner, Bill and Addison Wiggin, *Empire of Debt: The Rise of an Epic Financial Crisis* (Hoboken, NJ: John Wiley and Sons, 2006).

Borrough, Bryan and John Helyes, *Barbarians at the Gate* (New York: Harper Perennial, 1991).

Borrows, Edwin G. and Mike Wallace, *Gotham: A History of New York City to 1898* (New York: Oxford University Press, 1999).

Brands, H. W., *The Reckless Decade: America in the 1890s* (Chicago: The University of Chicago Press, 1995).

Brooks, John, *The Go-Go Years: The Drama and Crashing Finale of Wall Street's Bullish 60s* (New York: John Wiley and Sons, 1973, 1999).

———, *Once in Golconda: A True Drama of Wall Street 1920-1938* (New York: John Wiley and Sons, 1969, 1999).

Bruck, Connie, *The Predators' Ball* (New York: Simon & Schuster, 1988).

Bryce, Robert, *Pipe Dreams: Greed, Ego, and the Death of Enron* (New York: Public Affairs, 2002).

Bunting, Josiah III, *Ulysses S. Grant* (New York: Time Books, 2004).

Byron, Christopher, *Martha Inc: The Incredible Story of Martha Stewart Living Omnimedia* (Hoboken, NJ: John Wiley & Sons, 2003).

Calavita, Kitty, Henry N. Pontell, and Robert H. Tillman, *Big Money Crime: Fraud and Politics in the Savings and Loan Crisis* (Berkeley: University of California Press, 1997).

Cerami, Charles A., *Great Gamble: The Remarkable Story of Jefferson, Napoleon and the Men Behind the Louisiana Purchase* (New York: Source Books, 2003).

Chace, James, *1912: Wilson, Roosevelt, Taft and Debs—The Election That Changed the Country* (New York: Simon & Schuster, 2004).

Chernow, Ron, *Alexander Hamilton* (New York: Penguin Press, 2004).

———, *The House of Morgan: An American Banking Dynasty and the Rise of Modern Finance* (New York: Touchstone Book, 1990).

Colbert, David, *Eyewitness to Wall Street: Four Hundred Years of Dreamers, Schemers, Busts and Booms* (New York: Broadway Books, 2001).

Cowen, David, *The Origins and Economic Impact of the First Bank of the United States, 1791-1797* (London: Garland, 2000).

Davis, Margaret Leslie, *Dark Side of Fortune: Triumph and Scandal in the Life of Oil Tycoon Edward L. Doheny* (Berkeley: University of California Press, 1998).

Day, Kathleen, *S&L Hell* (New York: W.W. Norton & Company, 1993).

Dean, John W., *Warren G. Harding* (New York: Time Books, 2004).

De Borchgrave, Alexandra, *Villard: The Life and Times of an American Titan* (New York: 2001).

Ferguson, Naill, *Colossus: The Price of America's Empire* (New York: Penguin Press, 2004).

Fischel, Daniel, *Payback: The Conspiracy to Destroy Michael Milken and His Financial Revolution* (New York: Harper Collins, 1995).

Galbraith, John Kenneth, *The Great Crash 1929* (Boston: Houghton, Mifflin Company, 1951).

Geist, Charles, *Wall Street: A History* (New York: Oxford University Press, 1997).

Gordon, John Steele, *The Great Game: The Emergence of Wall Street as a World Power 1653-2000* (New York: Scribner, 1999).

———, *The Scarlet Woman of Wall Street: Jim Gould, Jim Fisk, Cornelius Vanderbilt, The Erie Railway Wars, and the Birth of Wall Street* (New York: Weidenfeld & Nicolson, 1988).

Hielscher, Udo, *Financing the American Revolution: The American Revolution and the Origins of Wall Street in Contemporary Financial Documents* (New York: Museum of American Financial History, 2003).

Hofstadter, Richard, *The Age of Reform: From Byran to F.D.R.* (New York: Vintage Books, 1955).

Hughes, Jane and Scott B. MacDonald, *Carnival on Wall Street: Global Financial Markets in the 1990s* (Hoboken, NJ: John Wiley & Sons, 2004).

Jeffers, H. Paul, *An Honest President: The Life and Presidencies of Grover Cleveland* (New York: Harper Collins, 2000).

Jeter, Lynne W., *Disconnected: Deceit and Betrayal at WorldCom* (Hoboken, NJ: John Wiley & Sons, 2003).

Jacobs, Jane, *Dark Age Ahead* (Toronto: Vintage Canada, 2005).

Jett, Joseph with Sabra Chartrard, *Black and White on Wall Street: The Untold Story of the Man Wrongly Accused of Bringing Down Kidder Peabody* (New York: William Morrow & Company, 1999).

Jorion, Philippe, *Big Bets Gone Bad: Derivatives and Bankruptcy in Orange County* (San Diego: Academic Press, 1995).

Josephson, Matthew, *The Robber Barons* (New York: Harcourt, Inc., 1962). Originally published in 1934.

Karabell, Zachary, *Chester Alan Arthur* (New York: Henry Holt and Company, 2004).

Kessner, Thomas, *Capital City: New York City and the Men Behind America's Rise to Economic Dominance, 1860-1990* (New York: Simon & Schuster, 2003).

Klein, Maury, *The Life and Legend of Jay Gould* (Baltimore: The Johns Hopkins University Press, 1986).

———, *Rainbow's End: The Crash of 1929* (New York: Oxford University Press, 2001).

Korda, Michael, *Ulysses S. Grant: The Unlikely Hero* (New York: Atlas Books, 2004).

Jenkins, Roy, *Franklin Delano Roosevelt* (New York: Time Books, 2003).

Jensen, Merrill, *The New Nation: A History of the United States During Confederation 1781-1789* (New York: Northeastern University Press, 1981).

Jones, Robert F., *"The King of the Alley" William Duer: Politician, Entrepreneur and Speculator 1768-1799* (Philadelphia: American Philosophical Society, 1992).

Lewis, Michael, *Liar's Poker* (New York: W. W. Norton & Company, 1989).

———, *Next: The Future Just Happened* (New York: Norton & Company, 2002).

Lowenstein, Roger, *Origins of the Crash: The Great Bubble and Its Undoing* (New York: Penguin Books, 2004).

———, *When Genius Failed: The Rise and Fall of Long-Term Capital Management* (New York: Random House, 2000).

Lowy, Martin, *High Rollers: Inside the S&L Debacle* (New York: Praeger, 1991).

Lynch, Denis Tilden, *"Boss" Tweed: The Story of a Grim Generation* (New Brunswick, N.J.: Transaction Publishers, 2004). Originally published in 1927.

Malik, Om, *Broadbandits: Inside the $750 Billion Telecom Heist* (Hoboken, NJ: John Wiley & Sons, 2003).

Mayer, Martin, *The Greatest-Ever Bank Robbery: The Collapse of the Savings and Loan Industry* (New York: MacMillan, 1990).

McFeely, William S., *Grant* (New York: W.W. Norton & Company, 1982).

McGerr, Michael, *A Fierce Discontent: The Rise and Fall of the Progressive Movement in America 1870-1920* (New York: Free Press, 2003).

McDonald, Forrest, *Alexander Hamilton: A Biography* (New York: W.W. Norton & Company, 1982).

———, *Insull: The Rise and Fall of a Billionaire Utility Tycoon* (Washington, D.C.: Beard Books, 1964, reprint 2004).

McLean, Bethany and Peter Elkind, *The Smartest Guys in the Room: The Amazing Rise and Scandalous Fall of Enron* (New York: Penguin Books, 2003).

Minnigerode, Meade, *Certain Rich Men* (New York: Books for Libraries Press, 1927).

Moreau-Zanelli, Jocelyne, *Gallipolis: Histroire d'un mirage American au XV-LLLe siecle* (Paris: L'Harmatton, 2000).

Morris, Charles R., *Money, Greed, and Risk: Why Financial Crises and Crashes Happen* (New York: Random House, 1999).

Noggle, Burl, *Teapot Dome: Oil and Politics in the 1920s* (New York: W.W. Norton, 1965).

North, Douglass C., *The Economic Growth of the United States 1790-1860* (New York: W.W. Norton & Company, 1966).

Partnoy, Frank, *Infectious Greed: How Deceit and Risk Corrupted the Financial Markets* (New York: Times Books, 2003).

Patterson, Jerry E., *The First Four Hundred: Mrs. Astor's New York in the Gilded Age* (New York: Rizzoli, 2000).

Perret, Geoffrey, *Ulysses S. Grant: Soldier and President* (New York: The Modern Library, 1999).

Phillips, Kevin, *Wealth and Democracy: A Political History of the American Rich* (New York: Broadway Books, 2003).

———, *William McKinley* (New York: Times Books, 2003).

Platt, Harold L., *The Electric City: Energy and Growth of the Chicago Area, 1880-1930* (Chicago: University of Chicago Press, 1991).

Randall, William Sterne, *Alexander Hamilton: A Life* (New York: Perennial, 2003).

Royster, Charles, *The Fabulous History of the Dismal Swamp Company: A Story of George Washington's Time* (New York: Random House, 2000).

Rugoff, Milton, *America's Gilded Age: Intimate Portraits from an Era of Extravagance and Change 1850-1890* (New York: Henry Holt & Company, 1989).

Sanders, Elizabeth, *Roots of Reform: Farmers, Workers, and the American State, 1877-1917* (Chicago: The University of Chicago Press, 1999).

Sinclair, Upton, *The Jungle* (New York: Airmont Publishing Company, Inc., 1965).

Smith, B. Mark, *Toward Rational Exuberance: The Evolution of the Modern*

Stock Market (New York: Farrar, Straus and Giroux, 2001).

Smith, Jean Edward, *Grant* (New York: Touchstone, 2001).

Sobel, Robert, *Coolidge: An American Enigma* (Washington, D.C.: Regnery Publishing, Inc., 1998).

———, *Panic on Wall Street: A History of America's Financial Disasters* (New York: Truman Talley Books, 1988). There is also a latter edition of this book: *Panic on Wall Street* (Washington, D.C.: Beard Books, 1999).

Stewart, James, *Den of Thieves* (New York: Simon & Schuster, 1991).

Stratten, David H., *Tempest Over Teapot Dome: The Story of Albert B. Fall* (Norman: University of Oklahoma Press, 1998).

Strouse, Jean, *Morgan: American Financier* (New York: Random House, 1999).

Taleb, Nassim Nicholas, *Fooled by Randomness: The Hidden Role of Chance in Life and in the Markets* (New York: Texere, 2004).

Toffler, Barbara Ley and Jennifer Reingold, *Final Accounting: Ambition, Greed and the Fall of Arthur Andersen* (New York: Broadway Books, 2003).

Walworth, Arthur, *Woodrow Wilson* (New York: Penguin Books, 1965).

Wiebe, Robert H., *The Search for Order 1877-1920* (New York: Hill and Wang, 1967).

Index